Selected Speeches and Writings on Foreign Affairs

Selected Speeches and Writings
on Foreign Affairs

by

L. I. BREZHNEV

PERGAMON PRESS

OXFORD   NEW YORK   TORONTO   SYDNEY   PARIS   FRANKFURT

U.K.	Pergamon Press Ltd., Headington Hill Hall, Oxford OX3 0BW, England
U.S.A.	Pergamon Press Inc., Maxwell House, Fairview Park, Elmsford, New York 10523, U.S.A.
CANADA	Pergamon of Canada Ltd., 75 The East Mall, Toronto, Ontario, Canada
AUSTRALIA	Pergamon Press (Aust.) Pty. Ltd., PO Box 544, Potts Point, N.S.W. 2011, Australia
FRANCE	Pergamon Press SARL, 24 rue des Ecoles, 75240 Paris, Cedex 05, France
FEDERAL REPUBLIC OF GERMANY	Pergamon Press GmbH, 6242 Kronberg-Taunus, Pferdstrasse 1, Federal Republic of Germany

First Edition 1979

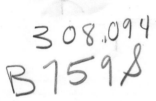

British Library Cataloguing in Publication Data

Brezhnev, Leonid Il'ich
  Selected speeches and writings on foreign affairs
  1. Russia – History – 1953 – Sources
  2. Russia – Politics and government – 1953 – Sources
  I. Title
  947.085'092'4   DK274   78–40614

  ISBN 0–08–023569–7

Phototypeset by Tradespools, Frome, Somerset
Printed by Aberdeen University Press

193294

CONTENTS

v

FOREWORD

I am delighted by this fresh encounter, through the good offices of Pergamon Press, with the English-language reader. It is my sincere hope that this book, containing as it does a selection of my speeches and addresses on foreign-policy matters over a number of years, will help the reader to a better grasp and fuller understanding of the nature and aims of the international activity of the CPSU and the Soviet state.

The basic aim of this activity has been and remains to exclude the threat of a new world war, and to achieve lasting peace and the growth of fruitful peaceful co-operation between countries under strict respect for sovereignty and without interference in one another's internal affairs.

Today we in the USSR regard the chief means to these ends to be the furthering of *détente* and the taking of realistic steps to check the arms race and proceed to disarmament.

The foreign policy of the Soviet Union has always striven to aid mutual understanding and *rapprochement* between peoples. May the appearance in Britain of this book lend support to this noble work.

L. I. BREZHNEV

1.
BASIC PRINCIPLES OF SOVIET FOREIGN POLICY

Lenin oriented the Soviet state on a consistent policy of peace in defence of the victorious revolution and the common cause of the working people of all countries. It was no accident that the first act of Soviet power written personally by Lenin was the historic Decree on Peace. It was Lenin who advanced the proposition for 'peaceful cohabitation' or, as we now call it, peaceful coexistence of states with different social systems, which, thanks to the consistent policy of the socialist states, has today become one of the cardinal principles underlying international relations. Also on Lenin's initiative one of the very first foreign-policy acts of the Soviet state in the world was to submit a programme for general disarmament and mutually beneficial economic relations with capitalist states.

For more than half a century the Soviet Union's foreign policy has been based on Lenin's ideas and precepts. Written into the decisions of our Party and of the higher organs of the Soviet state they remain the immutable, principled foundation of all the Soviet Union's actions in the international arena. Today, on this great Lenin centenary, we solemnly repeat to the peoples of the whole world:

True to the behests of the great Lenin, the Union of Soviet Socialist Republics shall continue to do everything in its power to enable the peoples of the socialist countries to live in peace and peacefully carry out the great work of building the new society, and to steadfastly strengthen the position of world socialism and the close co-operation and militant unity of the socialist states.

The countries pursuing an anti-imperialist policy and the peoples fighting for freedom, against imperialist aggression, shall always have in the person of our country a reliable and true friend and ally.

Realistically minded circles in the bourgeois countries, circles that really recognise the principles of peaceful coexistence, may be confident that in the Soviet Union they will have a partner prepared to promote mutually beneficial co-operation

We shall continue our active efforts to halt the arms race, which is ruinous to the peoples, to secure disarmament and to get outstanding issues between states settled on a reasonable foundation, by negotiation.

Socialist in content, the Leninist foreign policy of the Soviet state is consistently internationalist, genuinely democratic and profoundly peace-loving. It is one of the major sources of the strength and world-wide prestige of our socialist Motherland and world socialism. This is a powerful weapon

3

and we shall make the utmost use of it in our struggle for peace and communism.

> *Report at a joint celebration meeting of the Central Committee, the Supreme Soviet of the USSR and the Supreme Soviet of the RSFSR on 21 April 1970, to mark the centenary of the birth of Vladimir Ilyich Lenin*

Whenever the imperialists need to cover up their aggressive schemes, they try to revive the 'Soviet menace' myth. They seek to find evidence of this threat in the depths of the Indian Ocean and on the peaks of the Cordilleras. And, of course, nothing but Soviet divisions prepared for a leap against the West are to be discovered on the plains of Europe if these are viewed through NATO field-glasses.

But the peoples will not be deceived by the attempts to ascribe to the Soviet Union intentions which are alien to it. We declare with a full sense of responsibility: we have no territorial claims on anyone whatsoever, we threaten no one, and have no intention of attacking anyone, we stand for the free and independent development of all nations. But let no one, for his part, try to talk to us in terms of ultimatums and strength.

We have everything necessary – a genuine peace policy, military might and the unity of the Soviet people – to ensure the inviolability of our borders against any encroachments, and to defend the gains of socialism.

The period under review marked the end of the quarter-century since the rout of Hitler Germany and militarist Japan. The fruits of that great victory still live in international realities today. The Soviet people cherish everything that has been attained at such great cost.

For more than 25 years now, our people have lived in peace. We regard this as the greatest achievement of our Party's foreign policy. For a quarter-century now, mankind has been safeguarded from world war. That is another historic achievement of the peoples, to which the Soviet Union and its foreign policy have made a considerable contribution. However, the forces of aggression and militarism may have been pushed back, but they have not been rendered harmless. In the post-war years they have started more than 30 wars and armed conflicts of varying scale. Nor is it possible to consider the threat of another world war as having been completely eliminated. It is the vital task of all the peaceable states, of all the peoples, to prevent this threat from becoming reality.

The Soviet Union has countered the aggressive policy of imperialism with its policy of active defence of peace and strengthening of international security. The main lines of this policy are well known. Our Party, our Soviet state, in co-operation with the fraternal, socialist countries and other peace-loving states, and with the wholehearted support of many millions of people throughout the world, have now for many years been waging a struggle on these lines, taking a stand for the cause of peace and friendship among nations. The CPSU regards the following as the *basic* concrete tasks of this struggle in the present situation.

First

To eliminate the hotbeds of war in South-East Asia and in the Middle East and to promote a political settlement in these areas on the basis of respect for the legitimate rights of states and peoples subjected to aggression.

To give an immediate and firm rebuff to any acts of aggression and international arbitrariness. For this, full use must also be made of the possibilities of the United Nations.

Repudiation of the threat or use of force in settling outstanding issues must become a law of international life. For its part, the Soviet Union invites the countries which accept this approach to conclude appropriate bilateral or regional treaties.

Second

To proceed from the final recognition of the territorial changes that took place in Europe as a result of the Second World War. To bring about a radical turn towards *détente* and peace on this continent. To ensure the convocation and success of an all-European conference.

To do everything to ensure collective security in Europe. We reaffirm the readiness expressed jointly by the participants in the defensive Warsaw Treaty to have a simultaneous annulment of this treaty and of the North Atlantic alliance, or — as a first step — dismantling of their military organisations.

Third

To conclude treaties putting a ban on nuclear, chemical, and bacteriological weapons.

To work for an end to the testing of nuclear weapons, including underground tests, by everyone everywhere.

To promote the establishment of nuclear-free zones in various parts of the world.

We stand for the nuclear disarmament of all states in possession of nuclear weapons, and for the convocation for these purposes of a conference of the five nuclear powers – the USSR, the USA, the PRC, France and Britain.

Fourth

To invigorate the struggle to halt the race in all types of weapons. We favour the convocation of a world conference to consider disarmament questions to their full extent.

We stand for the dismantling of foreign military bases. We stand for a reduction of armed forces and armaments in areas where the military confrontation is especially dangerous, above all in Central Europe.

We consider it advisable to work out measures reducing the probability of accidental outbreak or deliberate fabrication of armed incidents and their development into international crises, into war.

The Soviet Union is prepared to negotiate agreements on reducing military expenditure, above all by the major powers.

Fifth

The UN decisions on the abolition of the remaining colonial régimes must be fully carried out. Manifestations of racism and apartheid must be universally condemned and boycotted.

Sixth

The Soviet Union is prepared to expand relations of mutually advantageous co-operation in every sphere with states which for their part seek to do so. Our country is prepared to participate together with the other states concerned in settling problems like the conservation of the environment, development of power and other natural resources, development of transport and communications, prevention and eradication of the most dangerous and widespread diseases, and the exploration and development of outer space and the world ocean.

Such are the main features of the programme for the struggle for peace and international co-operation, for the freedom and independence of nations, which our Party has put forward.

Report of the Central Committee of the Communist Party of the Soviet Union to the 24th Congress of the CPSU. 30 March 1971

As we see it, the purpose of our foreign policy is to strengthen peace, which we need for building communism, which is required by all socialist countries, by the peoples of all lands. This is why we shall continue to counteract the policy of aggression and help to eliminate throughout the world the conditions that breed aggressive wars.

As we see it, it is the purpose and mission of our foreign policy to help all the peoples to exercise their inalienable rights and, above all, their right to independent and sovereign development, so that they may benefit from the fruits of modern civilisation.

As we see it, the purpose and mission of our policy on the international scene is to side unfailingly with those who are fighting imperialism and all forms of exploitation and oppression, for freedom and human dignity, for democracy and socialism.

In short, we cherish the freedom, peace and well-being of our people, and we want all the peoples of the world to enjoy freedom, peace and well-being.

Our foreign policy has always been and will continue to be a class policy, a socialist one in content and aim. And it is precisely its socialist character that makes it a peace policy. 'We know, we know only too well, the incredible misfortunes that war brings to the workers and peasants,' Lenin stressed (*Collected Works*, Vol. 33, p. 148). Lenin's conclusion was crystal clear: to safeguard peace by all means; having started peaceful construction, to make every effort to continue it without interruption. The Soviet state has always followed this course charted by Lenin. From the first foreign policy act of Soviet power – the Decree on Peace – to the Peace Programme of the 24th CPSU Congress, our Party and state have steadily held to the main guidelines of struggle for peace and for the freedom and security of the peoples.

For nearly a quarter of a century – nearly half the life of the federal Soviet state – we have no longer been alone and have forged ahead together with the fraternal countries. We have repeatedly declared that we consider it our prime international task to consolidate and develop the world socialist

In the early and most difficult years of the People's Democracies, the Soviet Union played the decisive part in defending them against imperialist interference, and on many occasions gave them the necessary political and economic support. Later, too, joint defence against imperialism's hostile sallies, against its attempts to undermine the socialist system in one country or another, continued, and continues, to be one of the important prerequisites for the successful development of the world socialist system.

As a result of collective efforts and hard-fought battles against the class enemy we forged a lasting alliance of socialist states and a dependable system of all-round fraternal co-operation, which has become, as it were, the natural way of life for each of our countries. We have learned to carry on our day-to-day tasks successfully, to patiently arrive at suitable solutions of issues that cannot be resolved in capitalist conditions. And in doing this we have learned to harmonise the interests of each with the interests of all and to co-operate, sweeping aside everything that may hinder or complicate the joint progress.

When the question of uniting the Soviet Republics in a single Union of Soviet Socialist Republics arose 50 years ago, Lenin pointed out that the Union was necessary to withstand the military onslaught of imperialism, to defend the gains of the Revolution, and to achieve the peaceful creative tasks of socialist construction more successfully by common effort.

In principle, the same applies to the fraternal community of sovereign socialist states that belong to the Warsaw Treaty Organisation and the Council for Mutual Economic Assistance. This community was formed primarily to counter the imperialist threat, the aggressive imperialist military blocs, and to safeguard in common the cause of socialism and peace. And we have every reason to declare that never have socialism's positions been as firm as today, and that the cause of peace is gaining one victory after another.

The Soviet Union has been working for disarmament since the first years of its existence. In the past 10 years, a series of important treaties has been concluded with the most active participation of our country on such matters as the banning of nuclear weapons tests, nuclear non-proliferation, the banning of bacteriological weapons and so on. It stands to reason that all these are merely the opening pages of the chronicle of disarmament. We call on all governments, on all peoples of the world, to fill the succeeding pages of this chronicle jointly, including the last one – general and complete disarmament.

The adoption by the UN General Assembly – also on our initiative – of a resolution on the non-application of force in international relations and banning for all time the use of nuclear weapons was a big event in international affairs. Following up this UN resolution, we declare the Soviet Union's readiness to come to terms and appropriately formalise reciprocal commitments with any of the nuclear powers on the non-application of force, including the banning of the use of nuclear weapons against one another.

We are realists and are well aware that influential circles in the imperialist world have not yet abandoned attempts to conduct policy 'from positions of strength'. The arms race which they have started, and which is a threat to peace, is still continuing. Naturally, our allies and we cannot but draw the necessary conclusions. However, our peace-oriented foreign policy remains unchanged and in the present situation the potential of the peace-loving forces in their struggle against the forces of aggression and war is greater than ever. The Soviet Union will continue to work for *détente* and for consolidation of peace, persevering in its efforts to untie the knots of international tension, and working for stable good relations with countries with a differing social system. And if our policy evokes the appropriate response from them, then we shall say confidently that the *détente* will become stable, and peaceful coexistence – a universally accepted standard of inter-state relations. This means that peace on our planet will really become dependable and the danger of a new world war could be removed. And the foreign policy of our Party, of our Soviet state, is focused on this aim.

The CPSU has always held, and now holds, that the class struggle between the two systems – the capitalist and the socialist – in the economic and political, and also, of course, the ideological domains, will continue. That is to be expected since the world outlook and the class aims of socialism and capitalism are opposite and irreconcilable. But we shall strive to shift this historically inevitable struggle on to a path free from the perils of war, of dangerous conflicts and an uncontrolled arms race. This will be a tremendous gain for world peace, for the interests of all peoples, of all states.

While expressing its constant wish to co-operate in safeguarding peace with all governments willing to do so, the Soviet Union has been steadily expanding co-operation with the peace-loving public, with the peoples of all

9

countries. Ever new opportunities of promoting peace arise for public organisations and mass movements. And the Soviet public will continue to take an active part in their useful work. We are convinced that the forthcoming World Congress of Peace Forces will play a prominent part in the peoples' struggle for peace.

On this glorious jubilee of our state it is with a feeling of great pride for the Soviet people, for our Leninist Party, that we read the following evaluation of the country's foreign policy, which was formulated in the early period of the existence of the USSR: 'The federal state thus created on the basis of the fraternal co-operation of the peoples of the Soviet Republics sets itself the aim of preserving peace with all nations.' This was said in the Address of the Presidium of the Central Executive Committee of the USSR entitled 'To All the Peoples and Governments of the World', issued on the formation of the Soviet Union. It also said: 'A natural ally of oppressed peoples, the Union of Soviet Socialist Republics seeks peaceful and friendly relations, and economic co-operation with all nations. The Union of Soviet Socialist Republics sets itself the aim of promoting the interests of the working people of the whole world. On the vast expanses from the Baltic, Black and White Seas to the Pacific Ocean it carries forward fraternity among peoples and affirms the rule of labour, striving at the same time to facilitate friendly co-operation among the peoples of the whole world.'

Half a century has passed. The whole world has seen that they were not simply high-sounding words. The Soviet Union is faithful to the cause of socialism and peace, to which it pledged allegiance in the hour of its birth. And on the momentous day of the 50th anniversary of the Soviet Union we again declare to the whole world: The Communist Party, our state, the Soviet people shall continue to hold aloft securely the banner of its Leninist foreign policy, a policy of peace and friendship among the peoples!

Report at a gala joint meeting of the CPSU Central Committee, the USSR Supreme Soviet and the RSFSR Supreme Soviet, in the Kremlin Palace of Congresses. 21 December 1972

BASIC PRINCIPLES OF SOVIET FOREIGN POLICY

Today the principles of Soviet foreign policy are known to the whole world. It is a policy of promoting the fraternal unity of the countries of the socialist community, a policy of consolidating the alliance with peoples fighting for national and social liberation, a policy of peaceful coexistence of states with different social systems, and a policy of resolute action against aggression. It is a policy of active, straightforward diplomacy, of strict and unfailing fulfilment of commitments. This policy is consistent with the interests of socialism, and it fully accords with the interests of all peoples, with their aims and vital requirements.

In fulfilment of the behests of the great Lenin the 24th Congress of our Party put forward a realistic and, as developments have shown, fruitful Peace Programme. This programme is inspired by a lofty goal. It aims to silence the guns, to keep the sky clear and to ensure that rockets are used solely for peaceful purposes. The programme also aims at directing the inexhaustible forces of nuclear energy into constructive efforts to promote the good and the happiness of the working people. That is why our Peace Programme enjoys great esteem and recognition among workers and peasants, among all who are engaged in peaceful work, and is winning their growing and increasingly more effective support.

It has always been the position of Communists that the masses and their political parties and organisations should be active in solving questions relating to war and peace, and that in world politics they should be an active force and not passive onlookers. The voice of the people can be a detriment only to those who want to preserve international tension. And at the same time the authority of public opinion and its active support can only help those governments which consistently pursue a policy of peace.

Speech on receiving the International Lenin Peace Prize. 11 July 1973

A correct foreign policy is called upon to provide favourable peaceful conditions for our communist construction. Quite understandably, foreign-policy issues, just as the problems of our internal development, are of vital concern to the electors.

L. I. BREZHNEV ON FOREIGN AFFAIRS

The line of our Party and state in international affairs is well known. It stems from the very nature of socialism and is wholly subordinated to the interests of the peaceful constructive labour of the Soviet people and our brothers in the socialist countries. Being a consistently class policy, it serves the cause of peace, freedom and security of all peoples, the cause of their national independence and social progress, and meets the interests of the broadest masses throughout the world. The Soviet people enthusiastically and unanimously support this policy. We shall continue to pursue it vigorously and persistently in future as well.

Over the last few years belief in the possibility of and, moreover, the need for peaceful coexistence has been rooted in the consciousness of both the broad popular masses and the ruling circles of the majority of countries. The relaxation of international tensions has become possible because a new correlation of forces now exists on the world scene. Today the leaders of the bourgeois world can no longer seriously expect to decide the historical dispute between capitalism and socialism by force of arms. The senselessness and the extreme danger of the further fanning up of tensions are becoming increasingly obvious in conditions when both sides possess weapons of enormous destructive power.

The norms of peaceful coexistence between states have already been recorded in many binding official documents of a bilateral and multilateral character, as well as in political declarations. Of course, all this did not come about of itself. An enormous amount of political work had to be done to do away with the cold war and reduce the threat of a new world war. And it may be said that of decisive significance in attaining *détente* was the joint activity of the Soviet Union and the other countries of the socialist community, their consistent struggle against the forces of aggression and war.

Now the world is entering a period when the task of translating the principles of peaceful coexistence and mutually beneficial co-operation into daily practical actions is coming to the fore.

This is a crucial period. Those to whom the destinies of states and peoples have been entrusted should show that their deeds match their words. For politicians can be found who use the slogan of peace and pay lip service to the principles of peaceful coexistence and *détente*, while actually hoping to return to the policy of the cold war period, calling for a build-up of the arms race and displaying open animosity towards the socialist countries.

One can only be surprised at hearing certain apparently responsible

12

Western leaders speculating on whether *détente* is useful or harmful, that is, whether it is useful or harmful to live in conditions of a more stable peace and a reduced threat of war.

Sometimes we are told that attempts to question the benefit of *détente* are being made for purely internal political, tactical considerations, in order to win the sympathies of the right-wing circles in the country concerned. But, frankly speaking, we are convinced that the strengthening of peace is too serious a matter for the present and future generations of people to be subordinated to considerations of expediency or to one's mood.

Of course, we have our own ideology, our own convictions, but we proceed from the assumption that peace is equally needed by all peoples and that all states have a stake in removing the threat of a world nuclear war. Herein lies the main foundation for joint efforts to strengthen peace and security. Speaking of Soviet–American relations, US President Ford stressed recently that *détente* is advantageous to both sides. One, it seems to me, cannot but agree with this.

We firmly adhere to the view that *détente* can and must be further deepened. For this it is necessary that states should take due account of mutual, precisely mutual and not unilateral interests, and assume treaty obligations on a basis of reciprocity. Properly speaking, it was on this basis that international *détente* started, and on this basis it continues to develop.

Permit me, comrades, once again to declare from this rostrum that the Soviet Union, its Communist Party and the entire Soviet people are firmly and consistently coming out and will continue to come out for the invigoration of the international climate, for the strengthening of peaceful relations between states, for the consolidation of security in Europe, for the further improvement of relations with France, the United States, the FRG, Britain, Italy, Japan and indeed all countries which reciprocate in this matter.

Speech before the Electorate of the Baumansky District of Moscow. 13 June 1975

Struggle to consolidate the principles of peaceful coexistence, to assure lasting peace, to reduce, and in a longer term to eliminate, the danger of another world war has been, and remains, the main element of our policy towards the capitalist states. It may be noted that considerable progress has been achieved in this area in the past 5 years.

The passage from cold war, from the explosive confrontation of the two worlds, to *détente* was primarily connected with changes in the correlation of world forces. But much effort was required for people – especially those responsible for the policy of states – to become accustomed to the thought that not brinkmanship but negotiation of disputed questions, not confrontation but peaceful co-operation, is the natural state of things.

A big part here was played by the fact that our Party succeeded in accurately defining the main practical tasks of consolidating international security, and presenting them at its 24th Congress in the Peace Programme. The very first foreign-political actions of Soviet power, based on the platform of the peaceful coexistence of states with different social systems, showed the peoples of the world, as Lenin put it, 'the only correct way out of the difficulties, chaos, and danger of wars' (*Collected Works*, Vol. 33, p. 357). Invariably mindful of this platform, and acting on Lenin's behests and the half-century's experience of its foreign policy of peace, our Party advanced the Peace Programme at its 24th Congress. This Programme showed the realistic way to end the cold war and set clear objectives in the struggle to replace the danger of wars with peaceful co-operation.

Facts have borne out the Programme's timeliness and realism. And though world peace is by no means guaranteed as yet, we have every reason to declare that the improvement of the international climate is convincing evidence that lasting peace is not merely a good intention, but an entirely realistic objective. And we can and must continue to work tirelessly in the name of achieving it!

Report of the CPSU Central Committee to the 25th Congress of the Communist Party of the Soviet Union held in Moscow. 24 February 1976

Fundamental changes in the international position of the Soviet Union, the immense growth of its influence in world politics, and the close interrelationship of the internal and external factors of our development have made it necessary to include in the draft Constitution a special chapter on the foreign policy of the USSR. This is the first time such a chapter is being introduced into a Constitution.

It says that the Soviet state consistently follows the Leninist policy of peace and is for a strengthening of the security of peoples and broad international co-operation. The foreign policy of the USSR is aimed at ensuring favourable international conditions for building communism in the USSR, at strengthening the positions of world socialism, rendering support to the struggle of peoples for national liberation and social progress, preventing wars of aggression and consistently implementing the principle of peaceful coexistence of states with different social systems. This will be the first Soviet Constitution to explicitly state that the Soviet Union is a component part of the world system of socialism and of the socialist community. It develops and strengthens friendship, co-operation and comradely mutual assistance with the lands of socialism on the basis of socialist internationalism.

There is no doubt, comrades, that the adoption of a new Constitution of the USSR, the constitution of developed socialism, the constitution of communism which we are building, will be not only an historic event for our country, but also an event of tremendous international significance. Its implementation will have a profound long-term influence that will be felt far beyond the confines of our Motherland.

Our new Constitution will vividly show the whole world how the socialist state is developing and how it more deeply affirms and further strengthens socialist democracy. It will vividly show what socialist democracy means and wherein lies its essence. Our Constitution will show the diverse forms and the tremendous scope of the constantly growing effective participation of the broad masses of the people in administering the affairs of the state and society, something which is not known in the bourgeois countries where real power is exercised only by the numerically small class of capitalists.

In reading our new Constitution, people will see more clearly what extensive and diverse rights and freedoms are enjoyed by the citizens of a socialist society.

In its provisions the world will see a state which sets itself the goal of steady growth of the well-being and culture of the entire people, of all its classes and groups without exception, and which is actively working towards the attainment of this goal.

Finally, our new Constitution will show most convincingly that the first state of victorious socialism has for ever inscribed on its banner the word 'Peace' – peace as the highest principle of its foreign policy, which meets the interests of its own people and all the other peoples of our planet.

> *On the Draft Constitution of the Union of Soviet Socialist Republics: A report delivered at the Plenary Meeting of the CPSU Central Committee on 24 May 1977*

In all the 60 years of existence of the Soviet state, our foreign policy has been oriented on the ensurance of peace and security for our country, for all the peoples. To remove the danger of war, hold back the arms race, deepen and expand co-operation which would benefit all states – this is what the Soviet Union's initiatives on the international scene are aimed at today as ever. We intend to go on promoting the policy of *détente*, and working for its spread to all parts of the globe. I believe I shall not be wrong in saying that the dynamic, realistic and well-balanced nature of our foreign policy, and readiness to take the legitimate interests of others into consideration are recognised everywhere in the world, except, naturally, by those circles which deliberately, in pursuit of evil aims, give a distorted picture of this policy and deceive the public.

A word now about that part of your question concerning the competition of the two systems. I shall say, first of all, that since Lenin's days, we have been consistently following the line of peaceful coexistence with states belonging to a different social system, and of the settlement of outstanding issues not in the language of weapons, but at the negotiating table. With regard to the question as to whom the future belongs, we firmly believe in the advantages of the socialist system.

> *Replies to the Editor-in-Chief, Shoryn Hata, of the newspaper* Asahi Shimbun. *6 June 1977*

Foreign relations constitute, of course, an important area of the work of the Supreme Soviet of the USSR and its Presidium.

The Communist Party and the Soviet state are working persistently to strengthen peace, reduce the menace of another world war, curb the arms race, and build up the positions of socialism and all forces coming out for peoples' freedom and social progress, and for mutually profitable co-operation of all countries. These efforts rest on the determined stand of the Soviet people and meet with support and understanding from millions of people of goodwill in every corner of the globe.

The fundamental principles of Soviet foreign policy are clearly defined in the Draft Constitution. The Supreme Soviet of the USSR, its Presidium, the standing committees and deputies are called upon to make a substantial contribution to the implementation of these principles and promotion of contacts with other countries.

Speech in the Kremlin at a sitting of the Presidium of the Supreme Soviet of the USSR. 17 June 1977

Dear Doyen,
Gentlemen,
Comrades;

I am glad to welcome the heads of embassies accredited in Moscow who have gathered here. Some of you are old acquaintances of mine, while others I still have to get to know better.

First of all, allow me to thank you for the congratulations on the occasion of my election to the post of Chairman of the Presidium of the USSR Supreme Soviet, extended on behalf of you all by Ambassador Ford, doyen of the Diplomatic Corps.

I believe that today at this meeting there is no need to discuss the basic principles and directions of Soviet foreign policy. You cannot fail to know them. I have no doubt that you thoroughly study and analyse every move made by the Soviet Union in its bilateral relations with other countries, and closely follow our actions in the international sphere, whether in matters of world or of regional politics.

At the same time, you explain to us the policies of your states. This, too, is an important function of an ambassador, and we appreciate it.

Being aware of the range of your responsibilities and concerns, I should like to emphasise one point. It is only through profound knowledge of the policy of the state in which you work, only through carefully weighed and unbiased assessment of concrete proposals or actions by the Soviet Union, that it is possible to arrive at objective conclusions and find the right path towards the truth.

And who can have a more subtle and accurate perception of the political pulse of the country of their residence than ambassadors and their embassies? Who but they, through their contacts and their information, can help to dissipate the misunderstandings and misconceptions that sometimes arise between capitals? Who but they can see to it every day that the intentions of both sides are understood correctly, that the imaginary is not taken for the real and vice versa?

In a word, a lot depends on you, ambassadors, in creating an atmosphere of friendship and good will, of greater or lesser confidence in the relations between your countries and the Soviet Union. Of course, in discharging your important mission in the Soviet Union you will always meet with assistance from the Presidium of the USSR Supreme Soviet and the Soviet Government.

Today's international life is very dynamic. The opportunities to strengthen peace are growing, and growing constantly. At the same time the dangers threatening peace are growing as well. Evidently, one of the primary objectives of a far-sighted policy and sensible diplomacy is to do everything to expand the range of opportunities and reduce the size of dangers. As I see it, the role of ambassadors and embassies in achieving this objective, too, is a big one.

I shall tell you in passing that we exercise a similar approach to the work of Soviet ambassadors in foreign countries. So we do not apply any 'excessively high' criteria in your case.

I take this opportunity to ask you to convey the following to your heads of state and leaders of your countries:

There is no country or people in the world, in fact, with which the Soviet Union would not like to have good relations; there is no outstanding international problem to the solution of which the Soviet Union would not be willing to contribute; there is no centre of war danger, the removal of which, by peaceful means, the Soviet Union would not be interested in; there is no type of armaments and, first of all, weapons of mass destruction, which the Soviet Union would not be willing to limit or prohibit on a reciprocal basis, in agreement with other states, and then to remove from the arsenals.

The Soviet Union will always be an active participant in any negotiations or any international action aimed at developing peaceful co-operation and strengthening the security of peoples.

It is our belief, our firm belief, that realism in politics and the desire for *détente* and progress will ultimately triumph, and mankind will be able to enter the twenty-first century in conditions of peace, stable as never before. And we shall do everything in our power to see this come true.

Speech in the Kremlin at a reception for Heads of Diplomatic Missions accredited in Moscow. 8 July 1977

Soviet power was established under the sign of Lenin's Decree on Peace, and ever since our country's entire foreign policy has been one of peace. Objective historical conditions have dictated its concrete expression as the peaceful coexistence of states with different social systems.

In our day the principles of peaceful coexistence have by and large taken firm root in international affairs as the only realistic and reasonable principles. This is a result of the changed correlation of forces in the world – above all, of the growth of the strength and international authority of the Soviet Union and the entire socialist community. It is also a result of the successes of the international working-class movement and the forces of national liberation. And finally, it is a result of the acceptance of the new realities by a certain section of the ruling circles in the capitalist world.

At the same time, it is a result of the tremendous work done in recent years by the Soviet Union and other countries of the socialist community to reshape international relations in the direction of peace.

The Soviet Union is confidently pursuing a policy of peace. We actively and persistently call for the contest between socialism and capitalism to be decided not on the field of battle, not on munitions conveyors, but in the sphere of peaceful work. We want the frontiers dividing the two worlds to be crossed not by flight paths of missiles with nuclear warheads, but by threads of broad and diversified co-operation for the good of all mankind. By steadfastly pursuing this policy, we are giving practical expression to one of the main rallying cries of the October Revolution and carrying out one of Lenin's most important behests: Peace to the peoples!

If it should prove possible to solve the main problem – that of preventing another world war and establishing durable peace – new bright vistas would open before the inhabitants of our planet. There would then be the preconditions for solving many other vitally important problems confronting mankind today.

What are these problems?

One such problem, for example, is that of providing enormous numbers of people with food, raw materials and sources of energy. For according to the estimates we have, by the end of the century the population of the earth will have increased from 4000 million to 6000 million people. Another problem is that of ending the legacy of economic backwardness bequeathed by colonialism in Asian, African, and Latin American countries. This is necessary for normality in the future development of relations between states and generally for the progress of humanity as a whole. Finally, there is the problem of protecting man from the many dangers with which further uncontrolled technological development threatens him, in other words, the conservation of nature.

These are very real and serious problems. With every decade they will become more acute, unless a rational collective solution is found for them through systematic international co-operation.

Our world today is socially heterogeneous – it is made up of states with different social systems. This is an objective fact. By its internal development and by its approach to international relations the socialist party of the world is setting a good example of how the major problems facing mankind can best be solved. But, needless to say, it cannot solve them for the whole of humanity. What is needed is purposeful effort by the people of every country, broad and constructive co-operation by all countries, all peoples. The Soviet Union is whole-hearted in its desire for such co-operation. In this – if one looks deeper – lies the essence of the foreign policy course that we refer to as the policy of peaceful coexistence.

> *'The Great October Revolution and mankind's progress.' Report at a jubilee meeting of the Central Committee of the CPSU, the Supreme Soviet of the USSR, and the Supreme Soviet of the RSFSR to mark the sixtieth anniversary of the Great October Socialist Revolution. 2 November 1977*

Yet another aspect of the international importance of the new Soviet Constitution is that in both spirit and letter it serves the cause of peace, the security of the peoples, the strengthening of the anti-imperialist solidarity of all progressive forces.

All the aims and thoughts of our people revolve around peaceful, creative endeavour. In the USSR and other socialist countries, as distinct from the imperialist states, there are no classes or social groups that have any interest in the arms race, in military preparations. By including in the new Constitution a special chapter formalising the peaceful character of the foreign policy of the Soviet Union, our people have once again stressed their determination to follow the Leninist course of peace, the course of ridding humanity of the horrors of war, of the material hardships and mortal dangers implicit in the arms race. This chapter contains clauses corresponding to the fundamental obligations that the Soviet Union has undertaken as a participant in vital international agreements, including the Final Act of the Helsinki Conference. Indisputably this imparts additional weight to the efforts that are being made in the world for a further normalisation of the international situation, for the development of *détente*.

The Soviet Union is a component of the world system of socialism. A profound and consistent international solidarity unites our Party, the whole people with the progressive, liberation forces of the world, with the international Communist movement. It is natural therefore that the Constitution should clearly reflect the class character of the Soviet state's foreign policy, its

21

social ideals and political sympathies, its traditional support of the people's struggle for national liberation and social progress. It also reflects the positions that have been worked out by the CPSU on a collective basis together with the other Communist parties and have been recorded in their joint documents, for example, at the Berlin Conference of Communist and Workers' Parties of Europe.

In short, our Constitution elevates to the rank of a state law of the USSR that which constitutes the very essence of the foreign policy of the socialist state – its concern for peace, for the creation of international conditions consonant with the struggle for national freedom and social progress, for socialism and communism.

> *'A Historic Stage on the Road to Communism':* World Marxist Review, *No. 12, 1977*

It is easy to understand how I feel now. For me, a person who went right through the war from the very beginning to the very end and who, in the post-war years, was always connected with the life of our Armed Forces, being awarded the Order of Victory is a very great honour, a deeply stirring moment. From the bottom of my heart, I would like to thank our Party, its Central Committee, and the Presidium of the USSR Supreme Soviet.

While accepting this award, I am thinking, above all, about my comrades-in-arms, about infantrymen, sailors, officers and generals. Coming back to me now are those with whom I went through the war shoulder to shoulder, and with whom we arrived at the victory.

The victory was our people's greatest accomplishment. All the people, young and old, rejoiced on 9 May 1945. And literally that instant our Party and the Soviet Government put on the agenda the task of a lasting peace settlement aimed at conclusively ending the war which was just over.

However, it took colossal efforts to consolidate the victory won at so dear a price. It took three decades for Europe, as well as the United States and Canada, to recognise the inviolability of post-war borders. And this is truly the consolidation of the results of the victory.

While defending their homeland and fighting against fascism, our soldiers, our Soviet people, thought about peace. We fought so that there would be no more military conflicts. We fought so that mothers would not weep in mourning over their sons. We fought to uphold the freedom of our people and of the peoples of other countries, to uphold their right to life, to work in peace, to happiness.

Our Party and our people have always been and will always be faithful to the cause of peace. For us, the defence of peace is the defence of socialism, the defence of a happy future for the entire human race.

I would like to mention here one special and very important aspect of our peace efforts – the strengthening of the Soviet country's defence capacity.

I am proud, comrades, to receive this highest award on the days of the 60th anniversary of our Soviet Army, of our Red Army born in the flames of October. The Party is doing all it can so that the country's defence is at the required level.

But in strengthening our Armed Forces we in no way overstep the real needs of our security and the security of our socialist friends. We are not threatening anyone, and we are not imposing our will on anyone.

If *détente* continues, if other states are prepared for disarmament, we will not keep them waiting. Every year we have insistently, consistently and always more vigorously sought approaches to the solution of this problem right up to the most radical solution – universal and complete disarmament.

Speech in the Kremlin on being presented with the Order of Victory. 20 February 1978

The youth of your fathers passed in the firing lines of the Great Patriotic War. This had truly been, as the poet said, 'a fight not for fame but for life on earth'. Decades have passed. Today, more than half the population of our country knows about the war, its hardships and suffering, only from the stories of their elders, from books and films. But today, too, under different conditions, the fight continues for life on earth. To secure a lasting and stable peace – this is the aim of our foreign policy and of such of its fundamental principles as peaceful coexistence and *détente*.

Today, *détente* is neither theory, nor slogan, nor wishful thinking. It has to its credit quite a few good, perfectly concrete and tangible deeds. In Europe it has laid the groundwork for relations between states and has extended to various fields of their life. For all the ups and downs in Soviet–US relations, these too have a new appearance, more favourable to peace. The policy of *détente* has been recognised and is supported by the peoples as the only sensible policy in our troubled times.

The most essential and urgent task today is to secure a further easing of the war danger and to check the arms build-up. All peoples are conscious of this, and most of the governments in the world recognise it. This is also borne out by the fact that, for the first time in history, a session of the UN General Assembly specially devoted to arms limitation and disarmament will open in a few weeks. We wish it success, which we shall actively promote.

We are in favour of general and complete disarmament. It is not our fault that the talks on this problem, now nearly 20 years old, are deadlocked. And yet agreements on arms limitation in certain fields have been concluded during this period. And talks are under way on a number of questions.

The central goal of our struggle for peace in the present conditions is to reduce the threat of another world war and of mass extermination of people with nuclear weapons. For this purpose the Soviet Union is undertaking a set of major actions. One of them is the negotiations with the United States on the limitation of strategic offensive arms.

As you know, Moscow has just been visited by the US Secretary of State, Mr. Cyrus Vance, who came on President Carter's instructions. There was a thorough exchange of opinions. As a result, some progress was made in working out an agreement on strategic arms limitation. Not all problems by far have yet been resolved. We can by no means accept certain positions of the American side. I believe, however, that by reciprocal efforts based on sensible and realistic compromise we can complete the drafting of an agreement that will justly take into account the security interests of both powers. This will enable us substantially to bridle the arms race and therefore also help to strengthen peace.

For a number of years the Soviet Union has been pressing for an agreement on the general and complete banning of nuclear weapons tests. We are negotiating with the United States and Britain on banning tests in all media (i.e. including underground tests). And we are gratified to note that definite progress has been made in these talks of late. We would like to hope that the matter will be brought to a completion and that a treaty will be signed in the near future. This will be an appreciable achievement in the struggle for peace and security of the peoples.

Along with other peace forces in the world, the Soviet Union is taking active steps to prevent the development of the neutron bomb, which is a new, especially inhuman weapon of mass annihilation. Our stand on this issue is absolutely clear and radical: before it is too late, to conclude an agreement between the countries concerned, reciprocally renouncing manufacture of this weapon. And may mankind be delivered from it, once and for all.

Unfortunately, the United States, which is poised to develop the neutron bomb, has not yet agreed to our proposal. President Carter has recently declared, however, that he has put off a final decision on beginning the manufacture of neutron bombs. This, of course, does not settle the matter and is at best a half-measure. But I can inform you that we have taken the President's statement into account and that we, too, will not begin production of neutron arms as long as the United States does not do so. Further developments will depend on Washington.

In line with its fundamental policy aimed at reducing the nuclear war danger, the Soviet Union has also decided to accede in due manner to the international Treaty banning nuclear weapons in Latin America. Under this Treaty, the Soviet Union, like the other nuclear powers, will assume the commitment not to assist any Latin American state to gain access to nuclear weapons and not to use such weapons against the states who are party to the Treaty.

So, as you see, comrades, the work for peace is continuing, and our Motherland is taking ever newer and newer steps to this effect.

We intend that my coming visit to the FRG should also help not only to determine the prospects for further broad, mutually advantageous co-operation between our two countries (which is important in itself), but also contribute to the consolidation of *détente* and universal peace, especially in Europe.

Of late, the opponents of *détente* and disarmament in the NATO countries — all these generals dabbling in politics and all these war-like politicians — have been raising a propaganda howl and spreading fabrications about the allegedly threatening military superiority of the Warsaw Treaty states over the NATO bloc in Europe, about alleged Soviet aggressive intentions in Europe, and the like. Needless to say, all this is nonsense. Not harmless but malicious nonsense, however, because it serves to justify and camouflage actions that are really dangerous and potentially aggressive: precipitating another round in the arms race, building up military forces, and contaminating the international atmosphere with venomous fumes of fear, suspicion and hostility.

More than any other country the Soviet Union, which suffered the greatest ravages in the Second World War, wants peace in Europe never to be violated again and for Europe to be a continent of lasting peace and peaceful cooperation. And, to be sure, no other state has done more for this than our country.

For some years, at the talks in Vienna, we have been working for a considerable reduction in the armed forces of West and East in Europe – without prejudice to the security of any side – but have so far only encountered Western attempts at changing the relation of strength in its favour. True, a few days ago in Vienna the Western countries submitted slightly refurbished proposals. They take account of the standpoint of the socialist states in some respects, though the general imprint of a one-sided approach has clearly remained. Well, this means that the work will have to go on. We are prepared to do everything in our power to find mutually acceptable solutions and to relieve military tension in a region of the world where it is especially great and dangerous.

Everybody ought to know that, far from harbouring any aggressive designs and building up any 'strike forces' in Europe for action against the West, the Soviet Union to the contrary has always done and will continue to do everything it can to relieve tensions and facilitate agreement. Unlike the NATO countries, we have not enlarged our armed forces in Central Europe for a long time, and do not intend – this I want to stress most emphatically – do not intend to increase them by a single soldier, by a single tank.

And we call on the Western states to follow this salutary example.

Trying to distort the meaning and goals of Soviet foreign policy, imperialist propaganda maintains that there is a contradiction between our policy of *détente* and peaceful coexistence and our relations with countries that have thrown off the colonial yoke. The Soviet Union and other socialist countries are being falsely accused of interference in the affairs of young states. Our opponents go to the length of imputing an 'expansionist policy' and 'stoking up tension'. All this, of course, is an entire fabrication of the purest water with no basis in fact.

We want friendly co-operation with these countries on a basis of complete equality. We support their independence and their development on the road of peace and social progress. The Soviet Union invariably advocates strict respect for the sovereignty of these – and all other – states, for non-interference in their internal affairs, and for the inviolability of their frontiers.

It is the imperialist powers that continuously interfere – quite overtly or with but slight camouflage – in the affairs of independent newly-free states. They interfere in order to obstruct their progressive development. They infringe on sovereignty in order to secure the selfish interests of their monopolies or the plans of their military strategists.

As a rule, such interference leads to violence and encroachments on the rights of the peoples. This occurs either in the home life of the countries concerned, as, say, in the case of Chile, or in the form of undisguised external aggression, as in the case of the brazen conduct of the Israeli rulers.

The facts show that the peoples of the young states defend their independence and vital interests all the more successfully, the more solid their unity and solidarity, and the more solid their friendship with the countries of the socialist world, on whose support they can rely in their just struggle.

Here, too, there are many examples. It was thanks to the solidarity of the progressive forces that the attempts of the imperialists and their puppets to overthrow people's power in Angola and to dismember revolutionary Ethiopia were foiled.

Peace, non-interference in internal affairs, respect for independence and territorial integrity, equality, and mutually beneficial co-operation – all these are the indispensable and the most important elements of *détente* and lasting peace. Such is our policy in Europe, and it is the same in Africa, Asia, Latin America, and everywhere else in the world. And if anyone thinks that the Soviet Union can be diverted from this course by slander and threats, then he is deeply mistaken.

Comrades, analysing the world situation, we have arrived at the firm conviction that it is high time that thought should be given to putting a complete stop to any further quantitative and qualitative growth of the armaments and armed forces of states with a large military potential, and thereby create conditions for their subsequent reduction. Specifically, we are putting up for discussion a programme of the following measures, to be put into effect within a definite time limit:

– to stop manufacturing all types of nuclear weapons;
– to stop manufacturing and to ban all other types of mass-destruction weapons;
– to stop developing new types of highly destructive conventional arms;
– to renounce expanding the armies and increasing the conventional armaments of the permanent members of the UN Security Council and countries associated with them under military agreements.

Certainly, it is no simple matter to agree on these things. Probably, we could first tackle some one angle – say, the termination of nuclear arms manufacture, as we have already proposed. The main thing is that the problem as a whole is made easier to solve by the fact tha. these steps will not upset the balance of strength prevailing at present between states. Nobody would be the loser.

We must not, nor have we the right to forget that the nuclear peril is still hanging over the world and rousing alarm among nations for their future. Obviously, joint efforts of all the nuclear powers are needed to remove this peril. And each of them can and must do its bit. For its part, the Soviet Union declares unambiguously: we are against the use of nuclear weapons; only extraordinary circumstances, aggression against our country or its allies by another nuclear power, can compel us to resort to this extreme means of self-defence. The Soviet Union is doing and will do everything to prevent an atomic war, so that nations will not fall victim to atomic strikes – neither a first strike nor subsequent ones. This is our firm line, and we shall act accordingly.

To preserve our earth and to hand it over to the rising generation with all its wealth and beauty, unblemished by a nuclear holocaust – this, as we see it is the goal to which the thoughts of humanity should be directed. The Soviet Union is doing everything in its power to maintain and consolidate peace. We trust, our dear young friends, that your future will be one of happy free work on a peaceful planet.

Speech to the 18th Congress of the All-Union Lenin Young Communist League. 25 April 1978

2.
STABLE PEACE AND INTERNATIONAL SECURITY

For almost 30 years after the nuclear explosions in Hiroshima and Nagasaki mankind has been living with the awareness that somewhere, beyond the horizon, or perhaps somewhere rather close, the threat of a nuclear catastrophe was lurking. All these years peace-loving people have been demanding the removal of that threat from the life of mankind. Today, at last, we have made real progress in that direction.

Indeed, is it possible to overestimate the fact that the USSR and the USA, the two powers holding most of the world's stocks of nuclear weapons, have agreed to refrain from the threat or use of force against each other, against each other's allies and against other countries, and that they have agreed to act in such a way as to exclude the possibility of a nuclear war breaking out between them or between either of them and other countries? It is really impossible to overestimate this!

I have already said that if we had limited ourselves only to one agreement with the USA, the Agreement on the Prevention of Nuclear War, we would, even in that case, have accomplished a great deal.

Imperialism's forces of aggression will evidently not lay down their arms for a long time yet. There are still adventurists who are capable of kindling another military conflagration in order to further their own mercenary interests. We therefore consider that it is our sacred duty to conduct our policy in such a way as to avoid being caught unawares by any emergency and to firmly counter any attempt at returning the world to the 'cold war' days.

The best way of defending peace is to continue actively pursuing our policy of peace, to continue our – as people now call it – peace offensive.

Speech on receiving the International Lenin Peace Prize. 11 July 1973

International *détente* is opening favourable conditions for progress all along the front of struggle for stopping the arms race, for disarmament. The Soviet Union has been waging this struggle for many decades. Our efforts, the efforts of the other socialist states and of all peace-loving countries are already yielding fruit. But the main thing still lies ahead. The arms race still continues, which is fraught with serious danger for mankind. And this comes in ever greater conflict with the general trend in the development of international relations towards *détente* and the consolidation of peaceful coexistence.

The partial steps taken in the field of disarmament, such as a ban on some kinds of weapons, an end to all nuclear tests by everybody and everywhere, reduction of military budgets along with further measures for the limitation of strategic arms of the states most powerful in military respect will bring the world closer to achieving the final goal in this field, that is general and complete disarmament. The Soviet state has been struggling for this great goal since the first years of its existence. It has already made a considerable contribution to this cause. And I wish to assure the Parliament of friendly India that the Land of the Soviets will do its utmost to bring closer the day when the centuries-old dream of mankind's greatest minds to destroy the means of mutual extermination will come true.

Esteemed Members of the Parliament!

The changes for the better which have taken place in the relations between the Soviet Union and the United States of America in the last 2 years are undoubtedly of great importance for a stable change in the entire international situation – towards a more durable peace and security. Speaking of what is of primary importance for other countries, the essence of these changes consists in the fact that the two strongest powers – one socialist and one capitalist – have recognised mutually and in a binding legal form the principle of peaceful coexistence to be the basis of their relations. Moreover, they have pledged to pursue their foreign policy in a way as to prevent the eruption of a nuclear war.

I think there is no need to prove that all the peoples of the world interested in the prevention of a new world war stand to gain from such agreement. Taking these steps to improve relations with the USA, the Soviet Union acted in compliance with the well-known principles of its peaceable socialist foreign policy. We duly appreciate the fact that the leaders of the United States of America have shown in this case political realism, foresight and understanding of the requirements of the times.

Like all the significant changes in historical development, this change in the relations between the USSR and the USA is not proceeding smoothly; it is proceeding amid the struggle of different forces, with some zigzags and hitches. We clearly see that certain circles in the military-political bloc of Western powers, and also within the United States itself, are against the establishment of relations of lasting peace and mutually advantageous co-operation between the Soviet Union and the United States and are doing their best to prevent it. It is also known how active such circles are in the United States, although this activity, as we are deeply convinced, has nothing in common with the interests of the American people.

However, what has been achieved as a result of the Soviet–American summit talks in 1972 and 1973 as regards directing relations between the Soviet Union and the United States into a healthy normal course undoubtedly accords with the basic, long-term interests of both the Soviet and the American peoples and the interests of universal peace. And here, if I may, dear friends, I will be quite plain: we in the Soviet Union are convinced that nobody will be able to cancel out the peaceful gain of this constructive policy!

The Soviet Union firmly intends to continue to advance along the same road of *détente* and peaceful co-operation. We, of course, proceed from the assumption that the American side will act accordingly.

Speech in the Indian Parliament.
29 November 1973

'The future of mankind is peace,' said Cuba's glorious son, Jose Marti. 'There was a time', he added, 'when war was the first means used in settling conflicts. Today war is the last resort. Tomorrow war will become a crime.'

The 'morrow' of which Marti spoke has become our today. The Soviet Union, the Communist Party as well as other socialist countries, fraternal parties and all peace forces, are engaged in a constant struggle to put an end to wars of aggression and establish a lasting peace. In doing so we are following the line of policy laid down by Lenin.

We are not pacifists. We are not for peace at any price, and we are not, of course, for the freezing of socio-political processes taking place inside countries.

Peace, as we understand it, is unconditional respect for the right of the peoples of the socialist countries to build a new society without any

33

interference from outside. Peace is unconditional respect for the right of every state and every people to sovereign and independent development.

Peace, as we understand it, is ensuring that the Vietnamese people, who have won a historic victory in the struggle against imperialist aggression, have an opportunity to realise their national aspirations; peace is strict implementation of the Paris Agreement, firm opposition to any attempts by reaction to thwart efforts to improve the situation in South-East Asia.

Peace, as we understand it, is restoration of the legitimate and inalienable rights of the Arab peoples, rights that have been trampled upon by Israel's aggression; it means a constructive and lasting settlement of the Middle-East crisis.

That is precisely what the Soviet Union has firmly and consistently advocated.

The Geneva Conference must carry out its main mission: to achieve a thorough political settlement, and establish a lasting peace in the Middle East. But this aim can be attained only provided Israeli troops are withdrawn from all the Arab territories that were occupied in 1967 and the legitimate rights of the Arab people of Palestine are respected. The UN decisions on the Middle East must be carried out fully, in all their aspects and in the shortest possible period of time. The Soviet Union has made and will continue to make an active contribution to this important cause.

Peace, as we understand it, is refusal to settle inter-state disputes and differences, however deep and complex, by military means. Peace is the creation of conditions for equitable and fruitful co-operation between all countries.

In other words, we are for a stable and just peace that meets the interests of all peoples, the interests of social progress.

For a long time the statesmen of the capitalist world remained deaf to the proposals of the Soviet Union for building relations between the two systems on the principles of peaceful coexistence. They tried to crush the world's first socialist state by intervention, to strangle it by an economic and political blockade. They hoped to smash the Soviet Union in a big war. They wanted to intimidate us and other socialist countries with the cold war and hoped to impose their will on us with the help of a 'position-of-strength' policy. But all these hopes and attempts were in vain. The Soviet Union and the entire world socialist system have become a powerful invincible force.

Finally the capitalist world had to face the truth. It had to recognise the impossibility of solving by military means the historical dispute between capitalism and socialism. In these conditions, the more far-sighted of the leaders of bourgeois countries found it advisable to respond to the proposals of the socialist states for peaceful coexistence.

This has brought about, in recent years, a favourable turn in the relations of the Soviet Union and other socialist countries with France, the FRG, the United States and some other bourgeois states.

The consistent and active peace policy of the socialist states is producing ever more tangible results in Europe, a continent which is of such importance for the destinies of all mankind. Much of what our countries, together with all peace forces, had striven for in the course of the quarter-century has now become possible. The main thing is that the inviolability of the post-war frontiers in Europe and the independence of the socialist German state, the German Democratic Republic, have gained wide official recognition. This is very important for preventing the rise of revanchism in Europe, and a new aggravation of the situation; in short, this is important for creating conditions for a really stable peace.

But the concept of peaceful coexistence is not limited to a mere recognition that war is no longer acceptable as a means of settling disputes between states, especially between the two social systems. In our days there is a growing conviction that active and fruitful co-operation among all states is essential. It is not hard to see why this idea first struck root in Europe. It is on this continent that powerful armed forces of the two world systems face each other. In Europe it is particularly clear, because of purely physical conditions, that a war involving the use of modern means of mass destruction would be an utterly senseless undertaking.

A recognition of all this is at the heart of two very important initiatives in the international life of present-day Europe, initiatives that have come from the Soviet Union and its allies in the defensive Warsaw Treaty Organisation. I have in mind the All-European Conference on Security and Co-operation (which ought to be moving now towards its final stage) and the talks on troop and arms reductions in Central Europe which began comparatively recently.

The task of the All-European Conference is to consolidate the atmosphere of political *détente* on the continent and the possibilities opened up by it, to lay a firm foundation for long-term co-operation of European states in the field of strengthening peace, and in the spheres of economy, science and culture. The task of the talks started in Vienna is to ensure for the peoples of

Europe concrete fruit of *détente* in the sense of a certain lessening of the danger of military clashes in Europe and a certain reduction of spendings on defence.

It is the sincere wish of the Soviet Union and other socialist countries participating in these important undertakings that they end in complete success. We are actively seeking constructive solutions acceptable to all sides and beneficial to the cause of peace and *détente*. If we are to judge by words, all the other participants in the talks in Geneva and Vienna also appear to be engaged in this. In reality, however, there are coming to light in the positions of some countries features of quite another kind.

This concerns not only talks I have mentioned but also other important matters. Under various pretexts some people are dragging out the practical solution of ripe questions. Various reservations and 'conditions', most often having no relation to the matter under discussion, are being set forth. Attempts are even being made to openly interfere in the domestic affairs of other states. Time and again reactionary propaganda sows slander, strives to instil suspicions in people, to confuse them in order to poison the international atmosphere. Some military leaders and politicians find it possible to call for an intensification of the arms race. At the Vienna talks on the reduction of armed forces some NATO countries are obviously trying to replace an equitable and just agreement by one that would actually lead to a unilateral lessening of the defence capabilities of socialist countries.

All these facts cannot but put us on the alert. It is difficult to square them with the policy of *détente* and strengthening peace proclaimed by the governments of relevant countries.

What can be said on this matter? If these actions are planned as a means of pressuring the Soviet Union and other socialist states in the hope of securing unilateral advantages to the detriment of our principles and vital interests, this is a futile venture. This should be clear to all. It is much more serious if something bigger is concealed behind all this, that is, a hope to impede improvement of the international climate, to return the world to the infamous times of the cold war and to give new impetus to the arms race.

It is significant that not a single capitalist state now openly comes out as an opponent of *détente* and extension of peaceful co-operation. This is understandable since the ideas of peace have now struck too deep a root in the minds of the peoples. But there do exist forces that are irked by the strengthening of peaceful coexistence. These forces are still considerable and command certain influence. Imperialism has by no means changed its aggressive nature.

The policy of *détente* has scored considerable successes, but the world is far from being tranquil. The stockpiling and perfection of weapons, first of all nuclear weapons, go on as before. The danger of this situation is obvious. But mankind's future can be made secure only if the threat of nuclear war is fully eliminated. It is precisely towards this end that the Soviet Union has advanced its well-known proposals in the United Nations Organisation on questions of disarmament, on the non-use of force in international relations and on the prohibition of the use of nuclear weapons. It can only be regretted that the position of some states continues to prevent the implementation of these proposals.

It can be said on the whole, comrades, that recent years have brought many positive changes in international life. As a result, mankind has heaved a sigh of relief and hopes for a lasting peace have been strengthened. We believe that this process will go further. The task is to make irreversible the achievements in the field of *détente*. This calls for determined, I repeat, determined and vigorous struggle by peace-loving states, by all peace-loving forces.

The role of the popular masses in solving questions of international politics and first of all questions of war and peace has never been as great as now. The peoples demand a lasting peace and genuine security. This was eloquently confirmed by the World Congress of Peace Forces held 3 months ago in Moscow and attended by delegates from 143 countries.

It is becoming ever clearer that the only foreign policy that can hope for success in contemporary conditions is one which takes into account the will of the peoples and really expresses the aspirations of peace-loving mankind. Such is the policy of socialist countries, an honest policy free of selfish calculations. It should be openly said that if today mankind is closer to a lasting peace than ever before in the past, this is due first of all to the resolute and consistent efforts of socialist countries.

Speech at a mass rally of Cuban–Soviet Friendship, Havana. 29 January 1974

In recent years the Party has carried out exceptionally intensive and strenuous activities on the foreign-political front. And you understand what that was connected with. The situation in the world, and concern for the vital interests of the Soviet people, for the maintenance of peace on earth have led us to concentrate our efforts on the solution of acute international problems.

Let us recall what we had been faced with in the international arena in the comparatively recent past. Fierce battles raged in Vietnam. The situation in the Middle East was fraught with the danger of outbreaks of military conflicts. The 'cold war' weighed heavily upon the minds and life of peoples. Relations with the United States, the FRG, and many other big states of the capitalist world remained tense.

Our Party had never regarded such a state of affairs as inevitable, let alone normal. An appraisal of the general alignment of forces in the world led us several years ago to this conclusion, namely, that a real opportunity existed for bringing about a fundamental change in the international situation. The important thing was to furnish a broad basis for constructive discussion and solution of the problems that had accumulated. Those considerations and our policy were summed up in the peace programme proclaimed by the 24th Congress of the CPSU.

There is not a single person in the Soviet Union who would not regard this programme as an embodiment of his thoughts about the destinies of his country, about the present and the future. There is not a single person in the Soviet Union for whom war would not be hateful. All our projects, all our plans are connected with the maintenance of peace.

At present the first generation of Soviet people who did not have to live through war, to experience the hardships and sorrows of wartime, are in the prime of life. To put it simply, what we would like very much, comrades, is that our children and grandchildren will never know what war is. It is for the sake of this that the Party has put forward the peace programme and launched a struggle for a genuine normalisation of the entire system of international relations.

The results of our efforts are a matter of common knowledge. The main thing is that the foundations of peace and security of peoples have been consolidated to a significant extent, and the danger of nuclear war has been lessened. The Soviet people, all peoples of the world, regard this as a triumph of truly historic importance.

The favourable changes in the world situation are first of all due to the

38

impact of the world of socialism, its achievements, its might, and its example on international developments. This is a result of the purposeful and concerted policy of the community of socialist countries. One can confidently say that never before has the co-ordination of the foreign-political efforts of socialist states been so extensive and effective as in recent years. In the foreign-political arena the socialist states were in constant contact and showed complete mutual understanding. Development of co-operation with fraternal states in all fields, including the field of international affairs, has been and will continue to be a matter of unflagging concern for the Central Committee of our Party.

The termination of the aggressive war waged by US imperialism in Vietnam was one of the major achievements in the resolute struggle of the forces of peace and socialism. The Vietnamese people's heroic struggle was crowned with a victory which is of great fundamental significance. It is now important that a political settlement in South-East Asia should be carried through.

In many ways, owing to the policy of the Soviet Union and the socialist countries, owing to the change in the climate in international relations, there have emerged more favourable conditions for the struggle against imperialist aggression and for the elimination of the hotbed of war in the Middle East. Agreements on disengagement of troops in the Sinai Peninsula and the Golan Heights areas have been reached. At the same time it is necessary to realise that only the first steps have been made. The main questions of settlement are still to be considered at the Geneva Conference. This is an extremely complex task. It can be accomplished only through combined efforts of the states participating in the conference.

The Soviet Union contributes and will continue to contribute to this cause. Our stand with regard to a final settlement of the Middle-East crisis is well known. Progress towards a settlement will create conditions for the development of relations between the Soviet Union and all the countries of the Middle East. A durable and just peace should at last be established in the Middle East.

Thus, there is every reason to say that a major point of the peace programme concerning the elimination of the most dangerous hotbeds of war is being successfully implemented. Much has also been achieved in other directions of our foreign policy.

We are also for supplementing political *détente* with a military *détente*. In the field of arms limitation, as is known, a number of international agreements have been concluded and without them the international situation would probably be more grave, but regrettably the arms drive has not been stopped.

In these conditions the Central Committee and the leading bodies of our state continue to devote utmost attention to the strengthening of our socialist Homeland's defence capacity.

And I can assure you, comrades, that our defence is reliable, that it will remain at an adequate level.

At the same time we are working tirelessly for real progress in the field of disarmament. The advocates of the arms drive argue that limiting arms, to say nothing of reducing them, means taking a risk. But as a matter of fact, it is an immeasurably greater risk to continue an unrestrained stockpiling of arms. Proceeding from this we have again and again called on all states, all governments to put an end to the arms drive and to begin to advance to the great goal – universal and complete disarmament.

Being aware of the complexity of this task which is of tremendous scope we are ready to agree to partial measures on the limitation and reduction of arms. This determines in particular our position at the talks on the reduction of armed forces and arms in Central Europe. We think that there is a possibility of achieving in this field the first concrete results at an early date, if, of course, goodwill is displayed by all the participants in the talks.

An important factor in consolidating the positive political changes in the international arena and in creating a material basis for a lasting peace is the all-round development of economic and scientific–technical links. It meets the interests of all states and all peoples. However, there are circles in the West which hope to obtain from us, in exchange for such links, political and ideological concessions. That is a futile undertaking.

We are for the participation of every state in the international division of labour on an equitable basis and under conditions that are advantageous for all and that do not permit violation of sovereignty and interference in internal affairs.

This contributes to the general development of world economic ties whose significance is steadily increasing.

Another factor – the great activity of the general public – has acquired tremendous significance in the efforts to consolidate the positive changes in international relations. The policy of *détente* is acquiring at present a genuinely mass basis. We shall continue to pay constant heed to the development of contacts with the public of other countries, the development of links along parliamentary, trade union and other lines, the all-round extension of the front of peace champions.

The struggle for the triumph of reason in international relations can hardly be an easy one. Every gain on the road to lasting peace comes about through struggle, through fierce clashes with the most reactionary circles of imperialism and their accomplices.

A struggle between representatives of aggressive forces and supporters of realism is taking place in practically all the bourgeois countries. But whatever acute forms the struggle may assume, we are confident of one thing: the future is not with the advocates of cold war, not with those who would like to push peoples into the abyss of war.

The leadership of the People's Republic of China is acting contrary to the overall positive changes in the international arena. Whipping up militaristic, chauvinistic passions in that country they have subordinated their foreign policy to the tasks of struggle against the Soviet Union and the other socialist countries, to attempts at frustrating relaxation. The PRC leadership has recently gone so far as to openly team up with representatives of arch reaction, the Chilean junta, the leaders of the right-wing imperialist bourgeoisie in Britain, the FRG, the USA and other countries. These deeds, more than any words, reveal the real essence of Peking's policy.

As far as our relations with China are concerned we will naturally continue to rebuff anti-Soviet slander, to firmly protect the interests of our state and our security. At the same time we continue to advocate normalisation of relations with China, restoration of friendship with the great Chinese people on the reliable basis of proletarian internationalism. In other words, in this important issue we will consistently pursue the line of the 24th Congress of our Party.

The foreign policy of the CPSU, of our Central Committee is one of profound solicitude for the good of Soviet people. At the same time, this policy fully accords with the interests of all the revolutionary forces, the cherished aspirations of all peoples. It is a class, socialist and genuinely internationalist course.

Speech before the Baumansky constituency of Moscow. 14 June 1974

Efforts to end the arms race and to promote disarmament have been and remain — as the Peace Programme requires — one of the main trends in the foreign-political activity of the CC CPSU and the Soviet Government. Today, this objective is more vital than ever. Mankind is tired of sitting upon mountains of arms, yet the arms race spurred on by aggressive imperialist groups is becoming more intensive.

The main motive for the arms race given by its advocates is the so-called Soviet threat. They invoke this motive when they want to drag through a larger military budget, reducing allocations for social needs, and when new types of deadly weapons are being developed, and when they try to justify NATO's military activity. In fact, of course, there is no Soviet threat either to the West or to the East. It is all a monstrous lie from beginning to end. The Soviet Union has not the slightest intention of attacking anyone. The Soviet Union does not need war. The Soviet Union does not increase its military budget, and, far from reducing, is steadily augmenting allocations for improving the people's well-being. Our country is consistently and staunchly fighting for peace, and making one concrete proposal after another aimed at arms reduction and disarmament.

The Soviet Communists are proud of having undertaken the difficult but noble mission of standing in the front ranks of the fighters striving to deliver the peoples from the dangers ensuing from the continuing arms race. Our Party calls on all the peoples, all countries, to unite their efforts and end this perilous process. General and complete disarmament has been and remains our ultimate goal in this field. At the same time, the Soviet Union is doing all it can to achieve progress along separate sections of the road leading to this goal.

An international convention on banning and destroying bacteriological weapons, based on a draft submitted by the Soviet Union and other socialist countries, was drawn up, signed and has entered into force. In effect, it is the first real disarmament measure in the history of international relations. It envisages removal of a whole category of highly dangerous mass-annihilation weapons from the military arsenals of states.

The sphere of operation of the Treaty on the Non-Proliferation of Nuclear Weapons has expanded. Recently, other large states, including the FRG and Italy, have become party to it. But further effective measures to prevent the spread of nuclear weapons all over the planet are still a most important objective. The USSR is prepared to co-operate with other states in this matter.

Let me refer specifically to the current Soviet–US negotiations on further strategic arms limitation. We are conducting them in an effort to carry out the 1974 Vladivostok accord and to prevent the opening of a new channel for the arms race, which would nullify everything achieved so far. An agreement on this issue would obviously be of very great benefit both for the further development of Soviet–US relations and for building greater mutual confidence, and for the consolidation of world peace.

Since we attach the utmost importance to the whole of this problem, we have persistently and repeatedly proposed to the United States that the two sides do not stop at just limiting the existing types of strategic weapons. We thought it possible to go further. Specifically, we suggested coming to terms on banning the development of new, still more destructive weapons systems, in particular, the new Trident submarines carrying ballistic missiles and the new strategic B-1 bombers in the United States, and similar systems in the USSR. Regrettably, these proposals were not accepted by the US side.

But we have not withdrawn them. And need we say how beneficial their implementation would be for strengthening mutual confidence? Furthermore, both sides would be able to save considerable resources, and use them for productive purposes, for improving people's life.

Let me add one more thing. Of late, pronouncements have been proliferating in many countries against any of the powers setting up military bases in the region of the Indian Ocean. We are in sympathy with these pronouncements. The Soviet Union has never had, and has no intention now, of building military bases in the Indian Ocean. And we call on the United States to take the same stand.

Certainly, the time will come when the inevitable association of other nuclear powers with the process of strategic arms limitation will arise on the agenda. And those which would refuse would assume a grave responsibility before the peoples.

On our country's initiative the UN General Assembly has in recent years adopted a number of important resolutions on questions of restraining the arms race and banning development and manufacture of new types of mass-annihilation weapons, of new systems of such weapons.

The task is to have these resolutions implemented. Frankly, this is not easy to achieve, because a number of major states are still obviously reluctant to end the arms race. The opponents of *détente* and disarmament still dispose of considerable resources. They are highly active, operating in different forms and from different angles. Though imperialism's possibilities for aggressive action are now considerably reduced, its nature has remained the same. This is why the peace-loving forces must be highly vigilant. Energetic action and unity of all the forces of peace and goodwill are essential.

Therefore, special importance attaches to the proposal supported by the vast majority of UN member countries to convene a World Disarmament Conference.

Political *détente* needs to be backed up by military *détente*. The Peace Programme advanced a clear aim: to reduce armed forces and armaments in Central Europe. The Vienna negotiations on this issue have already been going on for more than 2 years. However, there has been no visible progress. For only one reason: the NATO countries refuse to give up trying to use the negotiations to secure unilateral military advantages. For some reason the West wants, even demands, concessions prejudicial to the security of the socialist countries. Yet we have not noticed any inclination on the part of the NATO bloc to make similar concessions to the other side.

Recently, the socialist states submitted new proposals in Vienna in an effort to get matters off the ground. For a start, we are prepared to accept a reduction of only Soviet and US troops in the course of this year, while the strength of the armed forces of the other participants in the negotiations remains 'frozen' and will not be subject to reduction until the second stage in 1977–8. We have also made perfectly concrete proposals concerning reduction by both sides of the number of tanks, nuclear-weapons-carrying planes and missile launchers along with a definite quantity of nuclear ammunition for these delivery vehicles.

Our proposals are based on the only realistic approach of preserving the existing relation of strength, in effect one of equilibrium, in the centre of Europe. Their implementation will not prejudice the security of either side. And it is to be hoped that all this will evoke the right response of the Western countries and it will at last be possible to go from discussion to actual measures for reducing armed forces and armaments.

The 24th Congress set this objective: renunciation of the use and threat of force in settling disputed questions must become the rule in international relations. Later, this principle was reflected in a number of treaties concluded by the USSR with other countries. It is included in the Final Act of the European Conference. To make the danger of war recede still further and to create favourable conditions for progress towards disarmament we now offer to conclude a world treaty on the non-use of force in international relations. Its participants, naturally including the nuclear powers, would undertake to refrain from using all types of weapons, including nuclear, in settling disputes that may arise between them. The Soviet Union is prepared to join other states in examining practical steps leading to the implementation of this proposal.

A great role and responsibility devolve on the mass public movement to consolidate peace. The past 5 years saw such milestones in the growth of this movement as the World Congress of Peace Forces in Moscow, the Brussels Assembly of Representatives of Public Opinion for European Security, and the World Congress of Women in Berlin. Our Party and the public in our country took an active part in all these events. In future, too, we shall not spare strength in drawing the broad popular masses into the efforts of consolidating peace.

In its foreign policy, the Soviet Union intends to search patiently and consistently for more new ways of expanding peaceful, mutually advantageous co-operation between states with different social systems, and more new ways leading to disarmament. We shall continuously augment our efforts in the struggle for lasting peace.

Assessing our country's international situation and world conditions, the Party's Central Committee considers that *further struggle for peace and the freedom and independence of the peoples now requires first of all fulfilment of the following vital tasks:*

—While steadily strengthening their unity and expanding their all-round co-operation in building the new society, the fraternal socialist states must augment their joint active contribution to the consolidation of peace.

— Work for the termination of the expanding arms race, which is endangering peace, and for transition to reducing the accumulated stockpiles of arms, to disarmament. For this purpose:

(a) do everything to complete the preparation of a new Soviet–US agreement on limiting and reducing strategic armaments, and conclude international treaties on universal and complete termination of nuclear weapons tests, on banning and destroying chemical weapons, on banning development of new types and systems of mass annihilation weapons, and also banning modification of the natural environment for military or other hostile purposes;

(b) launch new efforts to activate negotiations on the reduction of armed forces and armaments in Central Europe. Following agreement on the first concrete steps in this direction, continue to promote military *détente* in the region in subsequent years;

(c) work for a switch from the present continuous growth of the military expenditure of many states to the practice of their systematic reduction;

(d) take all measures to assure the earliest possible convocation of a World Disarmament Conference.

– Concentrate the efforts of peace-loving states on eliminating the remaining seats of war, first and foremost on implementing a just and durable settlement in the Middle East. In connection with such a settlement the states concerned should examine the question of helping to end the arms race in the Middle East.

– Do everything to deepen international *détente*, to embody it in concrete forms of mutually beneficial co-operation between states. Work vigorously for the full implementation of the Final Act of the European Conference, and for greater peaceful co-operation in Europe. In accordance with the principles of peaceful coexistence continue consistently to develop relations of long-term mutually beneficial co-operation in various fields – political, economic, scientific and cultural – with the United States of America, France, the FRG, Britain, Italy, Canada, and also Japan and other capitalist countries.

– Work for ensuring Asian security based on joint efforts by the states of that continent.

– Work for a world treaty on the non-use of force in international relations.

– Consider as crucial the international task of completely eliminating all vestiges of the system of colonial oppression, infringement of the equality and independence of peoples, and all seats of colonialism and racialism.

– Work for eliminating discrimination and all artificial barriers in international trade, and all manifestations of inequality, diktat and exploitation in international economic relations.

These are the main tasks, the attainment of which, as we see it, is essential at present in the interests of peace and the security of peoples, and the progress of mankind. We consider these proposals an organic projection and development of the Peace Programme advanced by our 24th Congress, *a programme of further struggle for peace and international co-operation and for the freedom and independence of the peoples.* We shall direct our foreign-policy efforts towards achieving these tasks, and shall co-operate in this with other peace-loving states.

Permit me to express confidence that the lofty aims of our policy on the international scene will be received with understanding and win the wholehearted support of all the peace-loving, progressive forces, and all honest people on earth.

Report of the CPSU Central Committee to the 25th Congress of the Communist Party of the Soviet Union held in Moscow. 24 February 1976

Esteemed comrades,

Gentlemen,

A treaty on underground nuclear explosions for peaceful purposes between the USSR and the USA is being signed today in Moscow and Washington. For the American side it has been signed by President Ford.

The decision to draft such a treaty was made during top-level Soviet–American meetings. It has now been carried out. This is highly gratifying for us.

It may be said with confidence that a good deed has been done. The new treaty aims to ensure that underground nuclear explosions are conducted solely for peaceful purposes and none other. It provides the necessary guarantees for this, including provisions concerning verification. The treaty will also help to promote co-operation between the USSR and the USA in the peaceful use of atomic energy and this will be of benefit to other countries as well.

In the context of agreements reached earlier, this treaty represents yet another step in a series of measures aimed at containing the arms build-up and bringing about the general and complete cessation of nuclear-weapon tests.

The political significance of the treaty undoubtedly also lies in the fact that this is a practical step towards the positive development of relations between the Soviet Union and the United States of America.

While speaking about the success achieved – the conclusion of a treaty on peaceful nuclear explosions – one cannot but note that there remain major problems which need to be solved. Among them is the problem of completing the elaboration of a new long-term agreement between the USSR and the USA on the limitation of strategic arms. In this connection I would like to emphasise once again that, as before, the Soviet Union is doing all it can – all that depends on it – to achieve this.

In co-operation with other states we are ready to promote vigorously a broad range of undertakings that would help curtail the arms race and achieve disarmament. There is no objective more noble and humane than that of strengthening peace and international security and definitely removing the threat of war from relations among states.

Guided by this objective, the 25th Congress of our Party advanced a programme of concrete actions, whose implementation would not only put an end to the dangerous arms build-up which is still continuing, but also ensure a resolute turn towards the actual reduction of existing stockpiles of weapons, towards genuine disarmament.

Governments and responsible statesmen must clearly realise that the urgent necessity to solve these questions is dictated by life itself.

Speech at the ceremony of the signing in the Kremlin of a Treaty on Underground Nuclear Explosions for Peaceful Purposes between the Union of Soviet Socialist Republics and the United States of America. 28 May 1976

You say that the opinion is being voiced in the West that a relaxation of international tension benefits only the Soviet Union and other socialist countries. Such a viewpoint seems to us strange, to say the least.

Certainly we did not, nor do we now, make a secret of the fact that the plans for the internal development of the Soviet Union rest on an expectation that there will be assured peaceful external conditions, and therefore *détente* is good for us. But does peace bode ill for other peoples? Is there really a people who can hope to gain something from unleashing a world war with the use of up-to-date means of mass destruction?

Let us take a closer look at what a relaxation of tension brings. This is the road from confrontation to co-operation, from threats and sabre-rattling to a negotiated solution of disputed issues and, generally, to a reshaping of international relations on the sound foundation of peaceful coexistence, mutual respect and mutual advantage.

All this creates conditions for fruitful contacts between states, the development of commercial and economic relations, and the expansion of scientific, technological and cultural exchanges. We are aware that this, too, is something referred to as a one-way street, supposedly benefiting the Soviet Union only. Thus it turns out that everything good, everything positive in international affairs benefits the Soviet Union alone. Thanks for a very flattering opinion, but, of course, the real situation is different.

Those who think we need contacts and exchanges in the fields of economy, science and technology more than anyone else are mistaken. Soviet imports from the capitalist countries account for less than $1\frac{1}{2}$ per cent of the country's gross social product. It is clear that this is not of decisive importance for the development of the Soviet economy.

It is quite obvious that a relaxation of tension is needed by all countries which take part in normal international intercourse. It is therefore no exaggeration to say that the attitude to *détente* is today a yardstick for evaluating the policy of any state and the true worth of any statesman.

I should like to emphasise that we assess international developments above all by the degree of progress achieved towards strengthening peace and eliminating the danger of a nuclear war. It is our opinion that definite positive results have been attained in this field in recent years.

Much has been done to make the necessity of peaceful coexistence of states with different social systems recognised. Clear-cut principles on which peaceful coexistence should rest have been worked out. A number of important inter-state agreements to this effect, both on a bilateral and a multilateral basis, including the Final Act of the European Conference, have been signed. Constructive co-operation in economic, scientific, technological and cultural fields is being established step by step.

But to ensure that these healthy trends become really irreversible, it is necessary to curb the arms race, to set a limit to it and then to scale it down.

Otherwise, much of what has been achieved as a result of great efforts may one day be lost.

Some progress has been achieved in arms limitation in recent years. But it cannot be regarded as satisfactory.

We are surprised at the stand taken on this issue by the governments of some Western countries. Nobody seems to deny, at least in words, that arms reduction is important, but in fact spokes are being put in the wheels, so to say. Some circles in Western countries persistently spread allegations about a Soviet menace, speculating on the fear they themselves assiduously incite.

Yes, the Soviet Union has impressive armed forces. But we declare clearly and unequivocally: the Soviet Union has never threatened and is not threatening anyone and is ready at any time to reduce our armed forces on a reciprocal basis.

We are forced to improve our defences; I repeat, we are forced to do so, because we are faced with an unbridled arms race. Every now and then one hears statements to the effect that NATO's leading power 'must be the strongest in the world' and that NATO as a whole must build up armaments so as to bring constant pressure to bear on the Soviet Union and other socialist countries. It is this that spurs on so vigorously the arms race in the world today.

If someone is really worried about the level of the Soviet armed forces, then, it would seem, there would be all the more reason for the other side to get down in earnest to reducing armaments and advancing step by step towards a great goal—general disarmament. We are ready to take part in the working out of binding international agreements and we have made specific proposals to this effect at the United Nations, in particular at the current General Assembly session, and at the Vienna talks. I will not repeat them here. I will only say that the struggle against the build-up of armaments has become extremely urgent. Therefore, it merits special attention from high-ranking leaders of states.

Interview on French television given in Moscow. 5 October 1976

Today there is no greater task in the struggle for lasting peace than *to put an end to the arms race,* unleashed by imperialist powers, and to go over to *disarmament.* The fact is, that the aggressive circles of the capitalist world in the face of their defeats in social battles, their loss of colonial possessions, the increasing number of countries rejecting capitalism, the successes of world socialism and the growing influence of communist parties in bourgeois states, are feverishly intensifying military preparations. Military budgets are swelling, new types of armaments are being created, bases are being set up, military demonstrations are taking place. Acting from the 'position of strength', imperialism seeks to preserve the possibility of dominating over other countries and nations, which is slipping away from it.

Striving to prop up their policy 'ideologically', so to say, the imperialist inspirers of the arms race resort to any means, and even do not particularly care for elementary logic. When they require new credits for armaments, they frighten their parliamentarians and the public with the 'superior Soviet might', but when they want to show the electorate their concern for defence, they assure them of the 'absolute military superiority of the West'.

As to our defence, we spend on it exactly as much as is necessary for ensuring the Soviet Union's security, safeguarding, along with the fraternal countries, the gains of socialism and discouraging the potential aggressors from attempting to settle in their favour the historical contest between the two opposite social systems by force. To maintain the country's armed forces at a high level also in the future, to see to it that Soviet soldiers will always have the most up-to-date weaponry, the power of which the imperialists could not ignore, is our duty to the people, and we shall fulfil this as our sacred duty!

At the same time we have no greater desire than to use the resources, which now of necessity are being diverted from the national economy, for raising the people's living standards, for constructive purposes. We are prepared, even starting tomorrow, to implement disarmament measures – be they large and radical, or, for a start, only partial – but only on a truly fair and reciprocal basis. On our part, we are ready!

Years ago Lenin spoke of disarmament as the 'ideal of socialism'. At that time there existed no real prerequisites for halting the development of militarism and for averting the threat of a world war. Today the situation has changed. The forces of socialism and peace exert such a strong influence that it has become possible to achieve progress in carrying out this task, which is so vital for all mankind, even if it is gradual and takes place only in individual

51

sectors. Moreover, among the ruling quarters of capitalist states there is a gradually growing awareness that in the nuclear age to count on unleashing a new world holocaust is as futile as it is disastrous and criminal.

In recent years the joint efforts of the peace-loving forces, with the most active contribution of our country, have led to substantial results in the matter of lessening the threat of a new, nuclear war. Concrete, binding international treaties and agreements have been concluded on such matters as putting an end to many types of nuclear tests, on taking measures against proliferation of nuclear weapons, on their non-deployment in space, on sea and ocean floor, on carrying on strategic arms limitation by the Soviet Union and the United States, on prohibiting and eliminating bacteriological weapons. Those are not bad results at all. They disprove the arguments of the sceptics who proclaim the struggle for disarmament as hopeless. But what has been achieved needs to be consolidated and further developed in order to effectively put an end to the new arms race.

You will remember, comrades, in what an urgent and principled way the question of disarmament was discussed at our 25th Party Congress. After the congress, the Political Bureau has repeatedly discussed ways of providing a new impetus for the struggle for this most important goal. It has been decided, among other things, to advance a number of concrete proposals at the current session of the UN General Assembly.

The Soviet Union proposed to conclude a World Treaty on the Non-Use of Force in International Relations. A detailed description of this document was given at the session of the UN General Assembly. Here I only wish to stress that our proposal on the non-use of force covers the inter-state relations without infringing the people's inalienable right to struggle for their social and national emancipation. We strictly distinguish between these two spheres.

The USSR also submitted to the UN a comprehensive document — a memorandum proposing a broad and all-round programme of disarmament measures, which are most topical at the moment.

In short, our country has again proposed to the world's nations a concrete programme for disarmament. So that this programme will be as realistic as possible, it contains essentially new elements. The positions of many states on a number of questions have been taken into account, of course, without prejudice to the interests of our security. To be flexible, we are prepared to start implementing either all the measures stipulated in the programme, or, for a start, only some of them, progressing step by step.

Disarmament must become the common cause of all states without exception. Our proposals to convene a world disarmament conference or, at first, as a step in this direction, to call a special session of the UN General Assembly, serve this purpose.

The Soviet Union's new proposals in the UNO have met with understanding and the support of dozens of states and the broad circles of peace-loving public. This pleases us and inspires us to new efforts in the name of lasting peace on earth!

I want to note specially that the Soviet Union continues to regard as a most important task a successful conclusion of the Vienna negotiations on reducing armed forces and armaments in Central Europe. We have made there some concrete proposals which would lead to a reduction of the military forces confronting each other in Europe without harming the interests of any of the sides. We are prepared to discuss counter-proposals based on the same principles. We are prepared to conduct jointly further constructive search (but really constructive and fair, and not aimed at getting unilateral advantages), to hold negotiations with our partners at any level, including the very highest.

Dear comrades, if we want to mention our main achievement in international affairs, we can say with a clear conscience: as a result of our efforts made in concert with the other socialist states and with the support of all peace-loving and realistically minded forces, we *have succeeded in lessening the threat of nuclear war, in making peace more reliable and stable.*

We can all rejoice and take pride in such a result, comrades! The winner here is the whole of mankind!

Speech at the Plenary Meeting of the Central Committee of the Communist Party of the Soviet Union. 25 October 1976

Everywhere our great nation is absorbed in peaceful creative work, it is engaged in an undertaking of tremendous scope and historical importance. And the Soviet people do not want the threat of war to weigh down on them like a heavy burden. The 25th Congress instructed the Central Committee to intensify efforts to ensure a lasting peace. And that is what we are doing, perseveringly and, I would say, consistently.

Soviet people fervently support the Party's foreign policy. They know that this policy is designed to safeguard their country against war and that it accords with the interests of all nations, that it opens vast vistas for promoting friendship and co-operation between nations and advances the cause of social progress on our planet. At many meetings and rallies, in thousands upon thousands of letters to the Central Committee of the CPSU, to newspapers, radio and television, they highly praise the Central Committee, its Political Bureau and the Soviet Government for their unremitting struggle for peace.

No other country has ever offered the world such a sweeping, clear-cut and realistic programme for lessening and then fully eliminating the danger of another war as the Soviet Union.

This programme includes such a global measure as the conclusion of a world treaty on the non-use of force in international relations. It encompasses all the key problems relating to the arms drive and maps out effective measures to curb it, to achieve disarmament. This programme is aimed at preventing the appearance of new types and new systems of weapons of mass destruction, and at putting a total ban on nuclear tests. The Soviet Union has proposed to the United States that they refrain, on the basis of reciprocity, from creating new types of submarines and strategic bombers.

All of our peaceful initiatives accord with the common political line of the fraternal socialist countries in the international arena. We are working together to promote these initiatives. The proposals advanced by the Soviet Union and its friends are supported by dozens of countries at the United Nations, by the popular masses on all continents.

Fresh convincing proof of the peaceful nature of the defensive alliance of the socialist states — Bulgaria, Hungary, the German Democratic Republic, Poland, Romania, the Soviet Union and Czechoslovakia — is the important proposals they set forth at a recent meeting of the Political Consultative Committee of the Warsaw Treaty Organisation. They call on the participants in the European conference to pledge not to be the first to use nuclear weapons against one another and not to take actions that could lead to an increase in membership of the Warsaw Treaty Organisation and NATO.

We believe that the noble ideas of peace upheld by the Leninist Party and the Soviet state will ultimately be translated into reality.

But this can be achieved only through struggle, precisely through struggle, comrades, because our constructive proposals often come up against mute opposition and at times open resistance.

When, for example, the members of the Warsaw Treaty Organisation raised the question of not being the first to use nuclear weapons, NATO's reply amounted to the following: no, that won't do, for we want to retain the ability to threaten the Soviet Union with nuclear weapons. We hope, however, that those who have the final say in matters of national policy will exercise realism with respect to our proposal.

Here is another example. At the talks on the reduction of armed forces and armaments in Central Europe we are told in effect: you should reduce more and we shall reduce less. This position certainly will not facilitate progress of the talks.

Behind all that one feels the pressure exerted by the more aggressive forces of imperialism, the military and the military-industrial quarters and politicians bogged down in the mire of anti-Sovietism, the 'hawks' as they are called in the West. It is precisely on their orders that intelligence agencies, military staffs and all sorts of institutes draw up bulky reports and treatises that interpret in a most arbitrary way the policy of the Soviet Union and its measures to strengthen its defence capability. And all that misinformation is, as if by command, circulated far and wide by news agencies, the press, radio and television. Frankly, we are tired of that blather. In the West, too, when serious politicians are asked whether they feel concerned over this alleged Soviet threat, their reply is an emphatic No.

Of course, we are improving our defences. We cannot do otherwise. We have never yielded, and shall never yield in matters of our own security or the security of our allies.

However, the allegations that the Soviet Union is going beyond what it actually needs for its national defence, that it is trying to attain superiority in weapons in order to deal 'the first blow', are absurd and totally unfounded. Not so long ago, at a meeting I had with a group of leading US businessmen, I said, and today I want to repeat it, that the Soviet Union has always been and remains strongly opposed to such concepts.

Our efforts are directed precisely at averting the first strike and the second strike, indeed at averting nuclear war in general. Our approach on these questions can be formulated as follows: the defence potential of the Soviet Union must be at a level that would deter anyone from attempting to disrupt our peaceful life. Not superiority in weapons, but a course aimed at reducing armaments, at easing the military confrontation – such is our policy.

On behalf of the Party and the entire people, I hereby declare that our country will never embark on the road of aggression, will never raise the sword against other nations.

It is not we, but certain forces in the West that are stepping up the arms race, particularly the nuclear arms race. It is not we, but those forces that are swelling military budgets by throwing money – hundreds of billions – into the bottomless pit of military preparations. It is those forces that represent an aggressive line in international politics today under the false pretext of a 'Soviet menace'.

Unless this line is duly rebuffed, the threat of war will grow anew. This line is dangerous to the peoples both in the East and in the West. The Soviet Union will do all it can to counter it and expose the danger it presents.

From the experience of recent years we know that the policy of capitalist states can sometimes be determined by other forces – forces which realise the danger of playing with fire and which are capable of reckoning with the realities of the present-day world. We hope that notwithstanding all the hesitations and an inclination towards phrasemongering which is often dictated by the domestic situation, reasonableness and a sober approach to the problems of world politics will prevail in those states.

Indeed, it is precisely such an approach that made possible a change in the relations between the USSR and France, the conclusion of the well-known treaties between the USSR and the Federal Republic of Germany, the quadripartite agreement on West Berlin, and important agreements between the Soviet Union and the United States and other capitalist countries, and the convening of the Conference on Security and Co-operation in Europe. In other words, *détente* was set in motion.

What is *détente*, or a relaxation of tensions? What meaning do we invest in this term? *Détente* means, first and foremost, ending the cold war and going over to normal, stable relations among states. It means a willingness to settle differences and disputes not by force, not by threats and sabre-rattling, but by peaceful means, at a conference table. It means trust among nations and the willingness to take each other's legitimate interests into consideration.

Practice has shown that the international atmosphere can be perceptibly changed within a short time. Contacts between countries in the political, economic, cultural and other fields have been broadened. And the most important thing, comrades, is that the danger of a new all-out war has been reduced. People are giving a sigh of relief and are becoming more hopeful about the future. This is *détente*; these are its obvious results.

What can the cold-war generals offer in place of *détente*? Higher taxes and greater military expenditure? A further cut in allocations for social needs? Building up stockpiles of weapons of mass destruction? A whipping up of war hysteria and of fear of the future? This will not be accepted by the peoples. Definitely not.

A relaxation of international tension, as we all know, has been achieved at the price of tremendous efforts. And it is not easy to preserve the political capital of *détente* that has been accumulated. But no difficulties and obstacles will make us retreat. There is no task more urgent and vital than making peace lasting and inviolable.

Statesmen who are aware of their responsibility before millions of people, of their responsibility for the destinies of nations, should keep in mind the desire of the peoples for peace. As for the Soviet Union, it will not fail to do its duty in this.

Speech in the city of Tula on 18 January 1977

In our foreign policy we and our socialist allies firmly adhere to the Leninist course of peace. Developing and deepening co-operation with countries which have freed themselves from the colonial yoke, and co-operating, where this is possible, with realistically minded circles in bourgeois states, the countries of socialism come forward with concrete initiatives directed at improving the world's political climate. Precisely such proposals were made by the members of the Warsaw Treaty Organisation at the November meeting of their Political Consultative Committee. The consistent struggle by the socialist community for peace and security for all nations is widely welcomed among the European and world public.

But there still exist in the world of capitalism influential political circles interested in disrupting the constructive international dialogue. The reactionary forces of the old world will not reconcile themselves to the growth and consolidation of the new.

For instance, they do not want to reconcile themselves to the free, independent policy and progressive development of African and Asian states that have freed themselves from colonial oppression. The latest instances of this are the interference of NATO countries in the internal military conflict in Zaire and the new campaign of slander against the People's Republic of Angola. It is also shown by the dastardly assassinations a few days ago of two prominent leaders of the national-liberation struggle – the President of the People's Republic of the Congo, Marien Ngouabi, and the Chairman of the Progressive Socialist Party of Lebanon, Kamel Joumblatt. The Soviet people wrathfully condemn these murders.

With no less persistence 'operations' are conducted against the world of socialism. Attempts are being made to weaken the socialist community, and various means are employed in an effort to undermine the unity of its members. Attempts are also made to weaken the socialist system.

Our opponents would like to find forces of some sort opposed to socialism inside our countries. Since there are no such forces, because in socialist society there are no oppressed or exploited classes or oppressed or exploited nationalities, some sort of substitute has been invented and an ostensible 'internal opposition' in socialist countries is being fabricated by means of false publicity. That is the reason for the organised clamour about the so-called 'dissidents' and why a world-wide hullabaloo is being raised about 'violations of human rights' in socialist countries.

What can be said about this? In our country it is not forbidden 'to think differently' from the majority, to criticise different aspects of public life. We regard the comrades who come out with well-founded criticism, who strive for improvement, as well-intentioned critics, and we are grateful to them. Those who criticise wrongly we regard as people who are mistaken.

It is a different matter when a few individuals, who have estranged themselves from our society, actively oppose the socialist system, embark on the road of anti-Soviet activity, violate the laws, and, finding no support inside the country, turn for support abroad, to imperialist subversive centres – those engaged in propaganda and intelligence. Our people demand that such so-called public figures be treated as opponents of socialism, as persons acting against their own Motherland, as accomplices, if not agents, of imperialism. Naturally, we take and will continue to take measures against them under

Soviet law.

And in this matter let no one take offence: to protect the rights, freedoms and security of the 260 million Soviet people from the activities of such renegades is not only our right, but also our sacred duty. It is our duty to the people who, 60 years ago, under the guidance of the Party of Lenin, embarked on the road of building socialism and communism, to the people who, defending their socialist Motherland, their right to live the way they want, sacrificed 20 million lives in the great war against the fascist aggressors – precisely for the freedom and rights of the peoples – and who will never depart from that road!

As for the Soviet Union, we do not interfere in the internal affairs of other countries although, of course, we have our own, quite definite opinion about the order reigning in the world of imperialism, and we make no secret of this opinion. In full accordance with the decisions of the 25th CPSU Congress, we strive to build our relations with capitalist countries on the basis of long-term mutually advantageous co-operation in various spheres in the interests of strengthening universal peace.

Now a few words on the problem of limiting arms and attaining disarmament, which was defined by the 25th Congress as the central problem of ensuring peace and the security of nations.

I have already touched upon the Soviet–American Strategic Arms Limitation Talks. Banning all nuclear weapon tests is an extremely important, pressing issue. Its settlement would exert a beneficial influence on our planet's life both in a direct, biological, and in a moral-political sense. It is no less important, also, that such a settlement should limit the possibilities of qualitatively perfecting nuclear arms and developing new types of such weapons.

For a long time the opponents of a complete ban on nuclear weapon tests had cited the difficulties involved in settling the question of control. We are still convinced, and our view is supported by specialists, that national means of detection are quite sufficient to exercise control. And yet, to remove the obstacles from the road to agreement, the Soviet Union has taken a serious step to meet the Western powers half-way. Our draft treaty on the complete and general prohibition of nuclear weapon tests now includes a provision for on-the-spot inspection, on a voluntary basis, should doubts arise about any country's failing to honour the treaty commitments. This is a reasonable compromise which takes into account the positions of all sides.

Naturally, a complete stop to nuclear weapon tests can be effected only when all nuclear powers accede to the treaty. Only then will the treaty truly serve its purpose.

We are closely following the reaction in various countries to the proposal by the Warsaw Treaty countries to the effect that all the participants in the European Conference should undertake not to be the first to use nuclear weapons against each other. We would like Western statesmen, and first of all members of NATO, to give serious thought to the meaning of this important proposal and abandon the formal, mechanical approach which is to reject a proposal as dangerous only because it comes from the other side.

It is high time to realise that a policy based on the nuclear threat and on the readiness to use nuclear weapons is becoming increasingly dangerous for mankind. From the first day of the advent of nuclear weapons the Soviet Union has come out for their prohibition and destruction. Such was its stand when the United States had a monopoly on nuclear weapons, and such is it now when the nuclear potentials of the USSR and the United States have been generally acknowledged as equal.

When disarmament questions are discussed one often hears talk about the possibility and usefulness of introducing the practice of reciprocal example, that is of a state taking constructive action in the hope that others will respond in the same spirit. Perhaps, such a method could also be used. But it will be effective only if there is mutual goodwill and mutual trust.

I will cite one concrete example. Talks on the reduction of armed forces and armaments in Central Europe began 4 years ago. On *reduction*. What could be more logical and natural, it would seem, than for the participants in the talks to refrain at least from increasing their armed forces in this area while the talks are in progress? Precisely this step has been proposed several times by the USSR and its allies. For a number of years now we have refrained from increasing the size of our armed forces in Central Europe. How have NATO countries reacted to this example set by us? They have continued to build up their armed forces in this region.

What are we to do now? Maybe the Soviet Union should follow the example of the Western powers? But this is a negative example and, frankly speaking, we would not like to follow it.

Today we declare once again: we are prepared to refrain from increasing the numerical strength of our troops in Central Europe till agreement on the reduction of armed forces and armaments in that area is reached, provided, of course, that the NATO forces there will not grow either. Accept this proposal, esteemed partners in the talks, accept it as the first real step on the road to reducing armed forces! To be sure, nobody stands to lose from this, while the cause of peace and the cause of the security of nations will only gain.

Comrades,

The Soviet people have weathered many trials. They have gone through the flames of war, experienced the agony of loss and the joy of victory. The happy life which the Soviet people have created for themselves by their own hands is a well-deserved reward. A well-deserved reward are also the 32 peaceful years which we have already had since the end of the war. This, I believe, is the longest period of peace in the entire centuries-long history of our country. At the same time wars and armed conflicts have flared up in the world more than a hundred times during the period since 1945 alone.

The Soviet people appreciate the peace-oriented policy of their Party. They are prepared to do, and are doing, everything that is necessary to make peace stable, lasting and reliable. And I can say, comrades, that for me, just as for every one of us Communists to whom the Party and the people have entrusted the country's foreign policy matters, there is no greater duty and no greater happiness than to work in the name of this wonderful, humane aim.

Speech at the 16th Congress of the Trades Unions of the USSR. 21 March 1977

As for the international situation as a whole, the main direction of the effort to consolidate *détente* and achieve a lasting peace still consists in the task of restraining the arms race and of going over to a real reduction of armaments. Progress in talks between the USSR and the USA on these problems can certainly have considerable significance in this respect.

We are continuing the talks with the aim of concluding a new, a second, agreement on limiting strategic offensive arms. The guidelines for such an agreement were determined by the well-known 1974 Vladivostok accords. Successful completion of this great work would be of fundamental significance from the point of view of the general climate of Soviet–US relations and would undoubtedly serve to stimulate new and still more far-reaching international actions to curb the arms race.

We are confident that this would definitely help to solve such important problems as the banning of all kinds of nuclear weapon tests, the banning of new types and systems of weapons of mass destruction, and the limitation of the development and testing of a number of other kinds of arms.

I feel that attempts should also be made to discuss in detail such questions as the abolition of foreign military bases in the Indian Ocean and the withdrawal of ships carrying nuclear weapons from the Mediterranean. These questions should be settled on a mutually acceptable basis for the benefit of peace and the security of peoples.

In short, one can see that there are good prospects here. We feel that these prospects are completely realistic if all the participants in the talks show a sincere desire to strengthen peace and a true readiness to seek solutions that do not damage the interests of some states and do not give unilateral advantages to others. This is precisely the direction in which the Soviet Union will act.

The struggle to strengthen peace is not a policy of the moment for the Soviet Union. It is our principled course. When we set forth proposals aimed at strengthening *détente* in contemporary conditions, we also think constantly about its future and work to ensure its long-range prospects for many years and even decades ahead.

It is necessary to combine efforts so that the indicator of the world's political barometer should not constantly waver but should always point to 'clear'. This places a great responsibility on all who initiated the process of *détente*, who safeguarded its first moves and who are introducing this policy into the broad arena of international life today.

Speech in the Kremlin at a dinner in honour of Urho Kaleva Kekkonen, President of the Finnish Republic. 17 May 1977

First of all I would like to emphasise that in the past 3 years the process of *détente*, the development of all forms of equitable co-operation in the interests of all states and peoples, and the establishment of the principles of peaceful coexistence in international relations have become a reality, and it is to an increasing extent determining the course and nature of world developments.

Moreover, the atmosphere of *détente* is gradually becoming part of the everyday life of people, it is becoming an everyday fact.

One only needs to look at how economic, cultural, sports and other ties have grown between dozens of countries and how international tourism has expanded in order to realise the progress achieved in the development of peaceful co-operation as compared to the period of the so-called cold war and sharp confrontation.

But nevertheless, we have never thought that everything has already been done and that one can calmly reap the fruits of *détente*. We are only at the beginning of a restructuring of international relations, which all of us will have to carry out together. I say 'all of us' because *détente* should be universal and all-embracing. In our time, when technology, including military technology, is developing so rapidly, when the interconnection of various areas of the world is becoming ever closer, any local conflict can easily develop into a global one.

You mentioned the arms race. Unfortunately, it is continuing and even mounting. The latest NATO recommendations aimed at increasing the military spending of the members of that organisation, the continuously swelling military budget of the United States and that country's constant efforts to create more and more new types of weapons – all this shows that the ground is being prepared for a new spiral of the arms race. We are deeply convinced that the task of limiting armaments is central for preserving peace and further developing *détente*. If this diabolical race is not stopped, we will all once again find ourselves on the brink of the unpredictable, as in the years of the cold war.

That is why our country is working so persistently and steadfastly for the adoption of effective measures for ending the arms race and ultimately achieving disarmament. No other country in the world has come forward with so many initiatives in this respect and advanced so many proposals as the Soviet Union. I declare with all responsibility that we are ready to support any proposal that would really lead to the termination of the arms race, but we definitely will not support proposals that contain only words about arms reduction and in reality are nothing but attempts to upset the balance of strength and to secure one-sided military advantages and thereby jeopardise the security of other countries.

We are realists and therefore, of course, we are clearly aware of the difficulties involved in solving these problems. However, it is precisely as realists that we declare that important prerequisites now exist in the world for making *détente* stable and irreversible, for concentrating the efforts of states on achieving a breakthrough on the question of disarmament.

Much depends here, of course, on public opinion. We know that in all countries, including France, broad sections of the public are deeply concerned about the question of disarmament. They have for a long time insisted that declarations in favour of disarmament be backed up by practical action, that a breakthrough on the matter of disarmament become a reality of world politics. We in the Soviet Union have deep respect for the views of these sections. They represent the aspirations of the peoples of the world and should be respected everywhere.

Answers to questions from Le Monde.
15 June 1977

Much has been said and written lately about the world situation becoming complicated. This is so, indeed. For it is a fact that the progress of the most important talks on restricting the arms race has slowed down. It is a fact that certain imperialist circles have unleashed a hostile propaganda campaign against the socialist countries, a campaign that is actually conducted in the cold-war spirit and does not contribute at all to promoting trust among the participants in international relations or to improvement of the international climate.

Propaganda is not the point, of course. It does not frighten us because we know that our ideas are right. The point is that the hostile propaganda campaign is being used as a smokescreen for another round of the arms race. This connection became particularly obvious after the United States took the decision to develop the production of cruise missiles and to allocate funds for the neutron bomb.

That decision has caused concern among the public all over the world, including in countries that are allies of the United States. There are serious grounds for such concern. It is important, however, that matters should not stop at expressions of regret. If humanity does not want the danger of war to grow it must act to strengthen peace, act energetically and without delay.

While we see negative features in the development of international relations, we do not at all consider that they alone determine the situation in the world. For successful and varied development of peaceful co-operation among dozens of states with different social systems is taking place now. This, it must be noted, is proceeding along the lines mapped out collectively at the European Conference in Helsinki.

Things may not be moving spectacularly here, but they are moving, and it would be a mistake to underestimate this process. It can be said that the results of the first stage of the Belgrade meeting of the representatives of the states which took part in the Helsinki Conference are a reflection of this trend.

Our foreign policy is well known. It is a policy of peace and international co-operation. The 25th CPSU Congress described it quite distinctly. I myself and other comrades, Members of the Political Bureau, have frequently spoken about it at various forums and meetings. I should like to stress one thing now: when a good initiative appears somewhere we are always ready to respond to it.

We are all familiar with the latest statements by US President Carter. He speaks, in particular, about the desirability of developing Soviet–American relations for the sake of a stronger world peace. Compared with previous moves by the US administration, these are positive-sounding statements. Well, if there is a desire to translate them into practical deeds we shall willingly search for mutually acceptable solutions.

In our time the destinies of the world increasingly depend on the possibility of creating in the world a healthy international climate, an atmosphere in which all forms of the policy of aggression and advocation of cold war are resolutely condemned and efforts to strengthen security and peaceful co-operation among nations are just as resolutely supported.

Speech in the Kremlin at a dinner for Josip Broz Tito, President of the Socialist Federal Republic of Yugoslavia and Chairman of the League of Communists of Yugoslavia. 16 August 1977

The changes for the better in the world, which have become especially appreciable in the 1970s, we refer to as international *détente*. These changes are tangible and specific. They consist in the recognition and enactment in international documents of a form of code of rules for honest and fair relations between countries, which erects a legal and moral-political barrier against those given to military gambles. They consist in the achievement of the first agreements – modest though they may be for the moment – for blocking some of the channels of the arms race. They consist of a whole system of agreements covering many areas of peaceful co-operation between states having different social systems.

International relations are now at a crossroads which could lead either to a greater trust and co-operation, or to a growth of mutual fears, suspicion, and arms stockpiles – one way leads ultimately to lasting peace, the other at best to the brink of war. *Détente* offers the opportunity of choosing the road of peace. To miss this opportunity would be a crime. The most important, the most pressing task now is to halt the arms race, which has engulfed the world.

Regrettably, the arms build-up continues and is acquiring ever more dangerous forms. New modifications and types of weapons of mass destruction are being developed, and it is well known on whose initiative this is being done. But every new type represents an equation having several unknown quantities in terms of political as well as military-technical or strategic consequences. Rushing from one type of arms to another – apparently with the naïve hope of retaining a monopoly on them – only accelerates the arms race, heightens mutual distrust and hampers disarmament measures.

In this connection I would like to reiterate, most forcefully, something I said earlier. The Soviet Union is effectively ensuring its defence capability, but it does not, and will not, seek military superiority over the other side. We do not seek to upset the approximate equilibrium of military strength existing at present, say, between East and West in Central Europe, or between the USSR and the USA. But in return we insist that no one else should seek to upset it in his favour.

Needless to say, maintaining the existing equilibrium is not an end in itself. We are in favour of starting a downward turn in the curve of the arms race and gradually scaling down the level of military confrontation. We want to reduce substantially and then eliminate the threat of nuclear war, the most formidable danger facing humanity. That is the objective of the well-known proposals made by the Soviet Union and other socialist countries.

Today we are proposing a radical step: *that agreement be reached on a simultaneous halt in the production of nuclear weapons by all states.* This would apply to all such weapons – whether atomic, hydrogen or neutron bombs or projectiles. At the same time, the nuclear powers could undertake to make a start on the gradual reduction of existing stockpiles of such weapons, and move towards their complete, total destruction. The energy of the atom for peaceful purposes exclusively! – this is the appeal of the Soviet state, in the year of its sixtieth anniversary, to the governments and peoples of the world.

There is another important task that has a direct bearing on the problem of reducing the danger of nuclear war, namely, that of seeing through to the end the work of banning nuclear weapons tests, so that such tests are banned entirely – underground as well as in the atmosphere, in outer space, and under water. We want to achieve progress in the negotiations on this matter and bring them to a successful conclusion. Therefore, we state that we are prepared *to reach agreement on a moratorium covering nuclear explosions for peaceful purposes, together with a ban on all nuclear weapons tests for a definite period.* We trust that this important initiative on the part of the USSR will be favourably received by our partners at the negotiations and that the road will thus be cleared for concluding a treaty long awaited by the peoples.

> *'The Great October Revolution and mankind's progress': Report at a jubilee meeting of the Central Committee of the CPSU, the Supreme Soviet of the USSR, and the Supreme Soviet of the RSFSR to mark the sixtieth anniversary of the Great October Socialist Revolution. 2 November 1977*

Such an important area of work in the foreign policy sphere as disarmament is always in the field of vision of the CPSU Central Committee and its Political Bureau. An important place in this respect is occupied, for understandable reasons, by the Soviet–American strategic offensive arms limitation talks. There is no lack of willingness on our part to bring these talks to a successful conclusion. In our opinion there exist opportunities, and very good ones, for this. To judge by some statements, the American side also expresses some optimism. We should wish this optimism to be backed by practical deeds. I think that a new agreement would be a good and important thing both for the USSR and the USA and for world peace.

The present disarmament talks cover a broad spectrum of issues – from termination of all nuclear tests and prohibition of chemical means of warfare to consolidation of relaxation of military tension in Europe and curtailing of military activities in the zone of the Indian Ocean. The initiative in raising these questions belongs, to a considerable extent if not overwhelmingly, to the Soviet Union. The main thing now is to pass over from the talks on disarmament to real steps that would mean the beginning of disarmament. This and this alone will really accord with the aspirations of the peoples who want lasting peace and who resolutely condemn actions aimed at increasing the threat of a new world war and condemn the arms race.

And such actions do occur. How else could one assess, for example, the persistent stepping up of the arms race in the NATO military bloc? This is an extremely dangerous tendency for mankind. It is becoming even more dangerous with the appearance of ever more barbarous means of warfare.

Take, for instance, the neutron bomb. This inhuman weapon, especially dangerous because it is presented as a 'tactical', almost 'innocent' one, is now being persistently foisted upon the world. In this way an attempt is being made to erase the distinction between conventional and nuclear arms, to make transition to a nuclear war outwardly unnoticeable, as it were, for the peoples. This is a downright fraud, a deception of the peoples.

The neutron bomb is being insistently recommended for deployment in Western Europe. Well, this may be an easy and simple matter for those who live far from Europe. But the Europeans, who live, figuratively speaking, under one roof, are presumably of a different opinion. They will hardly care to have an additional dangerous load placed on this common roof of theirs, which is sagging as it is under the enormous weight of weaponry.

The Soviet Union is strongly opposed to the development of the neutron bomb. We understand and wholly support the millions of people throughout the world who are protesting against it. But if such a bomb were developed in the West – developed against us, a fact which nobody even tries to conceal – it should be clearly understood there that the USSR will not remain a passive onlooker. We shall be confronted with the need to answer this challenge in order to ensure the security of the Soviet people, its allies and friends. In the final analysis, all this would raise the arms race to an even more dangerous level.

We do not want this to happen and that is why we propose reaching agreement on the mutual renunciation of the production of the neutron bomb so as to save the world from the advent of this new mass-annihilation weapon. This is our sincere desire, this is our proposal to the Western powers.

Replies to questions put by a Pravda *correspondent. 24 December 1977*

Question: There are – and not only in the FRG – apprehensions that the Soviet Union is building up its military strength qualitatively and quantitatively, systematically and consistently, to an extent surpassing defence requirements. Don't you also believe that *détente* calls for agreements in the military field as well – based on a balance?

Answer: To begin with, allow me to make the main point: the apprehensions you allude to are totally ungrounded. A Soviet military threat to Europe or any other part of the world does not and cannot exist.

First, let us look at the purely factual aspect of the matter.

Regarding Europe. The Western press and certain Western politicians and military figures often claim that in Europe, the Soviet Union and other Warsaw Treaty countries have created 'military superiority' for themselves over the NATO countries and are still building up their armed forces there.

To put it mildly, these claims are biased and misleading.

First of all, for a number of years now the Soviet Union has not expanded or built up its armed forces in Central Europe, that is, in the area which is now the subject of the Vienna negotiations. Moreover, we and our allies have persistently suggested to the Western side that an agreement should be reached there that both sides directly commit themselves not to build up their armed forces and armaments in Central Europe while the Vienna talks are going on. Unfortunately, so far the Western countries have not accepted this proposal, and, by their practical actions, are pushing in the opposite direction.

As for 'superiority', at the said Vienna negotiations the sides have exchanged official statistics from which it can be clearly seen that there is no 'superiority' or 'disproportion'. Both the West and the Warsaw Treaty countries maintain approximately equal numerical strength in Central Europe – something a little more than 980,000 men on each side.

Obviously, this equilibrium is not completely identical; each side has its own way its armed forces are structured. On our part, the ground troops are our chief missile carriers, for instance, while in the NATO bloc the air forces are the main carriers of missiles with nuclear warheads, etc.

It should be added to all this that Western politicians and top-ranking military often repeat the assertion about the qualitative superiority of, as they believe, Western armaments. The question arises: where, then, is the logic in the claim by these same circles of the imaginary 'threat from the East'?

On the whole, there is certainly a military equilibrium in Europe, where the principal forces of the two military and political groups confront each other at closest range. The question is whether this equilibrium should be maintained at the present high level, or whether it is possible to lower this level without upsetting the equilibrium in anyone's favour. We in the Soviet Union are firmly convinced that this level can and must be lowered.

As for the global balance of forces between the biggest powers – the participants in the two military–political groups, that is, the Soviet Union and the United States – an approximate parity, i.e. the equilibrium of strategic forces, has evolved and is being maintained, as both sides have officially admitted. This parity underlies the 1972 Soviet–American agreement on limiting strategic offensive arms and the one now being prepared.

I can add to this that the total numerical strength of the Soviet armed forces by no means presents any 'military threat' to the West, although it is quite sufficient for dealing, if necessary, a retaliatory blow against an aggressor – wherever he might be – in the West or in the East. By the way, objective observers, including those in the American press, are very well aware of this and admit it.

And now about our Navy. First I would like to remind you of a simple fact: the Soviet Union's sea frontiers stretch more than 40,000 km. In a situation where the NATO countries possess powerful offensive weapons at sea, we also have to think about the appropriate defence in this sphere. We have built up our ocean Navy which is in a position to meet the tasks of this defence. This Navy does not have a greater fighting capacity than that of the Western countries, and structurally, it is obviously defensive. It is no accident, for instance, that we do not have, and are not building, attack aircraft carriers.

Another pet topic of those who enjoy holding forth about the 'Soviet military threat' is the civil defence measures taken in the USSR. It sounds incredible, but it is a fact that specialists in anti-Soviet slander manage to interpret even these measures, aimed at ensuring the safety of the civilian population in the event of war, as a sign of 'aggressiveness', intimating that the USSR is preparing to deal 'the first blow' while hoping to take cover from retaliation in shelters.

It really takes pathologically distorted imagination to turn things upside down to such an extent! Do any normal people really believe such inventions?

We do not want war, and we are not preparing for war. But the Soviet people know from their own bitter experience what enormous losses to the population the aggressor's actions can cause. And we only too often hear claims made by the other side about a readiness to deal 'powerful, destructive, preemptive blows', etc., to take no defence measures. It is only the out-and-out slanderers who can interpret this as preparations for attacking anyone.

The callous quantitative approach popular in some other countries to the prospects of nuclear war – an approach according to which a certain percentage of civilian casualties is declared 'permissible' – is alien to us. We are not at all overjoyed at the predictions one can hear in the West that a world nuclear war will kill 'a mere 10 per cent' of the planet's population and that this is supposedly not so terrible, not the end of the world. We do not want anyone, not a single person, to be among those '10 per cent'.

As for the Soviet Union, our country, I repeat, does not think in terms of 'dealing the first blow'. On the contrary, it is well known that we have made an official suggestion to all those who took part in the All-European Conference, including the USA, to sign an agreement on not being the first to use nuclear weapons against each other. It is also known that the NATO countries reject this proposal, making it rather transparent that they do not wish to abandon plans of dealing the first blow against our country. So who is threatening whom?

This is the actual state of affairs.

Let us now deal with the political side of the question.

The Soviet Union is truly a mighty state; it is powerful politically, economically and militarily. But the Soviet Union is a peaceful state. Its love for peace stems from the very nature of our society, whose supreme goal, proclaimed by laws and by decisions at the highest political levels, is ensuring the steady growth of the people's material well-being and culture. There is not a single task which we intend to carry out by military means. There is not a single state against whom we have made territorial or any other claims that could result in a military clash. Besides this, the Soviet people – the Soviet leaders included – know very well and remember from their own experience what the contemporary image of war is like. People of the older generation living in the Federal Republic of Germany also have an idea of what this image is like, and perhaps they understand better than, let us say, people living in the United States, the Soviet people's ardent wish to live in peace.

Attributing some sort of sinister intentions to the Soviet Union because of its military capability is the main 'argument' in Western discourses on the overused 'Soviet war threat'. One example of this card-shuffling is the speculations about how many hours it would take the Soviet Army to reach the shores of the English Channel.

But the Soviet Union has no intentions of attacking any country either in the West or in the East, in the North or in the South. The Soviet Union has no intentions whatsoever of 'conquering' Western Europe. And our General Staff is not busily working on a time schedule for 'reaching the shores of the English Channel'. The scope of any Soviet military build-up is determined by the limits of necessary defence. And when assessing the USSR's defence needs, we should also remember our country's geographical position. The Soviet Union's genuine intentions are clearly stated in official Party and state documents. One can also judge them by the entire moral and political atmosphere in which the Soviet people live and are brought up. Propaganda of militarisation, calls for preparing for war and fanning mistrust of and hostility towards other nations are alien to this atmosphere.

The history of the Soviet state provides many examples of its love for peace. It also speaks eloquently of the real causes and sources of the danger of war. It also speaks of why we have to give serious attention to problems of the country's defence. When, in the initial post-October Revolution days, our state called for the establishment of peace, all the belligerent powers, the Western countries, responded with collective hostile intervention. When in the 1930s the USSR spoke from a high international rostrum in favour of collective security in Europe, the answer was the Munich agreement and the ensuing Hitler aggression. When the aggressor had been routed and the USSR began to rebuild its war-ravaged economy, the West launched the cold war against us and started to blackmail us with atomic weapons – apparently counting on the fact that the USSR, weakened by the war, would obey diktats from outside. And when now the USSR makes practical, realistic and far-reaching proposals for curbing the arms race, and for disarmament, the reply is the brandishing of neutron weapons.

By the way, anyone who knows post-war history will easily remember that the arms race developed according to the principle of 'action–counteraction': the West made the challenge and the Soviet Union had to accept it. It has been this way throughout – from the first A-bomb to today. And the beginning of each new spurt in the arms race has been inevitably accompanied by a new wave of cries about the 'Soviet threat'.

I would like the esteemed readers of your newspaper to remember one other thing. It was not us, but the United States of America, which established dozens of military bases, with bombers and submarines carrying both nuclear and other long-range weapons, stretching in a sinister chain along the boundaries of the USSR and of our allies in the South and in the North, in the West and in the East. I would like to propose that those who today spread far-fetched fears and hysteria about the USSR's natural defence measures, as well as those who believe these panic-mongers, imagine themselves if only for a short time in the place of the Soviet people. You see, these bases have surrounded our country for several decades now. It would be interesting to know what these nervous gentlemen would feel in a similar situation.

But the Soviet people have strong nerves. They will never panic, as they have never done before, but are only taking the necessary measures for defending the country from the threat that has appeared, and are carrying on a persistent, consistent struggle for a lasting peace, for lowering the level of military confrontation, first of all in Europe.

Frankly speaking, it seems to me that those who are busy fanning the far-fetched campaign in the West over the 'Soviet military threat' really have other things in mind. They do not want to accept the approximate equilibrium that has evolved in the two sides' military forces, but want superiority. And even that is dangerous, because that kind of approach would promote a new and unbridled race in arms production and carries the threat of military ventures. But it is time these people should finally realise one thing – the Soviet Union has always found the answer to any military challenge and, you can rest assured, will also find the appropriate answer in the future.

For its part, the Soviet Union believes that approximate equality and parity are sufficient for defence needs. We have not set ourselves the task of achieving military superiority. We also realise that the concept itself loses meaning with the existence of today's huge arsenals of stockpiled nuclear weapons and the means to deliver them.

The Soviet Union is solidly opposed to the 'balance of terror'. We favour the balance of trust. It is exactly because of this that we have so persistently proposed to develop *détente* in depth, to raise the level and enrich the content of international co-operation, to perseveringly seek an effective road first to end the arms race and then move on to disarmament.

We are prepared at any moment to sign an agreement in Vienna on reducing the level of armed forces and armaments of the sides in Central Europe by 5, 10, 20 or 50 per cent, if you so desire. But let us do this honestly – in a way that does not upset the existing correlation of forces, that does not give benefits to one side and damage to the other. Let us take the steps that are already realistic and acceptable to both sides, and let us not try to use the talks for gaining unilateral military advantages.

This is my answer to your question.

Replies to questions from Vorwärts, *weekly of the Social-Democratic Party of Germany. 4 May 1978*

3.
SECURITY AND CO-OPERATION IN EUROPE

The Peace Programme of the 24th CPSU Congress has proclaimed the Soviet Union's readiness to expand mutually beneficial co-operation in every sphere with countries also seeking such co-operation. As regards Europe, this point is stated still more explicitly: to bring about a radical turn towards *détente* and peace on that continent.

This completely accords with the common platform of the world communist movement. It is clearly stated in the Document of the 1969 International Meeting of Communist Parties that struggle for world peace is the main aspect of the joint action of Communists.

Only a little over 18 months have passed since the 24th Congress. But we can confidently say that our Party and the Soviet state have gone a long way in implementing the most important propositions of the Peace Programme.

Together with our friends and allies we have made great efforts to settle problems inherited from the Second World War, and to create a healthier political climate in the world. Our relations with many bourgeois countries, including most countries of capitalist Europe, have shifted towards *détente* and mutually beneficial co-operation.

Elements of realism in the policy of many capitalist countries are becoming ever more pronounced as the might and influence of the USSR and the fraternal socialist countries increase, as our peace-loving policy becomes more active, and as other important progressive processes successfully unfold in the modern world. First and foremost, this applies to France, whose leaders – General de Gaulle and, later, President Pompidou – some years ago took a definite course of mutually advantageous co-operation with the Soviet Union and other socialist states. This applies to the Federal Republic of Germany, the realistic foreign policy of whose government, headed by Chancellor Brandt, has had a considerable influence on the situation in Europe. This also applies to the United States of America in so far as it shows a willingness to depart from many of the cold-war dogmas that had for so long determined the orientation of all American foreign policy.

In other words, our consistent policy of peace and the entire course of events are gradually making the capitalist world recognise the necessity of dealing with the socialist states on the basis of peaceful coexistence.

The treaties between the USSR and the FRG, and between Poland and the FRG, which formalised the inviolability of the existing European frontiers, the set of agreements on West Berlin, and the treaty on the principles governing relations between the GDR and the FRG, which is being signed today in the GDR capital, the final breakthrough of the diplomatic blockade of the GDR – all these are important steps in Europe's progress towards peace and security. And all this is not any one country's gain alone, but a big victory for reason and realism in international relations.

To be sure, there remain international problems in Europe which still await a solution. Take problems like the invalidation of the Munich diktat, and the admission of the GDR and the FRG to the United Nations. Their solution would help successfully to complete the process of clearing international relations in Europe of all the elements that have burdened them throughout the post-war period.

Our people know that the two world wars burst into their homes from the West, from Europe. We remember 1941. Every Soviet citizen cherishes the memory of the 20 million compatriots who laid down their lives in the Great Patriotic War. We remember all this well as we complete the history-making work of finalising the immutability of the post-war European settlement. And we may rightly say today that none of the results of the anti-fascist liberation struggle of the peoples has been forfeited; the fruits of the great victory have been preserved and consolidated!

The Soviet Union will persevere in its policy of securing a durable peace in Europe, the policy which we have pursued throughout the post-war period and which is now yielding results that gladden the Soviet people and all who cherish peace. We value our good relations with France and will develop them in accordance with the Principles of Co-operation adopted by the two countries last year. We shall continue our efforts to improve and extend our ties with the FRG in various fields. We are prepared to develop all that is positive that has become or is becoming part of the practice of our relations with countries like Finland, our good neighbour, Italy, the Scandinavian nations and a number of other countries. We are also prepared to improve relations with those European countries with which they are as yet unsmooth – provided, of course, they show by deed a willingness to do the same.

The All-European Conference on Security and Co-operation, for which the socialist countries have worked for many years, should open a new chapter in European history. It appears that the conference will begin not later than the middle of 1973.

The peoples attach great hopes to the convocation of the all-European conference. They expect it to deal with the basic problems of strengthening European peace, to put an end to the suspicion and fear bred by the cold war, and give the Europeans confidence in the morrow. It seems that its success could introduce useful and sound elements into relations between the European countries and the non-European participants in the conference – the United States and Canada.

We shall strive to achieve meaningful results at the conference, which would be of benefit to all its participants.

Everybody knows the political principles which, in the opinion of the USSR and its allies, should constitute the basis for ensuring the security of the European nations. They are: inviolability of state frontiers, non-interference in the internal affairs of other countries, independence, equality, and renunciation of the threat or use of force.

The time has come, we believe, to put on the agenda the elaboration of a European programme of economic and cultural co-operation. This leads to the following question: is it possible to find a basis for some forms of businesslike relations between Europe's two interstate trade and economic organisations – the Council for Mutual Economic Assistance and the Common Market? It could probably be found, if the Common Market countries refrain from all attempts at discrimination of the other side, and if they help to develop natural bilateral ties and all-European co-operation.

One often hears that the West attaches importance to co-operation in the cultural domain and, especially, to exchange of ideas, extension of information, and to contacts between nations. Permit us to declare here in all earnest: we, too, are in favour of this if, of course, such co-operation is conducted with due respect for the sovereignty, the laws and the customs of each country, and if it promotes mutual spiritual enrichment of the peoples, greater trust between them, and the ideas of peace and good-neighbourliness. We are for broader tourist exchanges. We are for broad public contacts, for meetings between youths, people of related professions, for travel on a collective or individual basis. In short, the possibilities here are quite broad if the matter is dealt with in a spirit of mutual respect and non-interference in each other's affairs, and not in a cold-war spirit.

As is known, negotiations are also to be held on reducing armed forces and armaments in Europe, and, first and foremost, in the area of Central Europe. The Soviet Union favours serious preparations for, and effective conduct of, these negotiations.

The consolidation of European peace is an issue of great importance for the future of all mankind. We are doing our utmost, with all energy and determination, to make it impossible for Europe, which has long been a dangerous volcano, to give rise to another war. We are well aware that reaction, militarism, revanchists of all shades, have not abandoned attempts to reverse the course of events in Europe. But their efforts will fail. The balance of forces on the continent is in favour of peace and peaceful co-operation. And we believe that wars can be eliminated from the life of the European peoples.

Report at a gala joint meeting of the CPSU Central Committee, the USSR Supreme Soviet and the RSFSR Supreme Soviet, in the Kremlin Palace of Congresses. 21 December 1972

We Communists are fighting for a relaxation of tension not just in order to bring about a state of tranquillity in Europe for a limited time. Our ideal in international politics – and today we can say more, our practical aim – is an inviolable peace, the only way it is possible to ensure genuinely equal co-operation between sovereign European states, regardless of their social system, size and other differences. The establishment of a lasting peace will be a fitting tribute to the exploit of all who, in the years of World War II, selflessly fought on the side of the anti-Hitler coalition for the freedom and happiness of nations, to smash the Nazi tyranny. European peace must be based on a secure and reliable foundation so that not only the present but future generations, too, can enjoy the benefits of peaceful development.

In whatever they do the socialist countries go into it seriously and thoroughly. This fully applies to the treaties and agreements of recent years, which have largely determined the change for the better on the European continent. If we put our signature to treaties this means that we are firmly resolved to observe strictly and fully the letter and spirit of these documents. We expect the same approach from our partners who sign these treaties. Otherwise aboveboard businesslike co-operation is impossible.

Everybody remembers the feverish atmosphere in Europe when the 'cold war' architects were trying to build up an atmosphere of confrontation and enmity between the two German states. The coming into force of the Treaty on the Bases of Relations between the German Democratic Republic and the Federal Republic of Germany, which was endorsed by the West German Bundestag the other day, is to put an end to this abnormal situation. I trust that all of us agree this treaty is highly important not only for normalising relations between the GDR and the FRG as two independent sovereign states, but also for the further relaxation of tension in Europe and consolidation of international peace.

The aim that we have set of establishing relations of good-neighbourliness and co-operation between the East and West of Europe demands, of course, reciprocal efforts on the part of the other side. This cannot be achieved without political courage, without an awareness of the real interests of one's own country and of the broader interests of peace in Europe. Anyone who wants a lasting peace must necessarily pay due credit to all the steps which have been made in this direction.

Speech on the occasion of the presentation of the Order of Lenin to Erich Honecker, First Secretary of the Central Committee of the Socialist Unity Party of Germany. 13 May 1973

I believe it would not be amiss to recall today the important conclusion arrived at by the International Conference of Communist and Workers' Parties held in Moscow 4 years ago. This conclusion is: 'The struggle against a military danger, against a danger of a world thermonuclear war that continues threatening the peoples with mass destruction, the struggle for world peace remains the main issue in the joint activity of the anti-imperialist forces.'

Any desire to impose its own rules on anyone is alien to the socialist countries. Revolutions are not exported. But we always fight resolutely against the export of counter-revolution, against imperialist interference in the internal affairs of the peoples. Each nation must exercise its inalienable right to choose its own social system, to decide its own destiny.

For this the socialist countries have over many years been waging a consistent struggle for a firm and enduring peace, the benefits of which could be enjoyed not only by the present generation but also by generations to come. In the course of implementing its Peace Programme, the Soviet Union has since the 24th CPSU Congress taken a number of major steps towards the further strengthening of international security.

One of the most important steps has been the Agreement on the Prevention of Nuclear War, signed between the Soviet Union and the United States. We do not doubt that implementation of this agreement, as of the other Soviet–American agreements, is not only in the interests of the Soviet and American peoples, but also makes for a general improvement in the political climate in the international arena, is in the interests of the entire socialist community and is the cause of social progress.

The European Conference on Security and Co-operation has successfully begun its work in Helsinki. Given the good will of all its participants, it can and must become a milestone in the strengthening of European peace. The Soviet Union made a big contribution to the preparations for the all-European conference, and we shall strive to ensure that this important international cause reaches a completely successful culmination.

In short, the essence of the positive changes in world policy lies in that reorganisation of international relations on which a start has been made on the basis of the principles of peaceful coexistence, i.e. the very same principles Lenin advanced when socialism was first becoming established.

This, of course, is not a simple matter. It calls for political soberness, adherence to principle, and persistence, because relations between states with differing social systems are involved. We firmly adhere to Marxist–Leninist ideology, the ideology of the working class. The capitalist states have their own, bourgeois ideology. But we consider that this should not prevent specific steps to ease tension, the taking of agreed measures to relieve mankind forever of the threat of a nuclear war.

The Soviet Union deems it necessary to press step by step for practical measures towards not only political but also military *détente*. The depth and soundness of the basis created for the relaxation of tension, the entire cause of strengthening peace will largely depend on the solution of these problems.

Marching shoulder to shoulder with the fraternal socialist countries, the Soviet Union sees to it that the edifice of peace is erected on a firm foundation of respect for the sovereignty and independence of each country, each nation, and that the process of *détente* is of a global, all-embracing character.

Speech at a luncheon given by the CPSU Central Committee, Presidium of the USSR Supreme Soviet and Government of the USSR in honour of the Party and Government Delegation of the Vietnam Workers' Party. 10 July 1973

The climate in the world has noticeably changed. It has become warmer, and people are now living in conditions of greater tranquillity.

In such an atmosphere, it is easier to concentrate on the accomplishment of peaceful and constructive tasks, on deeds that are really worthy of man.

Such changes, taking place on the initiative and with the active participation of socialist states, are fully in line with the ideals of socialism, the communist ideals in the field of international relations, of which Marx and Engels, and later V. I. Lenin, vividly and convincingly wrote in their day. And we, comrades, may take pride in that it is our good fortune to contribute in some measure, through our work, through our efforts, to bringing about such a situation where these noble ideals have begun to be put into life.

All this, of course, does not mean, comrades, that the difference has vanished between the two social systems – socialism and capitalism. The bourgeois states remain bourgeois, while the socialist states continue to be socialist. We must not forget that there are states where influential quarters are out to see the world continue to live in a state of fever and tension, to see inflated military budgets and to see the arms race go on. We have been and remain principled opponents of imperialism. We firmly stand for an end to the arms race, we want political *détente* to be backed by a military one.

Competition, rivalry between the two systems in the world arena continues. The crux of the matter is only to see to it that this process does not develop into armed clashes and wars between countries, into the use of force or threat of force in relations between them, and that it does not interfere with the development of mutually advantageous co-operation between states with differing

83

social systems.

The beginning of the work of an all-European conference on security and co-operation is one of the recent developments in international life.

The idea of convening such a conference was put forward by the Soviet Union and other socialist states, which made detailed proposals concerning its aims and programme.

Our approach to European security is simple and clear. The experience of history convincingly shows what bloodshed wars — the two world wars in particular, which broke out in Europe — cost the peoples of this continent. One does not have to speak much about that here, in the Ukraine, the people of which, together with other peoples of our great homeland, experienced in full measure all the grimness and bitterness of the invasion, going through the fire of the sacred fight to rout the fascist aggressors. However, another war in Europe, now with the use of modern nuclear-missile weapons of an unprecedented destructive force, might result in the annihilation of a number of European states.

We Communists and all other citizens of the countries of the socialist community proceed from the firm conviction that international issues, including the most complex, arising between states with the same or differing social systems, can and must be resolved only by peaceful means, without the use of force or threat of force, without wars. We believe that such a path in the development of inter-state relations is all the more realistic, the more pronounced in international affairs is the influence of socialist countries — peaceloving by the very nature of their social system.

The preliminary consultations among 34 states, which continued in the Finnish capital for half a year, made it possible to draw up an agenda for the all-European conference, acceptable to all, to define the basic principles of approaching the questions to be discussed at the conference. One can, perhaps, say that these consultations were by themselves the first experience of political co-operation on the scale of a whole continent with the purpose of paving the way to a lasting peace. This alone can be regarded as a considerable achievement. I should like to say that we appreciate the constructive participation in this work, together with the European countries, of the United States and Canada, states of the Western hemisphere.

Now that the first stage of the work of the all-European conference itself is over, one can, perhaps, already speak about some first, if not results, then at least impressions. The Foreign Ministers of the participating states, big and small, on the basis of absolute equality, stated at the conference the fundamental views of their governments concerning the ways of achieving lasting peace and security in Europe, of promoting peaceful co-operation in the political, economic, scientific and cultural fields. The views, naturally, were not completely identical; moreover, they were very different on some points. And in the future, too, as it appears, there will still be discussions and arguments on a number of problems. Attempts might also be made to misuse this noble initiative, to use the all-European forum for some narrow interests or not quite seemly political manoeuvres.

However, on the whole, I think, one can say with confidence that the common denominator exists. It lies in a common desire that there should be no more wars in Europe and that reasonable conditions should be created for the development of peaceful co-operation among European states, useful to all nations. And if that is so, there is a hope for the success of the great cause, on which a start has been made, without unnecessary delay. In any case, the Soviet Union and other socialist countries will exert every effort towards ensuring such success.

Things have practically shaped up in such a way that the great and beneficial turning-point in the international situation, of which I spoke already, began largely from the improvement of relations between such big states of the socialist and capitalist world as the Soviet Union, on the one hand, and France, the Federal Republic of Germany and the United States of America, on the other. That was natural; moreover, it was necessary. If one takes, for example, the USA and the FRG, it was these countries' relations with the Soviet Union that, first of all, were characterized by tensions in the period of the 'cold war', affecting the world situation as a whole. From this point of view, as, incidentally, from many others, the improvement of relations between the Soviet Union and the FRG, between the Soviet Union and the USA is of great positive significance not only directly for the peoples of these countries, but also for each country, for each people that needs peace and that is interested in easing international tension.

One also cannot but note that now that the international climate has begun to improve, dozens of states, big, medium-size and small, are becoming more active in their policies, striving to make their own contribution to the common cause of consolidating peace. There are many illustrations of this in Europe, Asia, Africa and Latin America. And there is no need to prove that the constructive contribution of any state merits equal respect, attentive and well-wishing attitudes. And attempts to pit in this case the 'great' or even the 'super-great' (as some quarters put it) states against medium-size or small states are something absolutely unjustified, unnecessary and even harmful. We, the socialist countries, are for equal co-operation of all the states, based on complete mutual respect, on the strict observance of the sovereign rights and the inviolability of the territory of every state, and on non-interference in their domestic affairs. We are for ridding all countries, big and small, of the menace of war. Incidentally, small countries were often involved in wars againsttheir will, in the course of the world conflagrations that broke out in the past.

Speech at the joint celebration meeting of the Central Committee of the Communist Party of the Ukraine and the Supreme Soviet of the Ukrainian SSR, devoted to the presentation to the Republic of the Order of Friendship Among the Peoples. 26 July 1973

We can thus note with satisfaction that through the concerted efforts of all the peace forces the international climate has grown, on the whole, healthier in recent years, and the policy of peaceful coexistence, of peaceful co-operation between countries is yielding tangible results.

However, this is obviously only the beginning of the advance towards an objective, which, as I understand, unites all those present in this hall and all whom they represent, only the beginning of the advance towards a reliably peaceful future for humanity. We are only building up the conditions for the attainment of that objective. Our common duty is to move tirelessly forward along the chosen path, to move steadily, perseveringly along a wide front, resolutely breaking down the resistance of the adversaries of *détente* and the proponents of cold war. As we in the Soviet Union see it, the task is to make the *détente*, achieved in the decisive areas of international relations, stable, durable and, what is more, irreversible.

And in this respect, of course, much can be done, above all, in Europe. The peoples of that continent, more than of any other, have suffered from past wars, including the most terrible of all, the Second World War. On account of the present-day character of the productive forces, closed economic life in each of the 'rooms' of the 'European house' has become too crowded and uncomfortable. Besides, due to the modern means of mass destruction, the house has become an acute fire risk. As a result, maintenance of peace in Europe has essentially become an imperative necessity, and the utmost development of diverse peaceful co-operation among the European states – the only really sensible solution. A contributing factor is that an increasingly more active and important role in European life is being played by the socialist countries, which are profoundly and sincerely devoted to the cause of peace and international co-operation, while in the Western part of the continent there is a growing appreciation of the political realities, and the circles favouring these goals are winning ever more influence.

That is why we have faith in the ultimate success and the historic role of the European Conference, despite all the difficulties that are still to be overcome by those participating in that unique forum, which is now at a perhaps not very spectacular but extremely important stage of its work.

What do we expect from that Conference and what are we hoping for? To put it in the most general terms, we want to see well-defined principles of relations between European states formulated unanimously, sincerely, with heart and soul, as they say, without 'diplomatic' equivocations and misconstructions, approved by all the participants in the Conference and endorsed by all the peoples of the continent. I have in mind, for instance, such principles as the territorial integrity of all the European states, the inviolability of their frontiers, the renunciation of the use or threat of force in relations between countries, non-interference in each other's internal affairs and the promotion, on such a basis, of mutually beneficial co-operation in diverse fields.

We should like these principles to become accepted as a sacred and indisputable part of the day-to-day fabric of European life and the psychology of the European peoples. We should like these principles to be adopted by the governments and the peoples in order that they become reality.

We should like to see a dense all-European network of economic, scientific and cultural co-operation between states flourishing on the basis of these principles.

Trade has linked peoples and countries from time immemorial. The same is true of our day. But today it is disadvantageous and unreasonable to confine economic co-operation solely to trade. Broad international division of labour is the only basis for keeping pace with the times and abreast of the requirements and potentialities of the scientific and technological revolution. This, I should say, is now axiomatic. Hence the need for mutually beneficial, long-term and large-scale economic co-operation, both bilateral and multilateral. Of course, this applies not only to Europe, but also to all continents, to the entire system of present-day international economic relations. Another reason why we advocate such co-operation is that we regard it as a reliable means of materially consolidating peaceful relations among states.

We hope and believe that the political foundation worked out at the European Conference and the day-to-day peaceful co-operation will be supplemented and reinforced with measures aimed at achieving a military *détente* on the continent. This, as you know, will be the subject of the talks scheduled to open in Vienna in 5 days' time.

These talks are of considerable importance for Europe and for the entire world situation. The Soviet Union's attitude to them is serious, responsible, constructive and realistic. Our stand is clear and comprehensible. We hold that agreement must be reached on a reduction, in the region of Central Europe already specified, of both foreign and national land and air forces belonging to the states party to the talks. The security of any of the sides must not be prejudiced and none of them should gain any unilateral advantages. Moreover, it must needs be recognised that the reduction should also apply to units equipped with nuclear weapons.

How exactly the cut-back is to be effected and what method is to be applied – whether the reduction should be by equal percentages or by equal numbers – still remains to be settled by those participating in the talks. In our view it is important that the future reduction should not upset the existing balance of strength in Central Europe and on the European continent generally. If attempts are made to violate this principle, the entire issue will only become an apple of discord and the subject of endless debate.

How soon a start can be made to the actual reduction of armed forces and armaments also remains to be decided in Vienna. The Soviet Union would be prepared to take practical steps in this direction as early as 1975. A specific agreement on this score could be concluded in the immediate future. Such an agreement would unquestionably be a further major step improving the political situation in Europe and helping to foster an atmosphere of trust, goodwill and peaceful co-operation.

*Speech at the World Congress of Peace
Forces in Moscow. 26 October 1973*

The tendency towards relaxation of tension has now become a dominant feature of the development of the international situation. This is particularly noticeable in Europe, which is now justly referred to as a continent that may become an important link in the system of inter-state relations, based on the principles of peaceful coexistence, effective security, and equitable co-operation.

The growth of realistic tendencies in the policy of France and later of the FRG has played an important role in bringing about a change in the European climate. The credit for this undoubtedly belongs to such political leaders as de Gaulle, Pompidou, Brandt and the forces that supported them. They realised that a system of international relations oriented to the cold war presented a dangerous impasse, that it ran counter to the basic national interests of their countries. Their striving to develop constructive links with the East enhanced the prestige of their countries which they represented in the European and world political arena.

At present there is a new leadership in France and the FRG. In their first speeches President Giscard d'Estaing and Chancellor Schmidt said that they would preserve and carry on what was started by their predecessors. This policy of France and West Germany meets with understanding and reciprocity in the Soviet Union.

Tens of states – both large and small, those that belong and those that do not belong to military-political groupings – have now been drawn into the orbit of peaceful coexistence. Possibilities have emerged for a broadening of our relations with Italy. We are co-operating successfully with Finland, the Scandinavian countries, Austria and other states. Certain changes are beginning to take place in our relations with Britain.

The process now under way of turning Europe into a zone of stable peace and fruitful co-operation among nations should be supported in every way and

89

continued. With this aim in view it is necessary first of all to bring the all-European conference to a successful completion.

A considerable amount of work has already been done in Helsinki and Geneva. A way for the solution of a number of important and complex problems has been found.

It should be made clear that the delegations of some states are trying to complicate the situation by tabling first one, then another proposal, and some of their proposals sre obviously unacceptable or have nothing to do with the question under consideration.

Those who have adopted delaying tactics should ask themselves this question: exactly what alternative to a successful completion of the conference can they propose? A return to the past, to the tensions in the relations between states which the peoples of Europe were wearied of during the cold-war years? Do these politicians understand the responsibility they will bear if things should take such a turn? This would run counter to the vital interests of the peoples who want to live in peace and, therefore, expect from the conference important decisions that would strengthen peace and security in Europe.

We are convinced that given the desire, decisions that are satisfactory and beneficial for all can be found with regard to issues which remain to be settled. Only one thing is necessary for this: to preserve a sense of realism, to be guided by a concern for the peaceful future of Europe. We are also convinced that owing to the importance and the scope of the problems with which the conference deals, participation by top leaders at its concluding stage is necessary.

Speech before the Baumansky Constituency of Moscow. 14 June 1974

Esteemed Comrade Chairman,
Esteemed Conference participants,

All of us who take part in the final stage of the Conference on Security and Co-operation in Europe feel the unusual character of this event, its political scope. It can be said with confidence that the same feeling is shared by millions upon millions of people in all the countries participating in the Conference, and not only in those countries. Together with us they are in the process of comprehending what is taking place these days in the capital of Finland.

What has made the top political and state leaders present in this hall adopt such an attitude to the Conference?

The answer seems to be that the results of the Conference are linked with expectations and hopes never before engendered by any other collective action during the period following the well-known allied decisions of the post-war time.

The people who belong to the generation which experienced the horrors of World War Two most clearly perceive the historic significance of the Conference. Its objectives are also close to the hearts and minds of the generation of Europeans which has grown and is now living in conditions of peace and which quite justly believes that it cannot be otherwise.

The soil of Europe was drenched with blood in the years of the two world wars. Top political and state leaders of 33 European states, of the USA and Canada have assembled in Helsinki in order to contribute by joint effort to making Europe a continent which would experience no more military calamities. The right to peace must be secured for all the peoples of Europe. We stand, of course, for securing such right also for all the other peoples of our planet.

Being a focus of multiple and distinctive national cultures and one of the peaks of world civilisation, Europe is in a position to set a good example of building interstate relations on the basis of durable peace.

The Soviet Union regards the outcome of the Conference not merely as a necessary summing up of the political results of World War Two. This is at the same time an insight into the future in terms of the realities of today and centuries-old experience of European nations.

It was here, in Europe, that aggressors crowned themselves with questionable laurels many a time, only later to be cursed by peoples. It was here, in Europe, that a political doctrine was made of the claims to world domination which ended in a collapse of states whose resources had been used to serve criminal and inhuman purposes.

This is why the hour has struck for the inevitable collective conclusions to be drawn from the experience of history. And we are drawing these conclusions here, being fully aware of our responsibility for the future of the European continent which must exist and develop under conditions of peace.

One could hardly deny that the results of the Conference represent a carefully weighed balance of the interests of all participating states and, therefore, should be treated with special care.

Not an easy road had been travelled from the advancement of the very idea of the European conference to its culmination, the conclusion at summit level. In assessing soberly the correlation and dynamics of various political forces in Europe and in the world, the Soviet Union firmly believes that the powerful currents of relaxation and co-operation on the basis of equality, which in recent years have increasingly determined the course of European and world politics, will gain, due to the Conference and its results, a new strength and an ever greater scope.

The document which we are to sign, summing up the results of the past, is oriented, in its content, to the future. Understandings that have been reached cover a wide range of most topical problems, i.e. peace, security, co-operation in various fields.

Relations between participating states have been placed on the solid basis of the fundamental principles which are to determine rules of conduct in their relationships. These are the principles of peaceful coexistence for which the founder of the Soviet state V. I. Lenin fought with such conviction and consistency and for which our people are fighting to this very day.

The Conference has also determined directions and specific forms of co-operation in the fields of economy and trade, science and technology, environmental protection, culture, education and contacts between individuals, establishments and organisations.

Possibilities of co-operation now extend also to such areas where it was unthinkable in the years of the cold war: for instance, broader exchanges of information in the interests of peace and friendship among nations.

It is no secret that information media can serve the purposes of peace and confidence or they can spread all over the world the poison of discord between countries and peoples. We would like to hope that the results of the Conference will serve as a correct guideline for co-operation in these fields as well.

The Conference has adopted a number of important agreements supplementing the political relaxation by a military one. This is also a qualitatively new stage in building up confidence among states.

The Soviet Union has consistently supported the idea that the Conference should be followed by further developments in the sphere of military relaxation. In this regard, one of the first priority objectives is to find ways of reducing armed forces and armaments in Central Europe without prejudicing the security of anyone, on the contrary, to the benefit of all.

The special political importance and moral force of the agreements reached at the Conference lie in the fact that they are to be certified by signatures of the top leaders of the participating states. To make these agreements effective is our common, most important objective.

We proceed from the assumption that all the countries represented at the Conference will translate into life the agreements reached. As regards the Soviet Union, it will act precisely in this manner.

In our view, the sum total of the results of the Conference consists in the fact that international *détente* is being increasingly invested with concrete material content. It is precisely the materialisation of *détente* which is the essence of everything that should make peace in Europe truly durable and unshakeable. Therefore, uppermost in our mind is the task of ending the arms race and achieving tangible results in disarmament.

It is very important to proclaim correct and just principles of relations among nations. It is no less important to see that these principles are firmly rooted in present-day international relations, are put to practical use and are made a law of international life which is not to be breached by anyone. This is the aim of our peaceful policy and this is what we declare once again from this lofty rostrum.

The very meeting of the leading figures from 33 European states, from the United States and Canada, unprecedented in history, should, of course, become a key link in the process of relaxation, of strengthening European and world security and of the development of mutually advantageous co-operation. All that is so.

But if the hopes of peoples, pinned on this meeting and on the decisions of the Conference, are to be fully justified, and not frustrated at the slightest change of weather, what is required are the common efforts and day-to-day work of all the participating states in furthering *détente*.

The success of the Conference has become possible only because its participants continuously took steps to meet each other halfway and succeeded, overcoming often great difficulties, in working out, in the final analysis, mutually acceptable agreements on each of the issues before them. These agreements were conceived and reached not by way of imposing the views of some participants in the Conference upon others, but on the basis of accommodating the views and interests of each and every one and with general consent.

If there are compromises here, then these compromises are well grounded and of the kind that benefit peace without obliterating the differences in ideologies and social systems. To be more precise, they represent an expression of common political will of the participating states in a form that is feasible today, in conditions of the existence of states with different social systems.

The experience of the work of the Conference provides important conclusions for the future, too. The main conclusion which is reflected in the Final Act is this: no one should try, on the basis of foreign-policy considerations of one kind or another, to dictate to other peoples how they should manage their internal affairs. It is only the people of each given state, and no one else, that have the sovereign right to decide their own internal affairs and establish their own internal laws. A different approach is a flimsy and perilous ground for the cause of international co-operation.

The document that we are signing is a broad but clear-cut platform to guide unilateral, bilateral and multilateral actions of states in the years and, perhaps, in decades to come. What has been achieved, however, is not the limit. Today, it is the maximum of the possible and tomorrow it should become a starting-point for making further headway along the lines mapped out by the Conference.

Aspiration for continuity in endeavours and deeds is inherent in mankind. This is also true of the great cause which is now being initiated by the thirty-five states represented in Helsinki. This finds its reflection in the fact that further steps following the first conference on Security and Co-operation in Europe have been outlined to implement and develop its objectives.

Before this exceptionally competent audience we would like to stress most emphatically one of the inherent features of the foreign policy of the Soviet Union, of the Leninist policy of peace and friendship among nations – its humanism. The decisions of the 24th Congress of our Party are imbued with ideas of humanism as is the Peace Programme, a plank of which called for the convocation of an all-European conference.

We note with deep satisfaction that the provisions drawn up by the Conference with respect to the main problems of strengthening peace in Europe serve the interests of peoples, serve the interests of men and women regardless of their occupation, nationality and age: industrial and agricultural workers, working intelligentsia, each and every individual and all people together. Those provisions are imbued with respect for man, with care so that he would live in peace and look into the future with confidence.

Agreements we have reached expand the possibilities of peoples to increase their influence upon the so-called 'big politics'. At the same time they also touch upon worldly problems. They will contribute to better living conditions of people, providing them with work and improving conditions for education. They are concerned with care for health, in short with many things related to individuals, families, youth and different groups of society.

Like many of those who have spoken from this rostrum, we view the Conference on Security and Co-operation in Europe as the common success of all its participants. Its results can be of use also outside Europe.

The results of the prolonged negotiations are such that there are neither victors nor vanquished, neither winners nor losers. This is a victory of reason. Everyone has won: countries of East and West, peoples of socialist and capitalist states – parties to alliances and those who are neutral, big and small. This is the prize of all people who cherish peace and security on our planet.

We are convinced that a successful implementation of what we have agreed upon here not only will have a beneficial effect on the life of the European peoples, but will also become a major contribution to the cause of strengthening world peace.

And one more thought which is, perhaps, shared by many of those present here. The Conference has proved to be a useful school of international politics for the participating states, particularly useful in our time when incredible means of destruction and annihilation are in existence.

A powerful impetus provided by the meeting of leaders of 35 states participating in the Conference is intended to help everyone inside and outside Europe to live in peace.

In conclusion I would like to express profound gratitude to the people and Government of Finland, personally to President U. Kekkonen for the excellent organisation of the proceedings of the third stage, for exceptional cordiality and hospitality.

Speech at the Conference on Security and
Co-operation in Europe held in Helsinki.
31 July 1975

The 24th Congress set the objective of assuring European security through recognition of the territorial and political realities that resulted from the Second World War. And that was the direction in which our Central Committee worked.

The co-operation of the Soviet Union and other socialist countries with France developed successfully on this basis. Since the negotiations with President de Gaulle, Soviet–French summit talks have become a tradition. In the course of a series of meetings – first with President Pompidou and then with President Giscard d'Estaing – the positions of the two countries drew closer on a number of foreign-political questions, and diverse Soviet–French ties and contacts became more active. This was broadly supported by the French people, the majority of the French political parties. We highly value our relations with France and are prepared to extend the areas of accord and co-operation.

A significant shift occurred in USSR–FRG relations on the basis of the 1970 Treaty. They have been normalised, and this on the only possible basis – abandonment of the ill-founded intentions to tear down the existing European frontiers. Now the FRG is one of our major partners in our mutually beneficial business co-operation with the West. Our talks with Chancellor Brandt in Oreanda and Bonn, and likewise the negotiations in Moscow during the visits of Chancellor Schmidt and President Scheel, made it possible to improve mutual understanding and enabled us to further co-operation with the FRG in the economic and other fields.

The settlement with regard to West Berlin was one of the complicated questions. It will be recalled that crises upsetting the situation in Europe erupted over that city. But the four-power agreement concluded in the autumn of 1971, together with the agreements and understandings reached on a number of issues by the governments of the GDR and the FRG and the West Berlin Senate have, essentially, relieved the tension. We value the co-operation achieved in the matter with the United States, France and Britain. Conditions have been created to turn West Berlin from a source of disputes into a constructive element of peace and *détente*. All sides must only show true respect for the agreements reached. Unfortunately some of their signatories are doing far too little in this respect. We shall insist on strict and complete observance of all understandings. The Soviet Union favours a tranquil and normal life for West Berlin.

On the whole, our relations with the West European countries may be

96

described as positive. This also applies to our relations with Britain and Italy. We value and also want to develop and enrich our traditional good-neighbour relations with Finland, and our ties with the Scandinavian countries, Austria, Belgium and other West European states. The restoration of relations with Portugal and improved relations with Greece were, of course, a reflection of the big and welcome changes in the political climate on the continent. By and large, no state in the West of Europe has stayed out of the broad process of normalising relations with the socialist countries.

Comrades, in the interests of *détente* and lasting peace in Europe the 24th Congress of the CPSU called for ensuring the convocation and success of a *European conference*. Now this has become reality. Last August in Helsinki the leaders of 33 European states and those of the United States and Canada signed the Final Act of the Conference, whose work had lasted 2 years, and the political preparations for which took 10 years.

The results achieved are well worth the expended energy. The participants in the Conference have collectively reaffirmed the inviolability of the existing frontiers. A set of principles has been worked out for governing inter-state relations conforming fully — in letter and spirit — with the requirements of peaceful coexistence. Favourable conditions have thus been created for safeguarding and consolidating peace on the entire continent.

In many ways, the results of the Conference are projected into the future. Perspectives for peaceful co-operation have been outlined in a large number of fields — economy, science, technology, culture, information, and development of contacts between people. Some other measures, too, have been defined to promote confidence between states, covering also the military aspects. The main thing now is to translate all the principles and understandings reached in Helsinki into practical deeds. This is exactly what the Soviet Union is doing and will continue to do. Recently we made certain proposals for expanding all-European co-operation in a number of important spheres. We shall continue to apply our efforts in this direction, and expect the same approach from all the other participants in the European Conference.

Thus, comrades, there are gains, and substantial ones, in the matter of building peaceful relations in Europe.

But we should not overlook the negative aspects. There still exists in Europe, for instance, such a complex and dangerous source of tension as the Cyprus problem. We are convinced that sensible consideration for the interests and rights of both communities in Cyprus will — given unconditional respect for the independence, sovereignty and territorial integrity of the Republic of Cyprus and barring attempts to impose outside solutions alien to Cypriots – pave the way to a settlement of this acute problem to the advantage of peace, security and tranquillity in Europe.

There are also certain difficulties in our relations with a number of European capitalist states. They evidently derive from the reluctance of influential circles in these states really to reject cold-war psychology and consistently follow a policy of mutually beneficial co-operation and non-interference in the internal affairs of other countries.

In the FRG, for example, the course of normalising relations with the socialist countries is being attacked by Right-wing forces who essentially cling to revenge-seeking positions. And, evidently, their pressure is affecting certain aspects of the Bonn Government's policy. Far from promoting mutual confidence and international co-operation, a considerable section of the mass media in Western countries is inciting distrust and hostility towards the socialist countries. Certain quarters are trying to emasculate and distort the very substance of the Final Act adopted in Helsinki, and to use this document as a screen for interfering in the internal affairs of the socialist countries, for anti-communist and anti-Soviet demagogy in cold-war style.

In short, much persevering effort has still to be made to achieve truly lasting peace in Europe and to make the *détente* irreversible. The Soviet Union will apply these efforts in close co-ordination with the fraternal socialist states, with all the peace-loving and realistic forces in Europe. Before us, comrades, is the great aim of making lasting peace the natural way of life for all the European peoples.

> *Report of the CPSU Central Committee to the 25th Congress of the Communist Party of the Soviet Union held in Moscow. 24 February 1976*

Today our continent is a far cry from the Europe which emerged 30 years ago from World War II in ruins, covered with blood and ashes. It is not even the

Europe of a mere 10–15 years ago during the 'cold war'. The correlation of class forces, both internationally and within many states, has changed. The role which the working class and its vanguard – the Communist Parties – play in European social life has greatly increased.

What the peoples of Europe have achieved today is, above all, the fruit of the liberation struggle against fascist aggressors and enslavers. Tens of millions of people gave their lives in this struggle, making their own contribution to Europe's rebirth. We shall never forget that.

The Europe of today is, to a large extent, the fruit of the successful building of socialism and communism in several countries on the continent. It is also the fruit of a persistent and steady struggle for peace which the countries of socialism carry on in the international arena.

At the same time, Europe's new image is the result of the growing class struggle the working people, led by the working class, are waging in the bourgeois countries, and of the struggle for a lasting peace carried on by broad sections of society.

An important feature of the period we are living through is that these changes in today's Europe are happening against the background of a worsening general crisis of capitalism. It should be stressed here that this is far from just an economic crisis; it is a political and moral crisis as well. The masses are becoming increasingly convinced that capitalism is a society without a future, and therefore, the number of advocates of the other, the socialist way, is growing. This crisis cannot be ended by revitalising the imperialists' military–political blocs, or by the arms race, or by economic integration of the monopolies, or by apparent, but not real, social reforms, or by repression.

Today, it is clearer than ever that imperialism can no longer dictate Europe's destinies. The socialist states, the working-class and democratic movement in the capitalist countries today have a say in their determination. And it is specifically these forces which have made the decisive contribution to the fact that for more than 30 years Europe has lived in peace.

Many acute and explosive problems, which had troubled the continent since World War II, have finally been solved due to the new conditions that have taken shape in Europe. The important treaties and agreements of recent years between the socialist states and France, the FRG and other Western countries, and the quadripartite agreement on West Berlin, have changed the international situation in Europe for the better.

L. I. BREZHNEV ON FOREIGN AFFAIRS

The principles of peaceful coexistence have become the leading trend in relations among states. This was most completely reflected in the successful European Conference in which the USA and Canada participated. It is a tremendous political victory for the forces of peace.

The Conference's Final Act is a rich, multifaceted code for peaceful association and co-operation among states. We are striving to implement all its provisions. But what we value most highly is that this document is directed at achieving a lasting peace in Europe. That was the main goal of the European Conference – to help strengthen the peace and security of the European nations.

The success of international *détente* has inspired and strengthened the forces of peace and progress, and has heightened their prestige and influence among the people. It has shown that the positions of the realistically thinking representatives of the ruling circles in the bourgeois countries rest on solid ground. But it has also alerted and activated the forces of reaction and militarism, who would like to drag Europe and the entire world back to the 'cold war' and the time of nuclear brinkmanship. It has alarmed those who wax fat on the production of weapons of death and destruction, who cannot envisage any other political career except that of launching 'crusades' against the socialist countries, against Communists, and those who openly call for 'preparing for a new war', as the Maoist leaders in China are doing in the hope of benefiting from the setting of countries and peoples against one another.

These different forces oppose *détente* in different ways. However, their main objective is to further accelerate the arms race which is already of an unprecedented scope.

To do this, imperialism's aggressive forces and their henchmen have again resorted to the hackneyed myth about the notorious 'Soviet threat' supposedly looming over the Western countries. Fantastic assertions grossly distorting the policy of the Soviet Union and the other socialist states constantly appear in the mass media and are quite often made by prominent officials.

Against all common sense, the socialist countries are held 'responsible' for internal political events in other states and for civil wars, and wars of national liberation. Ordinary people are being intimidated by 'hordes of Russian tanks', and are being told that the USSR and the other Warsaw Treaty countries are building up arms on a tremendous scale, preparing a 'war against Western Europe'.

But these fabrications collapse like a house of cards as soon as we look at facts, at the realities.

In Central Europe there is not much difference in the size of the armed forces of the Warsaw Treaty and NATO countries. Their level has remained more or less equal (with certain differences in the types of forces each side has) for many years. And the Western powers know that as well as we do.

That is why the socialist countries propose that an equal reduction of armed forces and armaments for each side be agreed upon (say, starting with the USSR and the USA), not to change the correlation of forces, but to reduce the sides' military spending and lessen the risk of a clash. What could be more logical and fair? But no: the NATO countries are stubbornly trying to secure an unequal reduction, so that the correlation of forces would change in their favour and to the detriment of the socialist countries. Obviously, we cannot accept this, and our Western partners in the talks apparently realise it themselves. So their position can mean only one thing: slowing down the talks and impeding the reduction of armed forces and armaments in Central Europe.

It was the Soviet Union which proposed that the states taking part in the talks on the reduction of armed forces and armaments in Central Europe undertake an obligation not to increase the strength of their armed forces while the talks are in progress. But this proposal was not accepted by the West either. NATO continues to build up the numbers and the striking power of its combat units in Central Europe.

So who really wants to abate the threat of war in Europe and who is helping increase it?

The Soviet Union is the only great power which does not increase its military spending every year, and which is working for a generally agreed reduction in military budgets. At the same time, the United States' military budget is steadily growing, already exceeding 100,000 million dollars. And the West European NATO member-countries more than doubled their military spending in the 5 years between 1971 and 1975.

It is not that easy to defuse the powder-keg or, to put it more precisely, the atomic magazine into which present-day Europe has been turned. But it is important to start really moving in this direction. Any concrete measures that will preserve and multiply the elements of trust that are growing in relations between the states of the East and the West are valuable in today's conditions.

The Soviet Union, true to the spirit and the letter of the Helsinki agreement, makes sure to regularly inform the participants in the All-European Conference of military manoeuvres in the border zones and invites observers from neighbouring countries to attend them.

The socialist countries, as is known, have often proposed that the North Atlantic Treaty Organisation and the Warsaw Treaty Organisation be simultaneously dissolved, or, as a preliminary step, that their military organisations be abolished.

Naturally, we are far from equating these two organisations. The Warsaw Treaty is a purely defensive organisation. As for NATO, that bloc was established as a weapon of aggression and suppression of the peoples' liberation struggle. And it still is the same today, despite all the whitewashing. But we in principle are against the division of the world into military blocs and are prepared to do everything possible so that the activities of both these groupings can be terminated simultaneously.

The European peoples are heirs to and followers of noble traditions that cannot be separated from world culture. And so there is little need to point out that these great traditions place major responsibilities upon contemporary European people.

And there is another thing: Europe has been the starting-point of the most terrible wars in human history. Not less than 100 million human lives lost – such is the grim record in Europe's history up to our time. It is also Europe's contribution to history, but it is a terrible contribution, a warning and a responsibility. It demands that we think of the past in the name of the future.

Europe has entered a fundamentally new era, totally different from everything that went before. If the Europeans should fail to understand this they would be heading for a catastrophe.

An ancient maxim says 'All they that take the sword shall perish with the sword'. Whoever takes up the sword in contemporary Europe will not only perish himself; he cannot even imagine who else will perish in the flames – enemies, friends, allies or simply neighbours, both near and far.

To the Soviet people the very thought of using nuclear weapons anywhere in Europe is monstrous. The European 'house' has become crowded and is highly inflammable. There is not, nor will there be, a fire brigade able to extinguish the flames if the fire ever breaks out.

For Europe and its people, peace has become a truly vital need. That is why we Communists, who are partisans of the most humane, the most life-asserting world outlook, believe that it is now more important than ever to pave the road to military *détente* and to stop the arms race.

It is also exceptionally important to create, so to speak, the fabric of peaceful co-operation in Europe, the fabric that would strengthen relations among European peoples and states and stimulate their interest in preserving peace for many years to come. I am thinking of the different forms of mutually advantageous co-operation – trade, production co-operation and scientific and technological relations.

This task is quite feasible. Over recent years, in the course of strengthening *détente*, countries in both Eastern and Western Europe have gained much experience in this kind of co-operation. For example, the Soviet Union's trade with the European capitalist countries has more than trebled over the last 5 years. Co-operation in building large-scale projects on a mutually advantageous foundation is becoming more important.

I believe that the Communists of Europe think alike about the usefulness and the desirability of further developing such relations. They help build up the material foundations of a lasting peace. They are in working people's direct interests. It is enough to say that, according to data published in the West, the economic relations with the socialist countries are already providing work for hundreds of thousands, even millions of people in Western Europe in this time of crisis.

The USSR last year received 980 trade-union and workers' delegations from abroad, while 750 Soviet delegations visited other countries.

No, the socialist countries are not a 'closed society'. We are open to everything that is truthful and honest, and we are ready to expand contacts in every way, using the favourable conditions *détente* offers. But our doors will always be closed to publications preaching war, violence, racism and hatred.

We think that cultural exchanges and the information media should serve human ideals, the cause of peace, that they should promote international trust and friendship. But in certain European countries there are notorious subversive radio stations which have assumed such names as 'Liberty' and 'Free Europe'. Their existence contaminates the international atmosphere and is a direct challenge to the spirit and letter of the Helsinki agreements. The Soviet Union resolutely demands that the use of these means of 'psychological war' be stopped.

Speech at the Conference of the European Communist and Workers' Parties held in Berlin. 29 June 1976

103

L. I. BREZHNEV ON FOREIGN AFFAIRS

Question: In connection with the first anniversary of the Conference on Security and Co-operation in Europe and the signing of the Final Act, would you tell us how you assess the significance of this Conference?

Answer: The Conference has become an event of great import. The main thing, as we see it, is that it succeeded in expressing the will of the peoples of all the participating countries to secure peace.

The road to Helsinki was not an easy one. There were many difficulties along it. At the negotiation table there met states with different social systems and ideologies. But the desire to achieve general accord on the basic problems of European security and co-operation prevailed, and this assured success.

There were many attempts last year to cast aspersions on the accord reached at that Conference on different issues. But in assessing what has already been done and what is still to be done we should consider mainly, not this or that particular point, but the whole great undertaking that brought together 33 European countries, the USA and Canada.

It was such an approach that brought us all to Helsinki and led us to sign the Final Act. This collectively elaborated document, which consolidated the results achieved in improving the political climate of Europe, defined the long-term prospects for realistic and responsible handling of inter-state affairs, first of all as they apply in Europe, but also with account taken of their relevance and applicability in settling problems that concern the whole world. The document clearly points to the need for easing international tension, ending military conflicts in those parts of the world where they still exist and developing peaceful co-operation between states without interference in their internal affairs.

There is no doubt that the results achieved in Helsinki a year ago will have a long life and nobody will succeed in disrupting or belittling them.

It can be said with confidence that Europe, thanks to the Conference on Security and Co-operation, now stands on a higher plane than before. Europe has learned to be more persistent and effective in seeking solutions to burning international problems, to work in such a way as to achieve better practical results in the interests of easing tensions, broadening co-operation between states and establishing peace among nations.

Some people may say that these words are filled with optimism. And they would be quite right.

Interview given to a Pravda *correspondent in Moscow. 30 July 1976*

You have mentioned the Helsinki Conference in your questions.

On the whole, we assess positively what has been done over the period following the European Conference. New promising forms of co-operation emerge. The Soviet Union, guided by the principles worked out in Helsinki, has concluded a number of important agreements with countries that participated in the Conference. We can mention as an example the agreement with France on the prevention of an accidental or unsanctioned use of nuclear weapons, which was signed last July.

We have made it a practice to give prior notification of major military manoeuvres and invite foreign observers to attend them. This is essential if confidence among states is to be built up.

Far from everything, however, is running smoothly. Mention should be made of continuing attempts to distort the spirit and letter of the Final Act or to question its value altogether. This is done by those who advocate a return to the cold war, to tension. Such forces exist in the USA, the FRG and other countries. Therefore, the struggle to implement the provisions of the Final Act is at the same time a struggle against a return to the cold war, against the intrigues of the adversaries of *détente*.

As regards the Soviet Union, we respect and observe the Helsinki agreements in all aspects, I repeat, in all aspects. The most important thing concerning these agreements includes everything that contributes to a strengthening of security and peace. But, naturally, we do not underestimate in the least the importance of co-operation in the fields of economy, science and technology, culture and information, in promoting human contacts and in implementing confidence-building measures.

The Soviet Union is for the pooling of efforts on an all-European basis to solve outstanding problems in the fields of energy, transport and environmental protection. Our proposals to this effect are well known.

So facts show that the Soviet Union, displaying initiative and perseverance, together with other socialist countries, takes the lead in the great work of implementing everything that was agreed upon in Helsinki. We shall continue to act in this manner.

Interview on French television given in Moscow. 5 October 1976

The foreign policy of our Party is first of all struggle for a lasting peace. We consider it to be one of our most important tasks to make full use, and not only in Europe, of the favourable possibilities created by the holding of the European Conference and by the document on peaceful coexistence and co-operation of states which was solemnly adopted at Helsinki. In full conformity with the programme approved by the 25th Congress of the Party, we are continuing *the work of developing equitable and mutually advantageous relations with capitalist states.*

Every stage in this work has its own distinguishing features. Some 5 or 10 years ago our task was to create a basis for normal relations of peaceful coexistence with France, the FRG, the United States of America, Canada, Italy, Britain and other capitalist countries, to remove from our relations with these countries the main vestiges of the cold war. When this had been accomplished in the main, we went further and began developing ever more extensive co-operation in the fields of politics, economy, science, technology and culture.

Much that is positive has been done in this respect during recent months as well. For instance, agreements have been signed which fully accord with the spirit and letter of the Final Act adopted at Helsinki, included the 10-year agreement with Canada on promoting economic, industrial, scientific and technological co-operation, similar agreements with Cyprus and Portugal, the Soviet–Portuguese agreement on cultural co-operation, the agreements with France on preventing accidental or unsanctioned use of nuclear weapons, on co-operation in the fields of energy, civil aviation and aircraft manufacture, the agreement with Finland in the fields of public health and social security. As you see, things are moving forward. The whole world sees that the USSR is advancing along the road of peace and peaceful co-operation. And the world should know that we will continue to advance along this road!

It should be noted, however, that the development of our relations with a number of states has slowed down of late, and through no fault of ours. This was caused, to a considerable extent, by the complex political situation in some countries, in particular by the election campaigns in the United States and the Federal Republic of Germany.

We would like to see peaceful co-operation of states take place not only on a bilateral basis, but assume an ever wider, multilateral character, and become, so to say, a part of the fabric of lasting peace. The Soviet Union's proposals of holding European congresses on the problems pertaining to transport, energy, environmental protection were made with a view to accomplishing this aim in particular.

On the whole, the efforts to implement the Helsinki accords consist of scores and even hundreds of practical undertakings. Though not always conspicuous, they constitute the party and state work of an exceptional importance. And we the Soviet people appreciate the efforts of those who work in the same direction. For the cause of peace, so close to the heart of every Soviet person, is our common cause.

The so-called confidence measures: the practice of giving advance notice to other countries about forthcoming major military exercises and inviting foreign observers to such exercises, approved on our initiative at the European Conference, have played a constructive role in creating a calmer atmosphere in Europe.

We also consistently implement those provisions of the Final Act adopted in Helsinki, which deal with the extension of cultural and other ties and contacts among peoples, and the expansion of information exchanges. We proceed from the position that in the conditions of relaxation of tension the development of such ties and contacts is quite natural – of course provided that the principles of mutual respect for the sovereignty and non-interference in the internal affairs of the sides are strictly observed. But I'll have to say here, and some gentlemen may not like it, that we shall not allow anyone to violate such principles in conducting relations with the Soviet Union to act against the interests of the Soviet people and our socialist system.

> *Speech at the Plenary Meeting of the Central Committee of the Communist Party of the Soviet Union. 25 October 1976*

Our efforts, together with the efforts of other fraternal countries, to ensure lasting security and a durable peace in the world represent one of the main areas of Soviet–Polish co-operation.

It was largely the concerted policy of the Warsaw Treaty countries that several years ago gave an impetus to the process of *détente*.

We shall continue to take an active part in the further consolidation and deepening of this process. We consider it essential and realistic to take concrete and effective measures for curbing the arms race and for reducing armaments on the bases of reciprocity and the unimpaired security of any one country.

With elections being over in the FRG and the USA, we would like to look forward to more effective inter-state co-operation in solving major issues, concerning both bilateral relations and international affairs as a whole, that are important for strengthening peace and the security of all nations. We would very much like to see the full implementation of the spirit of Helsinki in international relations and will do our very utmost to promote this process.

We are fully aware, however, of powerful and well-organised forces which act with persistence in the capitalist world against *détente*, against the firm establishment of the principles of peaceful co-existence and certainly against an end to the arms race.

They are doing all they can to poison the international atmosphere with the venom of suspicion, mistrust and fear.

They are spreading slanders about Communists, socialist countries and national-liberation movements.

They would like to hamper the successful advance of our countries along the road of socialism and communism and seek to undermine our fraternal friendship and derange our united ranks.

This they would like to do — and indeed are trying to do in different ways. But their efforts are all in vain, for these gentlemen will not arrest the course of history — their hands are too short for that!

Actions by these forces demand of our countries a high degree of vigilance and still greater determination to carry out the struggle for a lasting peace. We regard it as our duty to strengthen our socialist community, our alliance which is a reliable means for defending the revolutionary gains of our peoples.

We shall develop close relations with the entire communist and working-class movement, the national-liberation struggle of the peoples, and democratic and peace-loving forces.

The surest way of frustrating reactionary attempts to interfere with a further deepening of the positive processes now taking place in the world lies in strengthening the alliance of the forces of progress and peace.

Speech at the dinner in the Kremlin in honour of the Party and State delegation of the PPR, headed by Edward Gierek, First Secretary of the PUWP Central Committee. 9 November 1976

Obviously, all of us, the fraternal socialist countries, will need to work closely with one another in preparing for the forthcoming Belgrade meeting of the participants in the European Conference. We would like to hope that this meeting will become not an arena of a propagandist wrangle, but a constructive forum of goodwill and a generator of positive ideas bearing on the further development of peaceful and mutually beneficial co-operation among the signatory states of the Final Act in Helsinki.

And, finally, I believe that the socialist countries, if they act all together, persistently and in a spirit of concord, will be able to do a great deal to bring nearer a solution to one of the most burning problems of our time – that of stopping the arms race and turning towards practical steps to reduce the level of stockpiled arms, that is, towards disarmament. Indeed in the solution of this problem lies the key to a really lasting peace, to a tranquil and creative life for the present generation and the generations to come, a life worthy of man.

On the side of peace and disarmament are powerful forces, the overwhelming majority of mankind. It is necessary that these forces should become more active and their actions be given a proper direction. And here a truly historic responsibility devolves on us Communists and on the socialist countries. So let us act, comrades, in such a way that none of us may ever have reason to reproach himself for not having done everything possible!

Speech at the Dinner in the Palace of the State Council of the Socialist Republic of Romania in Bucharest. 22 November 1976

The peace-loving foreign policy of the socialist states has been consistent and active and they have displayed constant internationalist readiness to support the just cause of the freedom and independence of the peoples. All this enormously multiplies the force of attraction of socialism in the present-day world.

Ours is a just cause, comrades. Our goals are noble. They meet the interests of the peoples of our countries and all peoples of the world. Our road is illumined by the unfading light of Marxist–Leninist teaching. The future is in our hands, a happy and bright future of our peoples. They are shaping it today by their creative labour. But one more thing is also needed for this future to be established – *lasting peace*. The foreign policy of our states is directed at ensuring peace.

We know that socialism has many enemies, because nowhere do the exploiting classes surrender their positions voluntarily. For this reason we maintain vigilance and are compelled to strengthen our defences in order to protect the peaceful work of our peoples and to defend socialism. Such a defence potential has been created and is being maintained through the joint efforts of the Warsaw Treaty countries that any attempt by imperialism to suppress socialism by means of military force is doomed in advance to a devastating failure.

By combining our strength with a consistent and sincere love of peace and by appealing to the common sense and realism of politicians in the capitalist world we have brought about a situation in which international tension, mistrust, hostility and intensive belligerent passions, typical of the cold-war period, have given way to a much calmer and healthier atmosphere. A constructive dialogue has begun between socialist and capitalist states. Mutually advantageous co-operation between them, rather exceptional not so long ago, has now become a widespread and firmly established feature. In short, what Lenin, the leader of the world's first socialist state, advocated has become a reality, namely, in conditions of relaxation of tension, relations between states with different social systems have begun to develop on the principles of peaceful coexistence.

This is a tremendous historic victory for mankind. Without any doubt, the decisive contribution to its attainment was made by the socialist countries, and they are continuing to make their contribution day after day.

Proceeding from the accords reached in Helsinki by 35 states of Europe and North America and sealed by the signatures of their leaders, including those of Comrade Ceausescu and myself, Ramania, the Soviet Union and other socialist countries of Europe are taking an active part in the development of peaceful relations between states. We are displaying a constant initiative in this matter. Scores of major political, economic and other treaties and agreements, intensively developing economic, cultural and scientific ties, contacts between mass organisations – all this is our asset, the asset of peace and good–neighbourly relations. Of course, the possibilities here are far from being exhausted. You obviously know about the Soviet Union's proposals for establishing all-European co-operation in such fields as transport, energy and environmental protection. We shall press insistently for their implementation. Mutually beneficial co-operation in many other fields is possible, of course, in conditions of peace. Europe is waiting for good, constructive initiatives.

Lasting peace, however, cannot be the privilege of Europe alone. Peace is indivisible, and today this truth is more correct than ever before. As long as the seats of war in the Middle East are not eliminated, as long as the Arabs are not given back their lands which were seized through aggression, as long as the Arab people of Palestine are denied the right to have a homeland, as long as the racialist régimes in Pretoria and Salisbury openly flout the rights of the indigenous population in the South of Africa and spill the blood of Africans, peace can nowhere be really secure.

To eliminate the centres of danger of war, to make the relaxation of tension universal – these are the truly pressing demands of our epoch. We are glad, dear friends, that in the struggle to accomplish these tasks the Soviet Union and Romania are marching together.

We also know, comrades, that peace cannot be secure until an end is put to the present arms race, to the inflating of military budgets, to the creation of ever more terrible means of mass destruction. Matters have already gone so far that were the weapons already stockpiled put to use, mankind could be totally destroyed. Where can we go to from this?

To continue or to end the arms race, to turn to disarmament or not – this is too serious a question to be left to be solved by the belligerent generals of the Pentagon and NATO and to the monopolies which batten on the manufacture of weapons. Responsible statesmen must act here and the masses of people, whose destiny, after all, is at stake, must have their say.

Aware of all this, we in the USSR consider it to be our duty to do everything within our power to put the speediest end possible to the piling up of the means of destruction and to start the process of arms reduction. The

111

Soviet Union's concrete proposals on the renunciation of the use of force in international relations, renunciation of the development of new weapons of mass destruction, reduction of military budgets, the complete end of nuclear weapons tests and on other relevant matters are known to the whole world. We are glad that in the struggle for these goals Romania, like other fraternal socialist states, goes along with us.

Our countries stand for the holding of a special session of the United Nations on disarmament and for the preparation of a world conference. We are working for progress at the Vienna talks on the mutual reduction of armed forces and armaments in Central Europe, which could lead to further steps in this respect already on an all-European scale. We would like to hope that after the change of administration in the USA the talks that we are conducting with the Americans to limit and then reduce strategic armaments will be continued and successfully concluded. A satisfactory solution of this problem – and we consider it quite possible, the more so since its main content has long been agreed on – would meet not only the interests of the Soviet and American peoples, but the interests of strengthening universal peace as well. This would be a good example to other countries.

Here in Bucharest 10 years ago, the socialist countries, united in the Warsaw Treaty Organisation, adopted a declaration on strengthening peace and security in Europe. This declaration set out major ideas on how to improve the European situation. Many of them have already been implemented. A regular meeting of the Political Consultative Committee of the Warsaw Treaty member-states is to open here tomorrow. We believe that this time, too, the decisions taken in the Romanian capital will help to safeguard a peaceful future for Europe and the whole world.

Speech at the Soviet–Romanian Friendship Meeting in Bucharest. 24 November 1976

This award, as well as the cordial words said here, I and my colleagues receive primarily as a new recognition of the correctness, fruitfulness and good prospects of the course towards sincere friendship, mutual trust and all-round co-operation between the Soviet Union and Finland.

As one thinks of the record of relations between our two countries, one finds oneself turning again and again to the role played by the founder of the Soviet state, V. I. Lenin, in establishing good-neighbourliness with Finland. It was Lenin who signed the historic decree on recognising the independence of Finland as a state. It was Lenin who stated – and he had every reason for making such a statement: 'Our socialist republic has done all it could, and continues to do all it can to give effect to the right of self-determination of Finland. . . .'

It is all the more appropriate to recall this today when our state and the Republic of Finland have entered the 60th year of their existence.

The development of Soviet–Finnish co-operation over the past few decades has become part of the political chronicle of the world, serving as a vivid example of the implementation of Lenin's principles of a new type of inter-state relations. These great principles, as has also been often mentioned by you, Mr. President, are embodied in the Treaty of Friendship, Co-operation and Mutual Assistance of 1948 signed between our countries. It is our firm conviction that the line defined in this treaty and in all its provisions has been and will continue to be the main direction in the development of relations between the USSR and Finland.

Another thing I want to say is this. Soviet–Finnish co-operation, which accords with the fundamental interests of the peoples of both countries, promotes *détente* and the consolidation of mutually advantageous ties on a wide international scale. It is not accidental that the code of principles governing inter-state contacts, adopted by the European Conference in Helsinki, has drawn upon the time-tested experience of relationship between the USSR and Finland. There is no doubt that in the implementation of the agreements reached in Helsinki our countries will also be able to set a good example.

Friendship and trust between the Soviet Union and Finland are a major gain of the peoples of our two countries and of their government leaders. This is our most treasured common asset.

The Soviet Union appreciates the concern which you, Mr. President, have constantly shown for strengthening Soviet–Finnish relations. We know that your activities in this area have the broad support of the progressive and democratic forces of Finland, of an overwhelming majority of the Finnish people.

For my part, I can say most definitely: the Communist Party of the Soviet

Union and the Soviet Government will continue to do everything possible to preserve good relations with Finland. We shall continue to expand in the Leninist way Soviet–Finnish friendship and to deepen the relations of peaceful and mutually advantageous co-operation with all states!

Speech in the Kremlin on being presented with the Grand Cross with Chain, the Order of the White Rose of Finland, the highest state award of the Republic of Finland. 17 December 1976

We would like to come as soon as possible to an agreement also on the reduction of armed forces and armaments in Central Europe. We have no objections to discussing the relevant questions at any level and at any venue – in Vienna, Bonn, Washington, Moscow – anywhere.

Occupying a central place in European politics today is the task of implementing to the full the accords reached by 35 states in Helsinki a year and a half ago. We regard the Final Act of the European Conference as a code of international obligations aimed at ensuring a lasting peace. To be sure, all of its provisions must be implemented, and that is our daily task. The Central Committee attaches much political importance to this work. Many of our ministries and agencies are involved in it.

It is quite understandable that at present much has been accomplished in some fields, while in others the necessary measures are being carried out gradually or are only being drafted. Much depends here on the overall state of political relations between states or, as it is sometimes said, on the level of *détente*. By poisoning the international atmosphere the opponents of *détente* are only impeding this work.

In Western countries attempts are often made to single out some elements from the Final Act and launch polemics over them. The purpose here is obvious: it is to obstruct the positive processes started by the European Conference. Judging by everything, those who make such attempts care little about ensuring a lasting peace in Europe. They are concerned with something else. They would like to put pressure on us, to have us live according to rules that are incompatible with socialist democracy, with socialist law and order. I would like to say that this is a lost cause.

In Helsinki, states with a socialist social system and states with a different social system worked together and achieved important results. This was serious, businesslike co-operation based on a common interest in making the conference a success. Now this co-operation should be carried forward. We are ready to work towards this and, as you know, have already made a number of concrete proposals, in particular on several economic problems.

We regard it as a big and important task to develop further bilateral relations with France, the FRG, Italy, Great Britain and other European and non-European states. We have built and will continue to build our relations with them on the basis of the principle of peaceful coexistence. This is a Leninist principle, and we shall preserve and augment Lenin's legacy, all of it, which we hold sacred.

Speech in the city of Tula. 18 January 1977

Speaking of our relations with West European countries, we must say that they are developing, on the whole, quite well. At one time the USSR and France were, so to say, the trail-blazers of *détente*, and their relations were described as 'preferential' ones. To a certain extent, this is still so: we are maintaining lively ties in the economic and cultural fields. We also co-operate in some foreign policy matters. The fact that the leaders of France, the FRG, Italy and Great Britain support the policy of relaxation of tension, the policy of peaceful coexistence, is appreciated in the Soviet Union. In relations between the USSR and the FRG, we believe, much can still be done and should be done. We have already covered some ground and should follow this through. As is known, I will be visiting France and the FRG this year. We hope that the forthcoming talks will give fresh impetus to the development of relations with these countries.

The recent restoration of the USSR's relations with Spain was a notable event in Europe's political life. Lately we have developed adequate co-operation with that country, mostly in economic matters. Now, it can be expected that our relations will be further developed. We are following the process of democratisation of political life in Spain with interest, and wish the Spanish people further success along this road.

Twenty months have passed since the day when the heads of state and government of 35 countries affixed their signatures to the Final Act of the European Conference on Security and Co-operation. During this period peace in Europe has strengthened, while economic, cultural and other ties and contacts among countries have become noticeably broader and richer. We in the Soviet Union welcome this. We want *détente* to continue. We will promote this in every way, because it is in the interests of the peoples.

In the countries which took part in the Helsinki Conference preparations have now started for the Belgrade meeting, the first full meeting of their representatives since Helsinki. We, for our part, want a constructive, businesslike discussion there by sovereign partners. The Helsinki Conference, as is known, was called the Conference on Security and Co-operation in Europe. We consider, therefore, that concern for peace and security in Europe, for developing co-operation between the nations of Europe, should be the main content of the Belgrade meeting. In our view, the main task of the meeting in the Yugoslav capital should be not simply to sum up what has already been done, but to reach agreement on some concrete recommendations and proposals on questions of further co-operation.

Speech at the 16th Congress of the Trades Unions of the USSR. 21 March 1977

The Soviet people have sincere respect for Finland and her friendly people. We treasure what has been achieved by our joint efforts in Soviet–Finnish relations over the last decades.

And our achievements are considerable. There is the establishment and constant strengthening of friendship and mutual trust between the peoples of

116

the Soviet Union and Finland. There is the large-scale development of economic, cultural and other ties and a high level of political co-operation. Finally, there is our joint fruitful work in the interests of international peace and security.

This year, which is an important anniversary year both for the Soviet Union and for the Republic of Finland, there is every reason to say that the good-neighbourly spirit cherished by our countries, in which Lenin firmly believed when he signed the decree recognising the independence of Finland as a state, has become firmly established in Soviet–Finnish relations and has become truly lasting and stable.

This is clearly seen in the Treaty of Friendship, Co-operation and Mutual Assistance that was concluded between our countries in accordance with the fundamental interests and desire of our peoples and with the experience of history. The peoples of our two countries, having such a treaty, feel confident about the future of Soviet–Finnish relations. This future is clear and certain.

We highly appreciate your statements, Mr. President, to the effect that the 1948 Treaty and the policy of full-scale development of friendship with the Soviet Union will continue to be the keystone of Finland's foreign policy.

We in the Soviet Union pay tribute to the political far-sightedness, realism and statesmanship which enable you, by relying on the support of the democratic, progressive and peace forces of Finland, consistently and successfully to pursue this realistic and independent policy.

Co-operation between the Soviet Union and Finland has become a major element in international life. This co-operation is, I would say, the material expression of the principled policy line concerning inter-state relations which the Soviet Union has consistently followed since the first days of its existence and a real embodiment of the just principles of international relations which are favoured today by all peace-loving states. It should be pointed out that the work done by the Soviet Union and Finland in this direction has often been far ahead of the times.

One cannot but recall in this connection that the Soviet Union and Finland were among the first states in post-war Europe not only to proclaim, but also to begin in practice to restructure their mutual relations on the basis of equality, mutual respect for independence and sovereignty, non-interference in internal affairs, and mutually advantageous co-operation. In short, the principle of peaceful coexistence was made the basis.

As a result of persistent and purposeful joint efforts, a new political climate has come about in relations between our two states. Friendship and trust, and a desire to understand each other's problems and to take into account each other's interests have come to the forefront. It is not fortuitous that a number of important initiatives and forms of co-operation have emerged and passed the test of time in relations between the USSR and Finland, particularly in recent years, initiatives and forms which have then been adopted on a wider scale in international practice.

We are confident that following the tried and tested course of good-neighbourly relations and co-operation, the Soviet Union and Finland will continue to contribute actively to the efforts of all peace-loving states to give a new look to Europe. As we see it, this is a promising trend in our joint policy, one which has good prospects.

Take, for example, the working out of a long-term programme for the development of trade, economic, industrial, scientific and technological co-operation until the year 1990. There is every reason to include the document which we shall sign tomorrow among the important documents of European politics and among the concrete moves in implementing the Final Act of the European Conference. This is the first time that states with different social and economic systems have defined the basic trends of their co-operation for such a long period, and have settled these questions within such a broad framework and on a concrete and practical basis.

All this reflects the optimism and confidence with which we approach the further development of our relations. There are many more areas in which co-operation between the Soviet Union and Finland can serve as a good example and in which their views and opinions may be necessary and timely.

Every state has its own history, its national features, and makes its own contribution in the field of international relations. It is easy to see that small countries can be more active and work for peace more effectively in conditions of *détente.*

An example is Finland, whose growing prestige in the world cannot but make all sincere friends of your country happy. It is a significant fact that the Final Act of the European Conference was signed in Helsinki and is to be in Finland's custody for all time.

The efforts which you, Mr. President, are making to strengthen peaceful conditions in the North of Europe are widely known. It is said that, unlike other parts of the world, the situation in this part of the European continent is fairly tranquil and stable. This is largely true, but one should not shut one's eyes to the fact that the activity of the North Atlantic bloc and the participation of individual Scandinavian countries in it make themselves felt here, too.

We are convinced that the ways of really strengthening security in the North of Europe should not be sought in the activation of the bloc policy here. The main thing is to find, through concerted efforts, solutions which are in accord with the objective interests of the peoples and which would promote peace.

Speech in the Kremlin at a dinner in honour of Urho Kaleva Kekkonen. 17 May 1977

Question: Are you satisfied with what has been done to implement the Helsinki accords?

Answer: I think no one doubts today that the Helsinki accords could exert a great, positive impact on relations between states, on the situation in Europe and beyond. More than that, the Final Act signed in Helsinki has already become an important political reality in international life and is being actively implemented. Much has been accomplished, though, naturally, the extent of progress made is not the same in all fields. The Final Act – and all participants in the All-European Conference agree with this – is a broad programme of action to be carried out by the participating states for strengthening peace in Europe, a programme projected for a long period ahead. I specially want to emphasise that this programme could be more successfully implemented in the future if fewer attempts were made to poison the atmosphere of relations between states.

Question: Both parts of Europe are now in a state of peaceful coexistence on the military and political planes. There is co-operation in the economic sphere and antagonism in the ideological sphere. How long do you think such a situation can last?

Answer: Indeed, substantial progress has been made in Europe in recent years in developing equal, mutually advantageous co-operation based on the principles of peaceful coexistence. Good headway has been made towards turning Europe into a continent of lasting peace and security. This aim, we believe, is attainable. But even then, we are convinced, the ideological struggle, that is, the struggle of ideas, will not cease. And there is no contradiction here. Since there exist or, to be more exact, coexist states with different social systems, the differences in views, ideas and ideologies inherent in these systems remain and cannot be removed by any agreements. But in our time it would be senseless and dangerous to try to ensure the victory of particular ideas, of a particular ideology, by means of force, by the use of weapons. The ideological struggle should not grow into a 'psychological war'. It should not be used as a means of interference in the internal affairs of states and nations, nor should it lead to political and military confrontation.

Otherwise this ideological dispute may develop into a catastrophe in which millions of people, and with them their ideas and concepts, so to speak, will perish.

The conflict between the two social systems and between their ideologies can be settled only by life itself, by historical experience, by the test of practice. We Communists, of course, are deeply convinced of the advantages of the socialist system. We hold that socialist, communist concepts better meet the vital aspirations and interests of society and of every person individually and the interests of universal peace and social progress.

Question: The USSR has somewhat softened its position of late regarding the European Economic Community. Can the USSR be expected to establish official relations with the Community?

Answer: We approach this question as one of the member countries of the Council for Mutual Economic Assistance. We regard the Common Market as a reality and consider it important that the West should assume a similar view in regard to CMEA.

CMEA, on behalf of the member countries' governments and acting in the spirit of the Final Act of the All-European Conference, has proposed that official relations be established between CMEA and EEC, and in April this year it set forth new proposals on this matter. So now it is for the Common Market to reply.

Answers to questions from Le Monde.
15 June 1977

Tomorrow, 22 June, will be another anniversary of Nazi Germany's treacherous attack on the Soviet Union. This date marked the beginning of the most tragic and at the same time heroic period in the life of the peoples of our country. This is why we were particularly moved when we laid a wreath at the Tomb of the Unknown Soldier today in honour of the memory of the French who gave their lives for the independence and honour of France and for our common victory over fascism. How many such monuments stand in towns and villages of the different countries of our continent! They stand as symbols of the heroism and grief of the people and as a reminder that until recently peace in Europe was only an interval between wars.

Europe has not known war for a third of a century now. People are looking to the future with growing hope. This does not represent a gift from heaven, but is the result of deliberate efforts and purposeful actions by statesmen, political figures and broad sections of people who are demanding lasting peace.

Peace in Europe, however, and still more in the world at large, is far from being as firm as one would wish it to be. It is threatened with many dangers, overt and covert. And the main danger is the uninterrupted and mounting arms race. The arms race is being instigated by the poisonous propaganda of militant opponents of *détente* whose aim is to sow distrust and hostility between peoples and between states.

Even though I risk being accused of repeating myself, still I shall say once again: There is no more urgent problem, no more important task, than that of ending the arms race and introducing real disarmament measures. How much will all the fine words and declarations of loyalty to peace and all that has been achieved so far in the field of *détente* and peaceful co-operation among nations be worth, if some day a spark flares up in a sensitive place and sets on fire all the stocks of the means of destruction capable of devastating the earth and of killing whole peoples?

The prospect for the further proliferation of nuclear weapons in the world, as well as the creation of new, perhaps even more terrible and even more destructive types and systems of weapons of mass annihilation, constitutes a particularly grave danger under the present conditions. The Soviet Union clearly sees the danger threatening mankind. Our country has been doing and will do everything in its power to prevent the development of such a dangerous situation. We would also like France to act vigorously in this direction.

It is important that all countries of the world take part in the examination and settlement of such a vital problem as disarmament and reducing the threat of a nuclear war. We believe that in order to ensure progress towards this objective all forums must be used – the United Nations and special international conferences, bilateral talks and broad public movements.

In short, in these matters, too, which literally affect the fate of the whole human race we count on the understanding and support of the French Republic.

Speech at a dinner in the Elysée Palace.
21 June 1977

As for Europe, the task of supplementing political *détente* with military *détente* assumes a special urgency. What can be done towards this end? As we see it, the following could be done:

To have the participants in the European Security Conference conclude a treaty undertaking not to be the first to use nuclear weapons against one another. The draft of such a treaty has already been proposed by the Warsaw Treaty countries. It is clear that provided all the parties to such a treaty observe it, this will rule out nuclear war in Europe, and also between European countries and the United States and Canada.

To agree, at least, not to enlarge the military–political groupings and alliances confronting each other in Europe by admitting new members.

Consistently to translate into life such measures as have already been stipulated in the Final Act of Helsinki – notification of major military exercises, invitation of observers to some of the exercises, and exchanges of military delegations. The experience of 2 yesrs indicates that these measures do to a certain extent promote greater trust and military *détente*. Bearing this in mind, we believe that it will perhaps be worth while to agree not to hold exercises above a level, of say, 50,000 to 60,000 men, since massive troop manoeuvres cause apprehension and look rather like military demonstrations.

Should the countries of the Southern Mediterranean wish that the military confidence-building measures envisaged by the Final Act would also cover that area, which is adjacent to Europe, we would regard this with sympathy.

Such is the programme of action which we are putting forward with the aim of achieving military *détente* in Europe.

It goes without saying that if other states have their own constructive proposals as regards this matter, we shall consider them seriously and with close attention.

All these problems could be discussed in detail in the near future – parallel with the current Vienna negotiations – through special joint consultations by all the states that took part in the Conference on Security and Co-operation in Europe.

Speech at a dinner given in the Kremlin in honour of Prime Minister of India Morarji Desai. 21 October 1977

Question: What opportunities do you see for concrete steps towards further *détente* in Europe?

Answer: Further *détente* in Europe depends in many ways on progress in resolving ripe, urgent questions of military *détente*. It can be even put in the following: we have reached a point at which the process of political *détente* should merge with the process of military *détente*. That is why the most important thing now is to take practical measures to reduce the arms race, to curb this race.

It is known that the Soviet Union has proposed a platform of measures for military *détente*. These include the renunciation of being the first to use nuclear weapons, the non-admittance of new members to existing military groups and limits on the strength of troops involved in military exercises.

Of course, the political aspect of the question cannot be overlooked for a minute. The climate in Europe which favours military *détente* is built on the foundation of a comprehensive development of relations among states, the strengthening of confidence among their leaders, respect for concluded treaties, and the consistent observance of agreements reached at the Helsinki meeting.

Many people in the West favour our suggestions for all-European congresses on co-operation in environmental protection, transport and energy. It would appear that it is possible to get down to business, but unfortunately even here our Western partners are slow and inconsistent.

Another point. We also do not want West Berlin to remain a white spot on the map of European *détente*. So far we have often come up against attempts to circumvent the quadripartite agreement. There have been actions showing a real unwillingness to accept that the city is not a part of the FRG. This all contradicts the spirit of *détente* and complicates the international situation. We cannot make any other appraisal.

So there are many factors determining the destiny of *détente*. One would like to hope that only those which facilitate its consolidation come into play.

Replies to questions from Vorwärts, *weekly of the Social-Democratic Party of Germany. 4 May 1978*

4.
RELATIONS WITH SOCIALIST COUNTRIES

The CC's attention has been constantly centred on questions of further cohesion and development of the world socialist system, and relations with the fraternal socialist countries and their Communist Parties.

The world socialist system has a quarter-century behind it. From the standpoint of development of revolutionary theory and practice these have been exceptionally fruitful years. The socialist world has given the communist and working-class movement experience which is of tremendous and truly historic importance. This experience shows:

Socialism, which is firmly established in the states now constituting the world socialist system, has proved its great viability in the historical contest with capitalism.

The formation and strengthening of the world socialist system has been a powerful accelerator of historical progress which was started by the Great October Revolution. Fresh prospects have opened up for the triumph of socialism all over the world; life has provided confirmation of the conclusion drawn by the 1969 International Meeting of Communist and Workers' Parties that 'the world socialist system is the decisive force in the anti-imperialist struggle'.

The world socialist system has been making a great contribution to the fulfilment of a task of such vital importance for all the peoples as the prevention of another world war. It is safe to say that many of the imperialist aggressors' plans were frustrated thanks to the existence of the world socialist system and its firm action.

The period under review was marked by important successes in *co-ordinating the foreign-policy activity* of the fraternal Parties and states. The most important international problems and events in this period were considered collectively by the representatives of socialist countries on various levels.

The Warsaw Treaty Organisation has been and continues to be the main centre for co-ordinating the foreign-policy activity of the fraternal countries.

The Warsaw Treaty countries displayed the initiative of putting forward a full-scale programme for strengthening peace in Europe, which is pivoted on the demand that the immutability of the existing state borders should be secured. The Political Consultative Committee has devoted several of its sittings to formulating and concretising this programme.

The Warsaw Treaty countries can also undoubtedly count among their political assets the fact that the plans which had existed within NATO to give the FRG militarists access to nuclear weapons have not been realised.

Joint efforts by the socialist states have also made it possible to achieve substantial progress in solving a task of such importance for stabilising the situation in Europe as the strengthening of the international positions of the German Democratic Republic. The so-called Hallstein Doctrine has been defeated. The GDR has already been recognised by 27 states, and this process is bound to continue.

Active and consistent support from the Soviet Union and other socialist countries is vitally important for the struggle of the peoples of Vietnam and the other countries of Indochina against the imperialist interventionists. The steps taken by the socialist states in the Middle East have become one of the decisive factors which have frustrated the imperialist plans of overthrowing the progressive régimes in the Arab countries.

In the United Nations and other international bodies, the socialist countries, acting together, have put forward many proposals of key international importance. These proposals have been in the focus of world attention.

As a result of the collective formulation and implementation of a number of measures in recent years, the *military organisation of the Warsaw Treaty* has been further improved. The armed forces of the allied powers are in a state of high readiness and are capable of guaranteeing the peaceful endeavour of the fraternal peoples.

In short, comrades, the socialist countries' multilateral political co-operation is becoming ever closer and more vigorous. We set ourselves definite aims and work jointly to achieve them. This is naturally of tremendous importance, especially in the present conditions of the contest between the two world social systems.

Of equal importance are *co-operation in the economic sphere* and extension and deepening of national–economic ties between the socialist countries. The period under review has also been fruitful in this respect.

> *Report of the Central Committee of the Communist Party of the Soviet Union to the 24th Congress of the CPSU. 30 March 1971*

Our foreign policy has always been and will continue to be a class policy, a socialist one in content and aim. And it is precisely its socialist character that makes it a peace policy. 'We know, we know only too well, the incredible misfortunes that war brings to the workers and peasants', Lenin stressed (*Collected Works*, Vol. 33, p. 148). Lenin's conclusion was crystal clear: to safeguard peace by all means; having started peaceful construction, to make every effort to continue it without interruption. The Soviet state has always followed this course charted by Lenin. From the first foreign policy act of Soviet power – the Decree on Peace – to the Peace Programme of the 24th Congress of the CPSU, our Party and state have steadily adhered to the main guide-lines of struggle for peace and for the freedom and security of the peoples.

For nearly a quarter of a century – nearly half the life of the federal Soviet state – we have no longer been alone and have forged ahead together with the fraternal countries. We have repeatedly declared that we consider it our prime international task to consolidate and develop the world socialist system.

In the early and most difficult years of the People's Democracies, the Soviet Union played the decisive part in defending them against imperialist interference, and on many occasions gave them the necessary political and economic support. Later, too, joint defence against imperialism's hostile sallies, against its attempts to undermine the socialist system in one country or another, continued, and continues, to be one of the important prerequisites for the successful development of the world socialist system.

As a result of collective efforts and hard-fought battles against the class enemy we forged a lasting alliance of socialist states and a dependable system of all-round fraternal co-operation, which has become, as it were, the natural way of life for each of our countries. We have learned to carry on our day-to-day tasks successfully, to patiently arrive at suitable solutions of issues that cannot be resolved in capitalist conditions. And in doing this, we have learned to harmonise ths of each with the interests of all and to co-operate, sweeping aside everything that may hinder or complicate the joint progress.

When the question of uniting the Soviet Republics in a single Union of Soviet Socialist Republics arose 50 years ago, Lenin pointed out that the Union was necessary in order to withstand the military onslaught of imperialism, to defend the gains of the Revolution, and to accomplish the peaceful creative tasks of socialist construction more successfully by common effort.

In principle, the same applies to the fraternal community of sovereign socialist states that belong to the Warsaw Treaty Organisation and the Council for Mutual Economic Assistance. This community was formed primarily to counter the imperialist threat, the aggressive imperialist military blocs, and to safeguard in common the cause of socialism and peace. And we have every reason to declare that never have socialism's positions been as firm as they are today, and that the cause of peace is gaining one victory after another.

But even in the present conditions, far from diminishing, the need for unity and the closest co-operation among socialist countries has become even greater. Today we require unity, co-operation and joint action chiefly in order to accomplish more quickly and effectively the tasks of developing socialist society and building communism. Moreover, we require unity, cohesion and co-operation in order to attain the best results in safeguarding and consolidating the peace, so vital for all the peoples, to further the international *détente*, and to effectively repulse all aggressive sallies of the imperialists, all attempts to impinge on the interests of socialism.

This is why the Soviet Union has always been and always will be an active champion of unity and co-operation among all the socialist countries.

Report at a gala joint meeting of the CPSU Central Committee, the USSR Supreme Soviet and the RSFSR Supreme Soviet, in the Kremlin Palace of Congresses. 21 December 1972

Nowadays we have a priceless possession that we share in common. For after the Second World War there came into being not only a whole group of socialist states, but also what we call the socialist community. This is an utterly new, hitherto unheard-of phenomenon. It is not an ordinary alliance of states but a socialist alliance based on common ideology and goals, on international solidarity of the working people, an alliance in which the working class and its tested vanguard, the Communist and Workers' Parties, became the leading force for the first time ever.

The establishment and development of the alliance took both time and a good deal of collective effort. It was necessary to find an answer to many fundamentally new questions of theory and practice; it was essential to react to various turns of events in a well-considered and timely way. Experience has convincingly shown that with the right Marxist–Leninist approach we have solved and are able to solve even the most complex problems, so as to promote the strengthening of each socialist country individually and the socialist community as a whole.

Today we have principles and forms of many-sided co-operation that have been tested in practice. Our collective organisations have acquired experience and become stronger. The Warsaw Treaty has become a reliable, effective instrument of peace and socialism. The activity of the Council for Mutual Economic Assistance contributes to the development of the highly important historical process of economic integration of socialist countries. We are all well aware of how beneficial co-operation and specialisation in production and exchanges in science and technology are for our countries. We are fully resolved to more actively utilise the opportunities and reserves of our co-operation and intensify the new type of relations that have evolved in the socialist community.

Socialism is, perhaps, the most influential factor in world politics. And we are proud of the fact that its impact on the peoples is wholesome. It is a fact, comrades, that at present practically all major steps to peace and to the development of mutually advantageous co-operation of states are directly or indirectly associated with the initiatives and active joint actions of socialist states. Mankind can see that the socialist community champions the peaceable foreign policy course handed down to us by the great Lenin!

Everyone knows how much has been done in recent years to achieve a turn in international relations from the cold war atmosphere poisoned with mutual animosity and distrust to normal, reasonable forms of inter-state intercourse based on the principles of peaceful coexistence. This process which requires constant political struggle has already resulted in substantial achievements which, we can safely say, are of historical significance.

The forces of war and reaction are far from giving up. The socialist countries cannot close their eyes to the intrigues of those who are opposed to peace, they cannot but draw relevant conclusions from this.

Significant and urgent problems need to be resolved, and without delay.

The Soviet Union, as well as other socialist countries, has repeatedly declared that it is ready to take decisive measures for limitation of the arms race and then the reduction of armaments. We reiterate again that we are ready, in particular, to agree on the reduction of troops and armaments in Europe. The task of more effective and universal application of the Treaty on the Non-Proliferation of Nuclear Weapons is becoming more urgent than ever. We have been ready for a long time now to sit down and negotiate at a World Disarmament Conference. We are ready to come to an agreement about the steps for slackening the confrontation between the existing blocs, and in the future bringing about their complete elimination. In a word, there will be no lack of co-operation on our part.

Comrades, for centuries almost every generation in Europe, and not only in Europe, had 'a war of its own'. Our generation had to bear the grim burden of the most destructive war in the history of mankind. Its scars have left its mark on millions of us, on our countries, in the memories of our peoples. They will not allow those of us who are alive to forget our duty to those who are no longer with us and those who are to come in order to continue our cause.

I have been once again made mindful of this high duty by the honorary award of fraternal Poland, the Order of Virtuti Militari. I will not conceal that I am moved by the fact that the State Council and the Government of the Polish People's Republic have honoured me with such an order – the highest award for military merits.

I accept this signal honour as a symbol of great friendship between our countries, between our people, which was forged in the grim days of fighting against the aggressor, and in the days of peaceful creative labour. I can say of myself that I have been and remain a soldier – a soldier of peace, a soldier of the great army of fighters for communism. There can be no greater happiness for a Communist than to serve the interests of socialism and peace, the interests of strengthening friendship and brotherhood among peoples. Never have I had, nor will I have, ideals that are nearer to my heart, dear comrades.

For ages humanity, striving for security, was guided by the formula: 'If you want peace, prepare for war.' In our nuclear epoch this formula presents a special danger. A human being dies only once but over the past years sufficient weapons have been accumulated to annihilate everything living on earth several times over. Fully realising this, we have said and repeat: 'If you want peace, pursue a peace policy, fight for it!' This was, is and will be the motto of our socialist foreign policy!

We Soviet Communists, the entire Soviet people are gratified to see that People's Poland, our nearest neighbour and good friend, is an active member of the fraternal family, an energetic participant in all creative undertakings of the socialist community. The Soviet people are proud of this friendship with the Polish people, a people who have a thousand-year history, a people rich in culture and talent, a people who have chosen for their Motherland the road of socialism for ever. On the day of the glorious thirtieth anniversary of People's Poland, we wish you, dear brothers, new great achievements, prosperity and happiness!

Speech at a ceremonial session of the Sejm of the Polish People's Republic to mark the 30th anniversary of the resurrection of Poland. Warsaw, 21 July 1974

This year and next are a time of remarkable anniversaries commemorating the establishment of people's power in a number of fraternal countries. It is a pleasure to realise that they approach their anniversaries with outstanding results in different fields of social, economic and cultural development. These results are particularly notable when viewed against the background of the unprecedentedly intensified economic, social and political instability in the capitalist world.

We are convinced that the greater the scope of the all-round co-operation between the socialist states, and the closer it brings them together, the more apparent the advantages of the new system will be.

And that is the way relations between the Soviet Union and the German Democratic Republic are developing. The militant comradely co-operation between our two Parties – the Communist Party of the Soviet Union and the Socialist Unity Party of Germany – keeps developing and becoming all the stronger. The peoples of our two countries are united by the close bonds of highly diversified relations and contacts in all fields involving literally millions of people. The GDR has long since become one of the USSR's biggest economic partners. And our people know from experience that they have a solid, reliable partner that conscientiously carries out its commitments. We also know that the GDR highly regards our assistance in supplying it with raw materials, machinery and other goods.

The multilateral co-operation of the fraternal countries within the framework of socialist economic integration is acquiring ever-growing significance. Projects connected with production co-operation, joint planning and collective research are already under way. And in the process such major problems as improving quality and technical standards in engineering, developing the raw-material and fuel base, and eliminating shortages of certain types of goods on the world socialist market come to the forefront.

I have no doubt that the German Democratic Republic, together with the other fraternal countries, will make a worthy contribution to solving these problems and ensuring that the socialist community is in the forefront of the scientific and technological progress.

We are living at a time when the prerequisites exist for a cardinal reconstruction of international relations, above all here, in Europe. The way is being paved for establishing good-neighbourly relations and mutually beneficial co-operation based on peaceful coexistence of states with differing social systems, which the Soviet country has advocated right from the first. And if today this task is being carried out in practice, we must declare outright: this has become possible, above all, thanks to the strengthening of world socialism and the immeasurably greater role played by the socialist states in the world arena.

For understandable reasons the socialist countries' relations with the Federal Republic of Germany occupy a special place in the complex of problems on which the durability of European peace depends. We all pay great heed to this. I feel there are grounds to speak highly of the progress attained in this respect in recent years.

It should be stressed that the policy of the German Democratic Republic, which is working for the normalisation and development of relations between the two German states on the basis of the principles of peaceful coexistence, is an important integral part of the general course pursued by the socialist countries and an important element in international *détente*, especially in Europe.

The transition, which has lately taken place in relations between the socialist countries and the FRG, from enmity and confrontation to peaceful, mutually advantageous co-operation, has the support of the people of Europe, including, as we understand it, the majority of the population in the FRG itself. We regard this as an assurance of further successes for the policy of peace and *détente.*

The socialist countries have done much in the struggle for the convocation and success of the All-European Conference. We were never under the illusion that it would be easy to hold such a meeting, the first of its kind in history. And, indeed, there were, and still are, difficulties at the Conference. Some stem from a natural divergence in views between the participants on individual questions, and others from the desire of some to obtain unilateral advantages for themselves. However, it is already clear that the interests of ensuring peace in Europe make it imperative for the All-European Conference to complete its work in the near future. The USSR, the GDR and other socialist countries are making every effort to ensure the success of the Conference so as to establish a firm foundation for security and peaceful co-operation in Europe.

We proceed from the assumption that the Conference decisions will facilitate the development of both bilateral and multilateral interstate co-operation on the European continent in the political, economic, scientific and cultural fields and other spheres of human endeavour. Our common task is to help to gradually bring about a new epoch in the life of old Europe – an epoch of good relations and mutual trust.

The policy worked out and pursued jointly by the countries of our community shows quite clearly that the socialist states are prepared to play an active part in achieving this goal. They extend the hand of peace and friendship to the other countries on the continent and hope for constructive co-operation.

And this not only applies to Europe, it also holds true on a world scale. Inspired by the principles of the Leninist internationalist policy which is geared to ensuring social progress in conditions of peace and security of nations, the USSR, the GDR and all the states of the socialist community are conducting a tireless struggle to reduce the danger of war, lessen the extent of military confrontation, limit the arms race and reduce the burden of expenditures on this race, and to achieve disarmament. This policy of ours is acknowledged and supported by all upright people.

Joint action by the socialist countries can, as before, play a useful and, I'd say, indispensable part in solving acute international problems in the interests of peace and security of nations. The co-ordination of our political efforts in the international arena for strengthening peace, and the fraternal co-operation of the armed forces of the Warsaw Treaty countries in the name of peace are all factors of the utmost importance. Here, as in fulfilling the tasks of internal development, the consolidation and unity of states of the socialist community is the real guarantee of our further success.

Speech at a meeting in Berlin dedicated to the 25th anniversary of the formation of the German Democratic Republic. Berlin, 6 October 1974

No impartial person can deny that the socialist countries' influence on world affairs is becoming ever stronger and deeper. That, comrades, is a great boon to mankind as a whole, to all those who aspire to freedom, equality, independence, peace and progress.

In socialist countries, the past 5 years have seen steady progress and confident advance to developed socialist society, to communism. Along with their further political consolidation, there have been rapid growth of social production and a rise in their people's material and cultural standards.

The ties between socialist states are becoming ever closer with the flowering of each socialist nation and the strengthening of their sovereignty, and elements of community are increasing in their policy, economy, and social life. There is a gradual levelling up of their development. This process of a gradual drawing together of socialist countries is now operating quite definitely as an objective law.

Of course, much depends on the policy of the ruling parties and their ability to safeguard unity, to combat isolation and national exclusiveness, to honour the common international tasks, and to act jointly in performing them.

Thanks to their unity, solidarity and mutual support, socialist countries have succeeded in fulfilling major tasks in the past 5 years, achieving what they had long been working for.

First of all, mention must be made of the victory of the Vietnamese people.

Imperialism's biggest post-Second-World-War bid to destroy a socialist state by armed force and crush a national liberation revolution suffered failure. The heroism and selfless dedication of the Vietnamese people, together with unremitting support from the socialist countries and the world's progressives, proved stronger than the armies of interventionists and their henchmen. The cause of freedom and independence triumphed.

The Soviet people take pride in having rendered considerable aid to Vietnam in its struggle against the imperialist invaders. Having won independence and national unity at a high price, the people of Vietnam are now working arduously to restore their country and are building the socialist future. Vietnam's victory has opened new horizons for all of South-east Asia. It was a glorious victory, and will be inscribed forever in the history of the peoples' struggle for freedom and socialism.

In Vietnam's wake freedom was won by Laos and Cambodia. We Soviet people send our most ardent fraternal greetings to the Communists, patriots and all working people of these countries, and wish them further success in the struggle for peace, democracy and social progress.

The worldwide recognition of the sovereignty of the German Democratic Republic, its entry into the United Nations, and the international confirmation of the inviolability of the western frontiers of the GDR, Poland and Czechoslovakia are an outstanding result of the concerted efforts of socialist states. Now the Munich diktat has been invalidated once and for all in legal terms as well. The most important results of the liberation struggle of the European peoples during and after the Second World War have been formalised. Conditions have been created for stable peace and good-neighbour co-operation in Europe and beyond it.

Socialism has taken deep root in Cuban soil. The efforts of US imperialism, still clinging to its policy of diplomatic and economic blockade, have been to no avail. On the contrary, Cuba's international situation has improved and her prestige has grown. The Cuban Communists' Congress, the Party's programme platform and the country's new constitution show that the first socialist state in the Western hemisphere is making steady progress. We rejoice fraternally over the achievements of our Cuban comrades and heartily wish them complete success in their efforts to assure the flowering of the socialist Republic of Cuba.

In its relations with the socialist countries, the CPSU firmly follows the tested rule of conducting affairs in the spirit of true equality and interest in

137

each other's successes, of working out decisions that meet international, as well as national, interests. No matter what problems arise, we believe that they must be resolved in the spirit of strengthening friendship, unity and co-operation. That is how we shape our relations with the fraternal socialist states – Bulgaria, Hungary, Vietnam, the German Democratic Republic, the Korean People's Democratic Republic, Cuba, Mongolia, Poland, Romania, Czechoslovakia and Yugoslavia.

The main basis of our close co-operation, its soul and the guiding, organising force, is the indissoluble militant alliance of the *Communist Parties of socialist countries*, the identity of their world outlook, their aims and will. The Central Committee, its Political Bureau, we can say with assurance, have all these years devoted unflagging attention to strengthening our fraternal friendship with these parties. And we can say with deep gratification that the fraternal parties have done likewise.

Today, the ties between the fraternal parties present an impressive picture of deep, varied and systematic contacts between thousands upon thousands of fighters for the common cause, builders of socialism and communism – from Party leaders to officials of local Party committees and Party branches at factories and collective farms. These ties ensure valuable exchange of experience, help us to advance with greater confidence, and add to our common strength. It is one of our Party's most important tasks, the Central Committee holds, to assure their continued all-round expansion.

I report to the Congress with deep satisfaction that the leaders of the Communist Parties of the socialist community maintain constant contact. There have been many friendly multilateral meetings of General and First Secretaries of Central Committees in recent years. Three of them took place in the Crimea. There have also been meetings during Party congresses, in particular, last year in Budapest and Warsaw. Regular multilateral and bilateral meetings enable us to consult on all major problems that arise, to share in each other's joys and sorrows, as the saying goes, and jointly chart our further advance.

On the whole, complete unity and fruitful co-operation are the hallmark of our relations with most parties of socialist countries. A few parties, as we know, have particular views on a number of questions, but the overall tendency is unquestionably characterised by a growing cohesion of socialist countries. We value this tendency highly, and shall, as before, promote it in every way. This requires joint efforts by the fraternal parties on the basis of the tested principles of Marxism–Leninism, socialist internationalism, equality and comradely co-operation.

The *Warsaw Treaty* Political Consultative Committee is an important form of co-operation among leaders of our parties and countries. The Treaty dependably serves the interests of peace and socialism. The significance of the initiatives advanced by our Political Consultative Committee in recent years is self-evident. Many of them have been the basis of decisions taken by major international forums or are reflected in a number of important bilateral inter-state acts.

We are firmly against the world's division into opposing military blocs and the arms race. Our attitude on this score is well known. But we must make it clear that as long as the NATO bloc continues to exist and as long as militarist elements continue their arms drive, our country and the other signatories of the Warsaw Treaty will continue to strengthen this political–military alliance.

The socialist countries are playing an ever more prominent part in the world economy as well. The socialist community has now become the world's most dynamic economic force. In the past 5 years the industry of its member countries grew four times as swiftly as that of the developed capitalist states. In 1975 the industrial output of the countries of our community was more than double that of the Common Market countries.

The Party Central Committee devoted unremitting attention to questions of *economic co-operation* with the socialist states, to its further development on the basis of mutual advantage and socialist internationalism. There have been many new developments in this field in the past 5 years.

The CC Political Bureau attaches special importance to the long-term programme of socialist economic integration adopted by us jointly with other CMEA countries in 1971. This programme, comrades, raises co-operation among socialist countries to a much higher level than ordinary promotion of trade. For example, it means joint development of natural resources for common benefit, joint construction of large industrial complexes to meet the needs of all the partners, and co-operation between our countries' enterprises and whole industries planned for many years ahead. Implementation of this Comprehensive Programme has already significantly deepened our economic interaction, and made our economies mutually complementary to a greater extent, to the considerable advantage of all concerned.

Already today socialism exercises a tremendous influence on the thinking and sentiment of hundreds of millions of people all over the world. It assures working people freedom, truly democratic rights, well-being, the broadest possible access to knowledge, and a firm sense of security. It brings peace, respect for the sovereignty of all countries and equal inter-state co-operation, and is a pillar of support to peoples fighting for their freedom and independence. And the immediate future is sure to provide new evidence of socialism's boundless possibilities, of its historical superiority over capitalism. Along with the other fraternal parties, the CPSU will continue to do everything to enhance the appeal of the example of victorious socialism.

In its relations with China, our Party firmly adheres to the course charted by the 24th Congress. This course has been proved correct. We shall continue the struggle – a principled and irreconcilable struggle – against Maoism.

At the same time, we should like to repeat once again that in our relations with China, as with other countries, we adhere firmly to the principles of equality, respect of sovereignty and territorial integrity, non-interference in each other's internal affairs, and non-use of force. In short, we are prepared to normalise relations with China in accordance with te principles of peaceful coexistence. What is more, we can say with assurance that if Peking returns to a policy truly based on Marxism–Leninism, if it abandons its hostile policy towards the socialist countries and takes the road of co-operation and solidarity with the socialist world, there will be an appropriate response from our side and opportunities will open for developing good relations between the USSR and the People's Republic of China consonant with the principles of socialist internationalism. The matter rests with the Chinese side.

Report of the CPSU Central Committee to the 25th Congress of the Communist Party of the Soviet Union held in Moscow. 24 February 1976

As always, the Political Bureau of the Central Committee is giving priority attention to the development of fraternal relations with the *socialist countries*.

We can state with satisfaction that the last few months have been marked by considerable successes in the further consolidation of the positions of world socialism.

The great community of socialist states is growing stronger and developing successfully. The 25th Congress of the CPSU gave a high assessment of the fraternal co-operation of our countries and Parties, and I will not repeat it now. The congresses of a number of fraternal Parties (Bulgaria, Czechoslovakia, the GDR, and Mongolia) already held after the 25th CPSU Congress, just as the congresses of the Communists of Hungary, Poland and Cuba, held somewhat earlier, asserted once again the unbreakable ideological unity and political cohesion of our close-knit family. Recently we played host to a Party and government delegation from Mongolia, headed by Comrade Tsedenbal. We had constructive talks and signed a number of important agreements. In November we are expecting to receive here a Polish delegation headed by Comrade Gierek. The visit to the Soviet Union of Comrade Ceausescu and our comradely talks with him have contributed to the development of our friendship with Romania and its Communist Party.

The economic co-operation between the socialist countries continues to progress. The 30th session of the Council for Mutual Economic Assistance held this summer adopted important decisions, in particular, on drawing up long-term special-purpose programmes for the individual branches of industry, such as the production of raw materials, electric power and food. In other words, socialist economic integration is gaining strength.

This time the session was attended by representatives not only of Yugoslavia, but also of Vietnam, the KPDR, Laos and Angola. This is indicative of the growing prestige of the CMEA and its expanding ties.

The Political Bureau of the Central Committee constantly maintains close *contacts with the leaders of the fraternal Parties of the socialist countries.* In this respect I also had to work much. Apart from the useful meetings in the course of the Berlin conference of Communist Parties at the end of June, including the meetings with Comrade Tito, I had talks, as you know, with Comrades Gierek, Husak, Zhivkov, Ceausescu, Tsedenbal, Honecker and Kadar in the Crimea. Those were detailed, truly comradely and frank discussions bearing on many topical questions of our co-operation and joint actions.

On the whole this year's round of the Crimean meetings turned out to be still another stage, as it were, in the development of our fraternal co-operation and in the further elaboration of our joint positions. The Political Bureau of the CPSU Central Committee has approved the work carried out during these meetings. A number of Parties also adopted special resolutions expressing a high appreciation of the importance of those meetings.

In a word, comrades, our great community of socialist states is living a rich, full life. This is a factor of major importance and our Leninist Party will do everything in its power so that this state of affairs will continue in future.

Of great significance is the fact that the *reunification of Vietnam has been completed and it has been proclaimed a socialist republic.* The Socialist Republic of Vietnam now has a population of over 50 million which makes it the third biggest socialist state in the world.

Vietnam, with its long history of heroic struggle against imperialist aggression, for freedom and independence, with its high revolutionary prestige, today has become an important factor of peace and progress in South-East Asia and, indeed, in all Asia. We wholeheartedly acclaim the historic victory of our Vietnamese friends and wish them every success!

As before, *our relations with China* are a question apart. Complicated political processes are taking place there. It is still difficult to say what will be the future political course of the PRC. However, it is clear even now that the foreign-policy line Peking had pursued for one and a half decades has been thoroughly discredited throughout the world.

As for the Soviet Union, it has consistently pursued a course of trying to improve relations with China. As it was stressed at the 25th Congress of the CPSU, 'in our relations with China, as with other countries, we adhere firmly to the principles of equality, respect of sovereignty and territorial integrity, non-interference in each other's internal affairs, and non-use of force. In short, we are prepared to normalise relations with China in line with the principles of peaceful coexistence.' More than that. It was clearly indicated at our congress that we stand for the restoration of good relations between the USSR and the PRC in keeping with the principles of socialist internationalism. I would like to underline that, in our opinion, there are no issues in relations between the USSR and the PRC that could not be resolved in the spirit of good-neighbourliness. We will continue working towards this goal. The matter will depend on what stand will be taken by the other side.

As to our relations with *Albania*, we, as it is known, are prepared to restore them and consider that there are no objective factors dividing us.

Speech at the Plenary Meeting of the Central Committee of the Communist Party of the Soviet Union. 25 October 1976

I regard the award of the highest decorations of socialist Czechoslovakia, above all, as a high appraisal of the activities of the Communist Party of the Soviet Union, its Central Committee and Political Bureau, aimed at consistently promoting all-round co-operation between our two countries and strengthening friendship between our peoples.

I regard this as a recognition of the efforts of the people who accomplished the Great October Socialist Revolution and built socialism; the people who bore the brunt of the hardest of wars in human history – the liberation war against fascism; the people who had the honoured but uneasy task of blazing the trail towards the building of communism.

I regard the high awards from fraternal Czechoslovakia also as a tribute to the heroic Soviet Army servicemen, those who are living and those who have fallen, who fought for the liberation of Czechoslovak soil from the fascist sway and for our common cause, for peace in the world.

In these days, when the 255 million Soviet people, under the guidance of the Communist Party, are carrying out all over the vast expanses of their great Homeland work that is unprecedented in scope and daring, a work aimed at creating their communist future, it gives the Soviet citizens a feeling of joy and encouragement to realise that they have in the lands of socialism brothers marching along side by side with them.

We are tackling the difficult tasks of building a new life, together, unselfishly helping each other and learning from each other's experience. Together, we are working to safeguard the security and the peaceful endeavours of our nations. Together, we are working for a lasting peace in the world. Never in history has there been a friendship that is closer and more open-hearted than this friendship of comrades, of people who share the same ideals and who are united in a common cause, the friendship of fraternal nations of socialism. It is this kind of friendship that links the Soviet Union and Czechoslovakia, and also the Communist Parties of our two countries.

The CPSU, as the recent Plenary Meeting of our Party's Central Committee has confirmed once more, will continue to pursue a consistent course towards the further strengthening of this brotherly friendship.

A cause can be considered really secure if it has a future. The relations between our two countries do have a future. This future is communism. It is guaranteed by the indestructible ideological unity of our Communist Parties and by their devotion to the teaching of Marx and Lenin. It is guaranteed by the identity of our system and of the will of the working class and all working people of our socialist countries.

> *Speech in the Kremlin on being presented with the title of Hero of the CSSR and the Klement Gottwald Order, the highest awards of the Czechoslovak Socialist Republic. 2 November 1976*

We have a firm basis for the further development of Soviet–Yugoslav friendly ties. This basis is a fairly high level of co-operation at present, the experience gained in working together in various fields, and our common adherence to the principles of equality and non-interference in each other's domestic affairs, combined with an internationalist approach to and careful consideration of the vital interests of both countries.

The position of the Soviet Union on the fundamental issues of present-day world politics is identical or similar to that of Yugoslavia. Our country, in close co-operation with the fraternal socialist nations, with its Warsaw Treaty allies, is doing everything it can to promote equitable peaceful relations among nations, whatever their social system, check the aggressors, reduce and eventually remove the threat of a new world war, and aid the just cause of freedom and independence of nations. Yugoslavia, a socialist country, is taking an active part in the non-alignment movement, which is also for peace and equal, peaceful co-operation and opposes imperialist diktat and arbitrary rule in international affairs.

We are convinced that wider co-operation between the socialist countries and the movement of non-alignment could effectively help to free mankind from the danger of thermonuclear war and from the attempts of imperialism to shape the destinies of peoples in accordance with its whims, to impose its will on them. Yugoslavia undoubtedly can greatly contribute to this.

In a word, Soviet–Yugoslav co-operation continues to develop successfully in all spheres and the prospects of its further development are good. This, I believe, can only be welcomed.

In some places in the West, however, it has recently become fashionable to besmear our good relations with you and to spread the most absurd stories about them. The authors of these fables try to paint Yugoslavia as a poor and defenceless Little Red Riding Hood whom the terrible, rapacious wolf – the aggressive Soviet Union – threatens to tear to pieces and swallow up.

I do not know what these fables are more indicative of – an absolute lack of understanding of the principles on which relations between socialist states are built, or a cynical view that the public will gobble up any lie if it is repeated persistently and often enough.

To make our position on this 'issue', so artificially created by our countries' enemies, clear-cut, I would like to take the opportunity offered by our friendly gathering here to say the following:

In its approach to relations with Yugoslavia the Soviet Union firmly proceeds from a desire to strengthen and develop friendly relations with it on the basis of full equality, mutual respect and trust and absolute non-interference in each other's domestic affairs. We want to develop these relations to the mutual advantage of the peoples of our two countries and for our common cause – the cause of peace and socialism.

I would like to add that our attitude towards Yugoslavia is certainly not determined merely by the standards of correct inter-state relationship and mutual benefit. No, at the core of our feelings towards the Socialist Federal Republic of Yugoslavia there also lie other, no less important factors. These are the historical, centuries-old traditions of deep mutual liking and friendship between our peoples, and also the memory of their soldierly brotherhood sealed with blood in the joint heroic struggle against fascism.

Speech at the supper in the Building of the Federal Executive Council of the SFRY in Belgrade. 15 November 1976

145

The lessons of war are binding lessons. They teach us to spare no effort to prevent a recurrence of the tragedy of the past and the flaring up anew of the peaceful skies of this planet in a world conflagration. And we are happy to know that the Soviet Union and Yugoslavia are acting jointly today in the great battle for peace, for a durable and stable peace.

The past decades have taught us well to value and cherish the friendship of the peoples of our two countries. It gives us a sense of profound satisfaction, as Communists, that our parties, countries and peoples, inspired by the Marxist–Leninist ideals, are closely co-operating in the accomplishment of the historic tasks of socialist and communist construction.

Our countries, being free, consistently defend the right of every people and every nation to free and independent development, and persistently work for a restructuring of international relations along the lines of equality and justice. We have every ground for sayi ag that we have been and remain faithful to the internationalist ideals which had inspired us in a most difficult struggle against the Nazi aggressors.

The world is changing and it is changing fast. But such values as the friendship and comradely mutual assistance of the peoples building socialism and communism not only retain their full significance, but are acquiring a still greater importance. And we are determined to go forward step by step, together with you, dear comrades, in strengthening the bonds of brotherhood which have long since linked the peoples of the Soviet Union and Yugoslavia.

May the brotherhood and friendship of the peoples of our countries continue to grow stronger and flourish!

May the internationalist solidarity of the Soviet and Yugoslav Communists become yet stronger!

Speech on being presented with the Order of Freedom, the highest military award of the Socialist Federal Republic of Yugoslavia in Belgrade. 15 November 1976

It was not very long ago, last summer in fact, that Comrade Ceausescu and I met and in a frank and friendly manner discussed questions concerning the further development and deepening of Soviet–Romanian relations. We both believe that those were very good talks and, what is more important, useful talks, since much of what we then discussed is already being put into practice. As to our joint plans and our wishes, they go further, of course. There are no major unsolved problems between our countries. Still it is in the interest of all of us that the opportunities offered by the traditional Soviet–Romanian friendship are used as fully as possible for the benefit of our peoples. This is, in fact, the chief purpose of our current talks in Bucharest.

Conditions for the expansion and deepening of Soviet–Romanian co-operation – and I think all comrades will agree with this – do exist, of course.

Of decisive importance here is certainly the strengthening of the ties between the Communist Party of the Soviet Union and the Romanian Communist Party. For it is our parties that are called upon to be the chief architects and builders of Soviet–Romanian friendship. Contacts between the leaders of the two parties, meetings between party officials, regular exchanges of delegations and ties between local Party bodies – all these are vitally necessary. For, indeed, we are not just close neighbours. Our shared ideology and aims, the Marxist–Leninist ideals and the experience of equal co-operation gained over decades – all this constitutes an objective foundation for the pooling of our efforts in carrying out the many tasks confronting us.

Economic co-operation is important and it can become still more important. Our relations in this field are growing from year to year and they are not just expanding but are acquiring qualitatively new features. This is taking place both within the framework of the Council for Mutual Economic Assistance and on a bilateral basis. I have in mind the steps that we are taking to organise co-operation in tractor building, in the manufacture of farm machinery and in machine-tool construction. An agrarian country in the past, socialist Romania has now become an exporter of many industrial goods. By improving the division of labour among the socialist countries we can create vast markets for the national industries of each fraternal state. This will be of tremendous benefit, for such markets will help accelerate the growth rates and improve the well-being of the working people.

Contacts in the ideological field are becoming an increasingly important part of our co-operation and a factor of great significance for our common struggle against imperialism. Ties between the ideological workers of our parties, between research institutions, the editorial boards of newspapers and magazines, unions of creative workers and between art workers are growing stronger. But the main thing is that the friendship between our socialist countries is becoming a matter of vital concern for millions upon millions of Soviet and Romanian working people. It reaches their minds and their hearts.

Happy as we are to see co-operation taking place between our peoples today, we are determined to continue our efforts so that Soviet–Romanian friendship will flourish and grow stronger. We have every right, comrades, to regard all this as an historic gain of our Communist Parties.

I would like to say here, dear Romanian friends, that we in the Soviet Union highly value our co-operation with the Socialist Republic of Romania in matters concerning international politics, when such co-operation takes place, and we believe that the broader this co-operation, the better it will be for the cause of peace and socialism and for our common objectives and ideals.

We successfully co-operated with our Romanian comrades during the preparations for the Conference of European Communist Parties this year. We are successfully co-operating now in the preparation for the forthcoming Conference of the Political Consultative Committee of the Warsaw Treaty Organisation, a conference which, we hope, will make a new substantial contribution to strengthening peace in Europe and hence in the world.

Speech at the Dinner in the Palace of the State Council of the Socialist Republic of Romania in Bucharest. 22 November 1976

I should especially like to thank Comrade Nicolae Ceausescu, General Secretary of the Romanian Communist Party and President of the Socialist Republic of Romania, for the kind words he said about our Communist Party and about the Soviet people. Comrade Ceausescu spoke highly of the results of our talks. We agree with this assessment.

The joint Soviet–Romanian 'Statement on the Further Development of

Co-operation and Fraternal Friendship Between the CPSU and the Romanian Communist Party and Between the Soviet Union and Romania' which we have just signed is yet another confirmation of this.

Our exchange of views has been both useful and fruitful. Our talks have deepened the understanding between our parties and have strengthened the atmosphere of trust which is so important for the further consolidation of our fraternal relations. We have succeeded in jointly outlining new frontiers for our co-operation in key directions.

Friendship between the Soviet and Romanian peoples goes back many centuries. The people cherish their memories of century-old events when the independence of Romania and other Balkan countries was re-established thanks to the joint struggle of our peoples. And can the Soviet people forget how the Romanian working people responded with all their hearts to the courageous revolutionary mutiny on the battleship *Potemkin* in 1905? The internationalist solidarity displayed by the Romanian workers saved the heroes of the *Potemkin* from being extradited to the tsarist authorities.

The thunder of the Great October Socialist Revolution reverberated in Romania. Lenin, speaking of the revolutionary actions of the Romanian proletariat and peasantry, said that the fire of the proletarian rising 'spread to Romania'. These actions were a prelude to the decisive battles fought by the Romanian working class with the Communists at their head against the power of the bourgeoisie and the landlords.

When the gloomy night of fascism descended on your country, it was the Communists who raised the banner of struggle in Romania against the Hitlerites and their accomplices. In the period of the offensive against Hitler's armies on the Soviet–German front, the Romanian Communists carried out the victorious August rising and otherthrew the fascist régime. Shoulder to shoulder with the Soviet Army and the anti-fascists and patriots of other countries, the best sons of the Romanian people took part in the concluding battles against the Nazi enslavers. It was quite natural, therefore, that after being born in the crucible of these hard trials, the new people's Romania established, from the very first days of its existence, relations of friendship with the Soviet Union. From the first days of its existence it felt the all-round, comradely support of the Soviet Union. From the very first days of its existence, it became an active and respected member of the close-knit family of states that set out on the road leading to socialism.

149

Soviet and Romanian Communists have drawn their conclusions from the experience of history. Today, our relations are recorded in our Treaty of Friendship, Co-operation and Mutual Assistance. This treaty is based on the immutable principles of equality, independence and non-interference in each other's affairs, combined with comradely mutual assistance and loyalty to proletarian socialist internationalism. It expresses the will of our Communist Parties and the determination of the Soviet and Romanian peoples to preserve and multiply the fruits of Soviet–Romanian friendship. We shall firmly adhere to the letter and spirit of this treaty.

The great concept of friendship is usually regarded as being a purely emotional one. But I think that friendship between socialist countries is a concept with a much deeper content. It is first of all a political concept. It manifests itself in the historically determined and deeply conscious line of behaviour of the broadest masses of the people.

The Communists of the socialist countries have the right to be proud of the fact that they provide a practical example of inter-state relations free of national egoism and full of consideration for the interests of foreign friends and comrades in the struggle for Marxist–Leninist ideals. Where exploiting ruling classes have for centuries planted discord and alienation among nations, we have succeeded in sowing seeds of friendship which have borne mighty and abundant fruit.

The great multitude of reciprocal ties which now unite the fraternal countries of socialism combine to form an amazingly rich and graphic picture of co-operation of parties, state bodies and production collectives. This involves the co-operation of millions upon millions of people united by common aims and ideals and by feelings of comradeship and mutual trust. Such friendship is good support in performing the national tasks of every socialist country. At the same time, it serves well to strengthen the joint positions of world socialism.

Our class opponents know this. That is why they are trying hard to exploit any complication in relations between socialist states, trying in every way to sow doubt, discord and mutual distrust, to slander our countries and to distort their policies and the essence of their mutual relations. In this respect the imperialists unambiguously abide by the cynical principle 'the worse, the better'.

We in the socialist countries, however, are not simple rustics either, so to speak. We shall not give Messrs. the Imperialists the pleasure they are dreaming of. The best reply to our common ill-wishers is to multiply our efforts in rallying the countries of socialism on the principles of Marxism–Leninism and proletarian internationalism and to deepen our co-operation in carrying out the major tasks of socialist and communist construction. Comrades, you and we are acting precisely in this way.

I have in mind not only the deepening of the many-sided co-operation between the countries of the socialist community – members of the Warsaw Treaty Organisation and the Council for Mutual Economic Assistance – but also the strengthening of friendly ties between all socialist states without exception. This task, as you know, is not always simple and easy at present, but, I believe, its tremendous historical importance is clear to all. It can be said with great satisfaction that both of our countries – the Soviet Union and Romania – and both of our Communist Parties are striving to do everything they can so that this most important aim may be achieved as is demanded by the interests of lasting peace, the interests of socialism and the interests of the freedom, independence and progress of all nations.

It is a very important fact that Romania, the Soviet Union and all the member-countries of the Council for Mutual Economic Assistance are now extending their work on long-term special programmes of mutually advantageous economic co-operation. Implementation of these programmes will help to satisfy more fully the requirements of all the fraternal states for energy, raw materials, foodstuffs, mass consumption goods, engineering products and transportation facilities. Such co-operation is a reliable material basis of our friendship.

At the same time, of course, none of us intends to fence himself off from the rest of the world. The Soviet Union, Romania and other socialist countries consistently come out for extensively developing equal and mutually advantageous economic co-operation between all states. We are against any discrimination whatsoever in trade and economic relations. Experience shows that discrimination is not infrequently practised by capitalist countries which, by the irony of fate, still call themselves supporters of 'free trade'.

The socialist countries consistently come out for the establishment of just international economic relations and for respect for the rights and interests of the nations that have been liberated from colonial oppression and are demanding with complete justification that imperialism repay what it has plundered. For our part, we have given brotherly assistance to the emerging nations and will help them to overcome the aftermaths of colonialism and neo-colonialism.

Speech at the Soviet–Romanian Friendship Meeting in Bucharest. 24 November 1976

How shall I regard this award? How in general do we Communists regard awards? This order means for me a recognition of the soundness, correctness and importance of the policy pursued by the Communist Party of the Soviet Union, its Central Committee and the Central Committee Politbureau, and of the greatness of the cause which I serve in the capacity of General Secretary of the CPSU Central Committee.

We Communists have dedicated our life, energy and knowledge to the building of communism, the most just, humane and happy society on earth. We give all our strength to developing fruitful and effective co-operation among the socialist countries in order to attain this great goal. We spare no effort to bring about the most favourable international conditions for socialist construction and the progress of all nations. In present conditions this means, above all, the necessity to eliminate the danger of a new world war, to work for disarmament and secure a truly lasting peace and good-neighbourly co-operation of all the nations of our planet, which after all is not so big.

As for Soviet–Romanian relations, I want to stress, in the light of these historic tasks, that we strive to do our utmost to strengthen our fraternal friendship and co-operation and to wage successfully the joint struggle for the common noble goals.

Advancing side by side along this road, the peoples of Romania and the Soviet Union will strengthen the traditions of fraternity and solidarity steeled in the flames of war against fascism and in the day-by-day building of socialism.

If our Romanian friends believe that to these great common undertakings I have also contributed as a Communist and a leader, I accept this award with gratitude.

May our socialist community, which plays a leading role in the movement for peace and progress, prosper!

May Soviet–Romanian friendship, our invaluable common asset, strengthen and become deeper!

Speech in Bucharest on being presented with Romania's highest order, the Star of the Socialist Republic of Romania. 24 November 1976

My biography is a small part of the biography of our great socialist Homeland. From the very start it is linked with the Leninist Party and its work to build communism. It is natural therefore that I should regard this high award not only and not so much as a recognition of my personal services, although this award is very dear to me, but above all as a recognition of the great role which my country and the Soviet Communist Party have played in the effort to carry out the great ideals of Marx, Engels and Lenin.

In undertaking this gigantic and historic endeavour we are working shoulder to shoulder. Soviet–Bulgarian co-operation is now so comprehensive and covers so many fields that it has no precedent even in the rich history of our friendship. This is a direct result of the fact that the CPSU and the BCP cherish and promote relations of complete mutual trust, great sincerity and effective co-operation characteristic of our contacts at all levels.

The process of drawing closer together of the Soviet Union and Bulgaria is steadily developing. The results of the conference of the Political Consultative Committee of the Warsaw Treaty member states, held recently, have shown that the unity and co-operation of all the countries of the socialist community are constantly growing. In this one sees once again the creative force of our fraternal relations and the great force of proletarian and socialist internationalism. That is why, in accepting, together with the Gold Star of Hero of the People's Republic of Bulgaria, the Order bearing the name of Georgi Dimitrov, an outstanding internationalist and revolutionary, I am deeply moved.

The Soviet people highly value the cordial and fraternal relations which link them to the Bulgarian people. And I want to emphasise that Soviet Communists, our Party's Central Committee and its militant headquarters, the Central Committee Politbureau, have been doing and will continue to do everything to assure that Soviet–Bulgarian co-operation develops and our time-tested friendship grows stronger and becomes deeper from year to year.

You may be assured, comrades, that on my part I, as before, will spare no effort to promote the steady strengthening of this friendship which meets the vital interests of the peoples of our countries, and the interests of peace, socialism and communism.

Speech in the Kremlin on being presented for the second time with Bulgaria's highest awards, the Gold Star of Hero of the People's Republic of Bulgaria and the Order of Georgi Dimitrov. 2 December 1976

The establishment of socialism on German soil was an historic event in the life of Europe. The German Democratic Republic has become a solid element of the strong socialist community. It participates actively in the struggle for a lasting peace and for security in Europe and the world and has won respect and a deserved prestige in the world arena.

When the leaders of the Communist Parties of Europe gathered in the capital of the GDR last summer to consider ways of further strengthening peace and promoting social progress on the continent, all of us, participants in the meeting, deeply sensed, I believe, the symbolic meaning of that event – a vivid confirmation of the noble role being played today by new, socialist Berlin.

Friendship and co-operation of the GDR with the Soviet Union and all fraternal countries are expanding and growing stronger. They are based on close political and ideological co-operation and comprehensive economic integration, and, what is most important, they have been fully understood and accepted by the millions of working people in our countries. I make no secret of the fact that I am proud that I, together with my comrades, have had the honour of doing what I can to promote this cause which is of historical significance.

I wholeheartedly wish our German communist friends, workers, farmers, intellectuals, all citizens of the GDR, new successes in their creative work and in the building of a happy life!

At this moment, which is so meaningful for me, I want to assure you that I shall continue to work for the development of fraternal co-operation between the Soviet Union and the German Democratic Republic and, as before, I shall devote all my abilities, knowledge and experience to our common cause – the struggle for peace and communism.

Speech in the Kremlin on being presented with the highest awards of the GDR, the Star of Hero of the German Democratic Republic and the Order of the Great Star of Friendship of the Peoples. 13 December 1976

I accept the Gold Star of Hero and the Order of Sukhe-Bator as a symbol of unbreakable friendship between our states, parties and peoples. I accept the awards well realising that many thousands of Soviet people share them with me by right.

They are those who did not spare their blood, indeed their very lives, in the battles for the freedom and independence of their brothers, the people of Mongolia.

They are Soviet workers, engineers, technicians, specialists in various fields who, in fulfilling their internationalist duty, have worked and are working shoulder to shoulder with their Mongolian comrades on the construction sites of Darkhan and Erdenet and who, with their knowledge and experience, are helping to create the material and technical basis of socialism in Mongolia.

The awards belong to the great Party of Lenin, which, alongside the Mongolian People's Revolutionary Party, is the creator and inspirer of inviolable Soviet–Mongolian friendship.

It is gratifying to know that the friendship and co-operation between our countries are becoming deeper and richer in content with each year. The decisions which we jointly adopted during the last visit to the Soviet Union of the Mongolian party and government delegation, which you, Comrade Tsedenbal, headed, open a new chapter of our co-operation, of closer relations between our parties, countries and peoples. Herein we see an effective embodiment of the letter and the spirit of the Treaty of Friendship, Co-operation and Mutual Assistance which we signed in Ulan-Bator more than 10 years ago.

The title of Hero of the Mongolian People's Republic carries a great responsibility. I want to assure you, dear Comrade Tsedenbal, that the Communists and all working people of my country will remain faithful to the cause of Soviet–Mongolian friendship. We shall do everything we can to promote closer ties between the Soviet Union and people's Mongolia and greater unity of the forces of socialism and peace in order to bring about the triumph of the immortal ideas of Marxism-Leninism.

As for myself, our Mongolian friends may be assured that I shall spare no effort to help achieve these great goals.

Speech in the Kremlin on being presented with the highest awards of the Mongolian People's Republic, the Star of Hero of the MPR and the Order of Sukhe-Bator. 14 December 1976

In accepting the high award of the Republic of Cuba, I see in it, first and foremost, an expression of the bonds of revolutionary solidarity and the pure brotherly friendship that link our parties and peoples. It is with these feelings that I offer my heartfelt gratitude to the Central Committee of the Communist Party of Cuba, the State Council and the Government of the Republic of Cuba.

I think that not a single adult Soviet citizen, and certainly not a single one of the sixteen million Soviet Communists, is indifferent to the destiny of revolutionary Cuba.

Cuba is loved and respected in our country as a symbol of selfless heroism in the struggle for freedom and independence, for the rights of working people, as the banner of a new, socialist life that has been held up high over the Western Hemisphere.

It is gratifying to know, comrades, that in the struggle of Cuba for her freedom and for socialism the Soviet people have invariably marched side by side with their Cuban brothers. Today our co-operation in diverse spheres has assumed very broad scope. This benefits our two countries and benefits the cause of peace and national freedom.

I want to assure you that the Communist Party of the Soviet Union and the Soviet people — and with them to the best of his ability, Leonid Ilyich Brezhnev — will continue to do everything possible in future as well to safeguard and develop the indestructible friendship between the Land of October and the Island of Freedom!

Speech in the Kremlin on being presented with the Order of Playa Giron of the Republic of Cuba. 15 December 1976

In accepting the Order of Renaissance of Poland I as a Soviet Communist with pride think of the proletarian solidarity and the assistance which our Party has invariably given to the struggle of its Polish class brothers. The renaissance of Poland as an independent state is connected with the October Revolution and with the name of great Lenin. The liberation of Poland from Nazi enslavement is connected with the victorious operations of the Soviet Army and with the brotherhood of Soviet soldiers and Polish patriots forged in the battlefields. I shall make no secret of the fact that it is gratifying for me to realise that I made a modest contribution to the liberating mission of our army, and marched in its ranks on Polish soil in the victorious year of 1945. In subsequent years, too, many things linked me to Poland, to the creative work of Polish Communists and to the great undertakings, joys and concerns of socialist construction on Polish soil.

It is good, comrades, that we have not only preserved our friendship and brotherhood born in the flames of war and in class battles for socialism, but have also made them still more versatile and rich. The broad, one may even say, all-embracing Polish–Soviet co-operation, the deep and strong bonds linking our Parties and peoples – these are the things which the Communists of our countries are rightfully proud of. Today I accept the award that has been conferred on me as an expression of this fraternity and I swear allegiance to the cause of strengthening this fraternity.

Speech in the Kremlin on being presented with the Order of Renaissance of Poland with the Grand Cross. 16 December 1976

Inspired by the noble ideas of proletarian internationalism Soviet and Hungarian Communists have cherished and preserved their combat alliance – this invaluable legacy of the October Revolution and of the first Soviet Hungarian Republic – through all the toil and battles of our stormy age. They have together inscribed many bright chapters in the chronicles of the world revolutionary movement. Following the defeat of fascism and the triumph of the socialist revolution in Hungary, this alliance, as it were, has been imbued with a new life and a new quality. It has become a vital necessity for both our peoples and finds expression today in the countless forms of co-operation and friendship between our socialist states.

I should like to point out, in this context, the particularly great role played in the development of our co-operation by the fine comradely relations which we Soviet leaders have with the Hungarian leaders and above all with you, Comrade Kadar, the tried and tested internationalist and revolutionary, who enjoys the well-deserved prestige and trust of his Party and the people as well as of Communists in other countries.

Our Party highly appreciates the fact that we are marching together with our Hungarian colleagues and friends, shoulder to shoulder, in the united ranks of the fraternal socialist nations, in carrying out the manifold tasks of socialist and communist construction and in the work for a lasting peace on earth and for making the international climate healthier. There can be no doubt that the concerted efforts of the Soviet and Hungarian Communists and effective co-operation of our countries will bear yet more plentiful and good fruit.

Speech in the Kremlin on being presented with the Banner Order of the Hungarian People's Republic, the highest award of the HPR. 17 December 1976

Turning to foreign-policy matters, I want to stress that the entire work done by our Party and the Soviet state in the international field, extensive and intensive work, has been determined by the programme of further struggle for peace and international co-operation adopted by the 25th Party Congress. This programme, of course, is intended to span a period of more than a year. But even within one year much has already been accomplished.

This applies, first of all, to the strengthening of the unity of the fraternal socialist states, and the deepening of their all-round co-operation.

Ties and contacts between the leadership of the socialist countries are becoming increasingly intensive. In the time since the 25th CPSU Congress, the leaders of the fraternal parties have met collectively three times – in Berlin, Bucharest and Moscow, not to mention the discussions in the Crimea. The most recent of the regular meetings – already the fourth – of secretaries of central committees for international and ideological questions has just been held in Sofia. A conference will be held of the secretaries of central committees for organisational-party work and there will also be a first meeting of the Committee of the Foreign Ministers of the Warsaw Treaty countries.

In the year 1914, now distant from us, in a world engulfed by the imperialist war, split by hostility and hatred, Vladimir Ilyich Lenin, thinking about the future, wrote: 'The socialist movement . . . creates new and superior forms of human society, in which the legitimate needs and progressive aspirations of the working masses of *each* nationality will, for the first time, be met through international unity...'.

Today this has become a living reality with the big, close-knit and equal family of socialist states. Drawn into the all-embracing work to develop the co-operation of fraternal countries are not only the central guiding bodies, but also virtually all elements of our party, state and economic organism, and also an extensive network of public organisations, including, of course, the trades unions of our country.

Today hundreds, thousands of Soviet people are working in the fraternal countries, helping our friends create important economic projects such as, for instance, the huge 'Katowice' metallurgical complex in Poland, and many workers and specialists from fraternal countries are also working in our country. The gas pipeline project from Orenburg to the western border of the USSR being jointly constructed by the socialist countries advanced last year by 1200 kilometres. This represents a big success for the international collective of 15,000 workers on the project. The day is now not far distant when the pipeline laid by them, the biggest in Europe, will be operating.

All CMEA member-countries are taking part in developing the nickel industry in Cuba. The first steps being taken by the CMEA member-countries in specialisation and co-operation in the manufacture of equipment for nuclear power stations are of great importance.

All this we are accustomed to and regard as something quite natural, and this is good. It is good when close co-operation becomes a very part of our consciousness, of our entire life.

The recent wonderful initiative of the collective of 'Red Csepel', this glorious enterprise in people's Hungary, shows how powerful and vivifying are the roots of the fraternal relations linking the peoples of socialist countries. The workers of Csepel have started a socialist-emulation movement in honour of the 60th anniversary of the Great October Revolution and assumed concrete pledges to fulfil export deliveries to the Soviet Union ahead of schedule. There have been similar initiatives made by workers in Bulgaria and the German Democratic Republic, Poland and Czechoslovakia.

Permit me from the rostrum of this congress to extend heartfelt gratitude to the working people of the fraternal countries for such an effective and moving expression of solidarity with the cause of the October Revolution, with our country, with our communist work. I believe I am speaking for all of us when I say that the Soviet working class, all Soviet working people, will respond worthily to the noble initiatives of their foreign comrades, will respond with new deeds in the building of communism, in developing our close co-operation.

If we think about it, comrades, what we have here is a qualitatively new phenomenon – an international movement of millions and millions of builders of the new world inspired by a single aim. This is a great beginning, and it has a great future.

Speech at the 16th Congress of Trades Unions of the USSR. 21 March 1977

Comrade Fidel, you have just visited a number of African countries. It was with much comradely interest that we followed this visit. It clearly showed that the policy pursued by socialist Cuba had broad international recognition. This policy, which has nothing in common whatever with any interference in the internal affairs of other states, is imbued with a noble striving to strengthen peace, and to help the peoples who have thrown off the hateful yoke of colonialism to uphold their gains and consolidate the independence of their countries.

We have already had an opportunity today to have a thorough exchange of views on Soviet–Cuban co-operation and to outline jointly some important steps to develop it further. I think you will agree, Comrade Fidel, that these conversations have again confirmed our full understanding and the unity of our parties' views.

During our talks the following thought occurred to me: what a mighty force is inherent in the ideas of Marxism–Leninism and in the noble principles of internationalism. Within a period of less than two decades since the victory of the Cuban revolution, our relations in all fields – and they were built virtually from scratch – have acquired a profound and many-sided character, and Soviet–Cuban friendship has flourished and become a powerful factor in creative work and mutual spiritual enrichment.

This has not happened of its own accord. It is the result of tremendous and purposeful work by our parties, the result of the work of millions of Cubans and Soviet people.

The following thought also occurred to me: as we carry out the decisions of the congresses of our parties – I mean the 25th CPSU Congress and the First Congress of the Cuban Communists – we realise ever more clearly that the work we are doing jointly or in close co-operation has become an important and inalienable part of our national efforts. And it is our common task to make use of all the available possibilities for developing fraternal co-operation, for developing it more effectively.

Speech in the Kremlin at a dinner in honour of Fidel Castro Ruz, First Secretary of the Central Committee of the Communist Party of Cuba and Chairman of the State Council and the Council of Ministers of the Republic of Cuba. 5 April 1977

Today's talks have reaffirmed an important truth: the capacities of our countries are growing, and so are the opportunities for extending Soviet–Bulgarian co-operation. This concerns everything – politics, culture and the economy. It is a very good thing that we have undertaken to work out a master plan of specialisation and co-operation in production for our countries for the period up to 1990. This, our first attempt at long-term planning of economic co-operation, will undoubtedly be of great practical value.

We see co-operation between the Soviet Union and Bulgaria as an integral part of the genuinely fraternal and truly internationalist relations that have been firmly established in the great community of socialist states.

These relations now encompass virtually all aspects of life. But although their scope is an important factor, this is not the only one. The very nature of these relations is such that not only parties, not only state bodies, but also the working people are taking a direct part in developing them. Millions upon millions of people are becoming increasingly aware that their destinies are linked together and are coming to feel an ever greater mutual sympathy and respect.

This is what makes the big family of socialist countries close-knit and strong.

Let our opponents harbour no illusions: the solidarity of the socialist community is indestructible. All that the enemies of socialism have so far been doing to split our ranks and to disrupt our joint efforts has had the opposite results. The unity of the socialist countries has only been made stronger. This is the way it is going to be in the future, too.

The socialist countries have achieved a high level of co-ordination of action in international affairs. New forms of co-operation have appeared. The Committee of Foreign Ministers of the Warsaw Treaty Organisation has started its work. The results of the Committee's first meeting reaffirmed that the socialist countries are confidently following the course of strengthening peace and security in Europe, a course charted by the Helsinki Conference, and are confidently going ahead with this historic undertaking. The meeting in Belgrade, we believe, should build a bridge into the future and broaden the opportunities for new initiatives to strengthen peace in Europe and throughout the world.

I would like to say a few words about China. We should like to have normal, good-neighbourly relations with that country. We have said this before, and we say it again. But relations between any states are built up from two sides.

China is now going through a complicated period. Perhaps, this has some bearing on the position adopted by the Chinese leadership at present. We, however, have no intention of discussing the internal situation in the People's Republic of China. This concerns first of all the Chinese people themselves. On the other hand, there are forces inside and outside China that are attempting to drive Soviet–Chinese relations into an impasse and aggravate them still further. They are the same forces that seek political advantages in mounting international tensions. They have dangerous, adventuristic designs which we must, and shall, fight against. At the same time we should like it to be understood in Peking that acting against the aspirations of people and attacking everything that is good and sound in international relations is a thankless and hopeless undertaking.

I do not intend to discuss all aspects of our foreign policy. We have thoroughly discussed it recently.

I should like to emphasise that we are profoundly pleased with the energetic support which our Bulgarian friends give us in our international affairs. The Soviet people greatly appreciate Bulgaria's active role in strengthening peace in Europe and the rest of the world. We support its consistent efforts to make the Balkan Peninsula a region of equitable co-operation between all the Balkan states, as well as their neighbours.

> *Speech in the Kremlin at a dinner for the Party and Government Delegation of the People's Republic of Bulgaria, headed by Todor Zhivkov, First Secretary of the Central Committee of the Bulgarian Communist Party and Chairman of the State Council of the People's Republic of Bulgaria. 30 May 1977*

Co-operation between our countries has been increasing in recent years. It has assumed a stable and planned character.

This fully applies to the mutually beneficial ties that make it possible to strengthen the economic base of both countries. The Soviet Union is now in the lead among Yugoslavia's trade partners, and the products of Yugoslav enterprises are in growing demand on the Soviet industrial and consumer markets. Specialisation and co-operation in production are deepening. And the main thing is that both sides are willing to deepen economic and scientific–technical links. Thus, the prospects in that area are good.

Permanent contacts at state level, co-operation between public organisations, cultural exchanges, and direct contacts between working people have become the daily practice of Soviet–Yugoslav relations.

Without a doubt, the strengthening of comradely ties between the Communist Party of the Soviet Union and the League of Communists of Yugoslavia is the basis of the favourable development of our co-operation. Our Parties are in a leading position in our countries, and it is contacts and co-operation between them that provide conditions for the strengthening and development of Soviet–Yugoslav relations for the benefit of our peoples and for the benefit of the cause of peace and socialism in the world.

Of course, problems sometimes arise in the practice of our relations. There is, however, nothing wrong with that if we have a reliable mechanism for settling them on a reasonable, comradely basis. I think you will agree, Comrade Tito, that we have jointly managed to find a key to the approach to questions concerning Soviet–Yugoslav relations which enables us to ensure their steady development. What I have in mind here is a sincere and honest desire for mutual understanding and trust, respect for each other's experience, and strict observance of the principles of independence and equality.

I want to say in this connection that the standards about which I have just spoken fit very well into a comprehensive formula that combines the independence of every revolutionary contingent with their solidarity and cooperation for the sake of attaining common goals. We adhere to this principle in our relations with all the fraternal Parties, with all the socialist countries. It is of decisive importance, of course, to be prepared to respect both parts of this formula which, we believe, fully accords with the spirit of the great internationalist teaching of Marx, Engels and Lenin, and with the interests of every fraternal Party and of the whole communist liberation movement.

The forthcoming Soviet–Yugoslav talks will give us an opportunity for a broad and fruitful discussion both of bilateral relations and outstanding international issues. Our exchange of views does not start from a blank page. On more than one occasion the positions of the USSR and Yugoslavia have been seen to coincide on such problems as European security, a Middle East settlement, the popular struggle against racialism in South Africa, and on a number of other issues. Nor have we had any difference of opinion in our general assessment of the international situation.

Speech in the Kremlin at a dinner for Josip Broz Tito, President of the Socialist Federal Republic of Yugoslavia and Chairman of the League of Communists of Yugoslavia. 16 August 1977

No event in world history has had such a profound and lasting effect on mankind as the Great October Socialist Revolution. The flashes of the

October storm illuminated the way into the future for the peoples of many countries. History began to advance literally in seven-league strides.

The most important of the international consequences of the October Revolution, which have shaped the face of our epoch, has been the emergence and development of the world socialist system. At one time, the bourgeoisie, terrified by the victory of the October Revolution and its powerful influence on the minds of millions, sought to uncover 'the hand of Moscow' in every revolutionary event in the world. Nowadays, few people give credence to such fairy-tales. Revolutions start and triumph by virtue of each country's internal development and the will of its people. The series of triumphant socialist revolutions in Europe, Asia and America signified a continuation of the ideas and cause of the October Revolution.

As a result, the practice of world socialism has been extended and enriched. Each of the countries that have taken the socialist road has, in some respects, dealt in its own specific way with the problems of socialist statehood, the development of socialist industry, the drawing of the peasantry into co-operatives, and the ideological re-education of the masses.

There is no doubt that the transition to socialism by other peoples and countries with different levels of development and national traditions will invest socialist construction with an even greater diversity of specific forms. That is quite natural.

However, life provides confirmation that the general fundamental and inalienable features of socialist revolution and socialist construction continue to apply and retain their force.

The sum total of experience in the development of world socialism provides convincing evidence, among other things, of the following:

the question of power continues to be the main issue in a revolution. It is either the power of the working class, acting in alliance with all the working people, or the power of the bourgeoisie. There is no third possibility;

transition to socialism is possible only if the working class and its allies, having gained real political power, use it to end the socio-economic domination of capitalist and other exploiters;

socialism can be victorious only if the working class and its vanguard, the Communists, are able to inspire and unite the working people as a whole in the struggle to build the new society, to transform the economy and all social relations along socialist lines;

socialism can consolidate its position only if the working people's power is capable of defending the revolution against any attacks by the class enemy (and such attacks are inevitable, both internal and, most of all, external).

Those are only some of the lessons of the development of socialism today. They once again confirm the great international importance of the experience of the October Revolution, despite the specific conditions attaching to it. They once again confirm the great truth expressed by Lenin in these words: 'It is the Russian model that reveals to *all* countries something – and something highly significant – of their near and inevitable future.'

But world socialism also has experience of a different kind, which confirms that a departure from the Marxist–Leninist course, a departure from proletarian internationalism inevitably leads to setbacks and a hard time for the people.

It is well known what grave consequences have been brought about in China by attempts to ignore the economic laws of socialism, by the departure from friendship and solidarity with the socialist countries, and by alignment with the forces of reaction in the world arena. The Chinese people's socialist gains have been gravely endangered.

Some leaders of capitalist countries now obviously count on the present contradictions and estrangement between the People's Republic of China and the Soviet Union and other socialist countries continuing for a long time and even growing more acute in the future. We think that this is a short-sighted policy. Those who pursue it may well miscalculate.

There is no point in trying to guess how Soviet–Chinese relations will shape up in the future. I would merely like to say that our repeated proposals to normalise them still hold good.

The new relations that have been established – thanks to the internationalist policy of the fraternal parties – between the socialist countries, above all between the countries of the socialist community, are a great contribution by the world socialist system to the life of the contemporary world.

We can say with a clear conscience: our alliance, our friendship and our co-operation are the alliance, friendship and co-operation of sovereign and equal states united by common aims and interests, held together by bonds of comradely solidarity and mutual assistance. We are advancing together, helping one another and pooling our efforts, knowledge and resources to move forward as rapidly as possible.

We have taken the course of jointly tackling the problems of raw materials, fuel and energy, food and transport. We have been intensifying our specialisation and co-operation, especially in engineering, on the basis of the latest scientific and technological advances. We intend to solve these problems reliably, economically and for a long term. We intend to solve them with due consideration for the interests and needs of each fraternal country and the community as a whole.

In the distant days of October 1917 the workers and peasants of Russia fought alone against the old world, the world of greed, oppression and violence. They built socialism in a country surrounded by the hostile forces of imperialism. They built and defended it successfully. Today we are not alone. Our country has become part of a great family of socialist nations. Can we Soviet Communists and all the Soviet people cherish anything more in the world around us than this socialist family? For its prosperity, for our common well-being we have been doing everything we possibly can!

> *'The Great October Revolution and Mankind's Progress': Report at a jubilee meeting of the Central Committee of the CPSU, the Supreme Soviet of the USSR, and the Supreme Soviet of the RSFSR to mark the sixtieth anniversary of the Great October Socialist Revolution. 2 November 1977*

5.

RELATIONS WITH GREAT BRITAIN, FRANCE AND THE FRG

The improvement in Soviet–French relations has had important positive consequences for the whole course of European affairs. As a result of the recent talks in Moscow with the President of France and the signing of a Protocol on Political Consultations, the possibilities of Soviet–French co-operation have been extended. Our peoples' friendship rests on sound historical traditions. Today, our states also have an extensive sphere of common interests. We stand for the further development and deepening of relations between the USSR and France, and regard this as an important factor of international security.

New prospects in Europe are opening up as a result of a substantial shift in our relations with the FRG.

Throughout the whole post-war period, we, like our allies and friends, have proceeded from the fact that lasting peace in Europe rests above all on the inviolability of the borders of European states. Now, the treaties of the Soviet Union and Poland with the FRG have confirmed with full certainty the inviolability of borders, including those between the GDR and the FRG, and the western border of the Polish state.

There is a sharp demarcation of political forces in West Germany over the ratification of these treaties. One would assume that realistic-minded circles in Bonn, and also in some other Western capitals, are aware of this simple truth: delay over ratification would produce a fresh crisis of confidence over the whole of the FRG's policy, and would worsen the political climate in Europe and the prospects for easing international tensions.

As for the Soviet Union, it is prepared to meet the commitments it has assumed under the Soviet–West-German treaty. We are prepared to cover our part of the way towards normalisation and improvement of relations between the FRG and the socialist part of Europe, provided, of course, the other side acts in accordance with the letter and spirit of the treaty.

Report of the Central Committee of the Communist Party of the Soviet Union to the 24th Congress of the CPSU. 30 March 1971

We all are pleased at the positive shifts taking place lately in the situation in Europe. We give due credit to those governments of capitalist countries that respond to our efforts to have European affairs progress along the road of *détente*, peaceful co-operation and the strengthening of security on the continent. In this connection, I would like to dwell on the importance of the treaty between the USSR and the FRG, signed on 12 August 1970.

Claims are made in the West that in this treaty the FRG is making 'concessions' to the Soviet Union. But we think that our commitments under the treaty of 12 August are just as important for the FRG as the FRG's commitments are for the Soviet Union, if not more so. This applies also to the question of renunciation of the use of force, to observance of the inviolability of borders and to the undertaking to adhere in mutual relations to the provisions of the United Nations Charter. What matters are not unilateral concessions – there are none on either side – but the treaty's political essence and general trend.

To those in West Germany who engage in political speculations about the treaty with the Soviet Union we want to say one thing: the inviolability of the frontiers of the USSR, the GDR, Poland, Czechoslovakia and other fraternal countries is guaranteed irrespective of the existence of this treaty; it is guaranteed by the joint might of the Warsaw Treaty member-states.

On coming into force, the treaty with the FRG can and must open a new page in the FRG's relations with the Soviet Union, provide scope for extensive, mutually advantageous economic and other kinds of co-operation. But it does not stop there. On coming into force the treaties of the Soviet Union and Poland with the FRG will largely create a new political climate in Europe. This, one would think, will considerably improve the prerequisites for the establishment of West Germany's normal relations with the European socialist countries, for the development, in general, of fruitful co-operation between countries of Eastern and Western Europe, for the solution of important problems of European security.

Speech at the 8th Congress of the Socialist Unity Party of Germany. 16 June 1971

The Soviet Union and France are connected by numerous links of contacts, exchanges and co-operation in the economic, scientific, technological and cultural spheres. Ever-broadening friendly relations exist between the Soviet and the French peoples.

I fully share your appraisal, Mr. President, of the importance of Soviet–French co-operation. We have come to Paris in the firm belief that our new meeting will help to develop Soviet–French relations still further. This is in keeping with the interests and wishes of the Soviet people and – we are firmly convinced – with those of the people of France. We see the main task of our talks as being to express and, as fully as possible, give material form to the mutual desire of our peoples for accord, co-operation and friendship.

Our talks are being held against the background of a number of new developments in international affairs which affect both the sphere of political relationships between many states and the sphere of trade, economic and other relations between them.

We are meeting with you at a time when Europe is, perhaps, at a turning point in its history. The forces standing for a *détente*, for security and for a better future for the European peoples have grown and become stronger on the continent. The way to this lies through recognition of the inviolability of frontiers, respect for the principles of renunciation of force or the threat of force, equality, independence and non-interference in the internal affairs of other countries.

Among the indications of change are such recent moves as the conclusion of the treaties by the Soviet Union and the Polish People's Republic with the Federal Republic of Germany and also the recent four-power agreement on West Berlin. The time is approaching for the normalisation of relations between the German Democratic Republic and the Federal Republic of Germany as independent sovereign states, and of their relations with other countries, and so is the time for their admission to the United Nations.

Realistically assessing the situation, we see that forces are still active in Europe which are trying in every way to obstruct the relaxation of tension on our continent. They are prepared to use any dubious means in order to reverse this process and, in particular, to put difficulties in the way of calling an all-European conference. But we are convinced that through the efforts of peace-loving states and of broad public circles, the people's hope that peace will cease to be for Europe merely a pause between two wars, but will become its natural state, will be realised.

One of the most important problems of the day agitating the peoples of all countries is that of disarmament. The similarity of the positions of the Soviet Union and France on the most important aspect of this problem, namely, that the nuclear arms race must be stopped first of all, is a matter of great satisfaction to us. We highly appreciate the fact that France, like the Soviet Union, stands for the convocation of a conference of the five nuclear powers and that she has supported the proposal for holding a world conference on disarmament which has been put forward at the current session of the United Nations General Assembly.

We note with satisfaction the closeness of the positions of the USSR and France on such a major question, too, as that of overcoming the division of the world into military–political groupings. The Soviet Union and also our Warsaw Treaty allies have proclaimed in no uncertain terms their readiness to work precisely in this direction.

Here in Paris we are also conscious of the atmosphere of frankness and goodwill which was characteristic of our talks with you in Moscow, Mr. President. This gives us grounds for believing – already after our first talk – that the negotiations will be helped by mutual trust and mutual understanding and that their results will raise Soviet–French co-operation to a still higher level.

Speech at a dinner at the Grand Trianon
Palace in Versailles. 25 October 1971

Mr. Chairman and Members of the Municipal Council,
Men and women of Paris,

May I, first of all, take this opportunity to thank the residents of the beautiful capital of France for the warm welcome accorded us everywhere in Paris.

We all are still under the spell of your wonderful city: the monuments of 20 centuries of history which has influenced the destinies of many peoples, the arena of the sombre events of medieval times, the cradle of great revolutions, the glorious deeds of a freedom-loving people; the treasure-house of unique works of art and architecture; the mighty centre of modern industry, science and culture; the city inhabited by energetic, industrious, gay, witty, and if necessary, also heroic, people. All this is Paris. Can anyone possibly be indifferent to such a city? My companions and I certainly cannot. We, the envoys of Moscow, fell in love with Paris at first sight, and we have become attached to it in the brief time we have been here.

Meeting Paris face to face, one realises in a new way the significance of the heroic exploit of August 1944 when an armed uprising of Parisians prevented the Nazi occupiers from carrying out their criminal plan to destroy this city. Twenty million Soviet people sacrificed their lives for the liberation of their country and of Europe from fascist slavery, and the Soviet Union is proud of the fact that many Soviet men and women, courageously fighting shoulder to shoulder with the patriots of France against the common enemy, were among the members of the French Resistance movement. I would like to convey the deep gratitude of the Soviet people to all municipalities and communes of France who cherish the memory of the Soviet soldiers who fell in your country and are buried in its soil.

During the war, we bowed our heads before the graves of heroes, hoping that future generations would not know wars, bloodshed, and sacrifices. The young people who were born after the war are now starting out on their active life. The heritage that we pass on to the new generation of Europeans largely depends on us and on you, on the concerted actions of our countries.

We bear the historical responsibility of ensuring that this generation and others following it will never have to bear such burdens and make such sacrifices as fell to the lot of our generation in your country and ours. It is our task to safeguard their future, to channel their creative activity into exclusively peaceful creative work and the strengthening of mutual contacts and understanding.

We also bear another kind of historical responsibility — a tremendous intellectual and economic potential is concentrated on the European continent and history will not forgive us if this potential is not realised for the good of mankind. With the scientific and technological revolution now in progress, there is a great need to pool the experience in the field of industrial development and scientific research which has been accumulated throughout the centuries in European countries. Through joint effort it will also be easier to solve the problems of our time such as the protection of the natural environment and the combating of particularly dangerous diseases.

In brief, ahead of us lies a highroad of co-operation for peaceful, constructive purposes, which accord with the interests, not only of our two countries, but also of all Europeans – indeed, of all the peoples of the world.

Dear friends, an important part of the friendly co-operation between France and the Soviet Union is made up of the contacts and bonds between the capitals of our countries, Paris and Moscow. These contacts are important at the present time but we are sure that they can become much more active, extensive and fruitful. This is bound to happen.

I would like to wish the people of glorious Paris peace and prosperity, good health and happiness!

Speech at the Town Hall, Paris. 26 October 1971

We attach special importance to Europe. There are more than 30 states with an ancient and glorious history here in Europe. A tremendous economic potential is concentrated here and science and culture are highly developed. At the same time Europe is a territory where many wars started in the past. Here states have arisen and disintegrated, whole empires have grown up and collapsed. And, finally, the last war came, bringing in its wake the horrible atrocities of fascism, a tremendous toll of human lives and millions of cripples, and destroying towns and villages and priceless monuments of culture.

Twenty-six years have passed since the end of the war. It is our desire that Europe should at last become really peaceful, that threats and the use of force have no place in relations between European states, that respect for the sovereignty of every state and the inviolability of its borders should be secured. We want a reduction in the strength of the armed forces confronting each other, we want to develop cultural and technological co-operation and mutually advantageous trade. This is what is in the Soviet people's minds, it is to this that we are directing our efforts.

The independent foreign policy of France and her constructive contribution to ensuring international peace enjoy great sympathy in our country, and contribute to the strengthening of the long-standing and deep feelings of friendship the Soviet people have for the talented and freedom-loving French people.

Speech over French television. 29 October 1971

Considerable progress has been made in our relations with the Federal Republic of Germany. This has been made possible by the signing of the Treaties between the USSR and the FRG and between Poland and the FRG.

These Treaties are now in the process of being ratified. Debates on the matter are being held in the USSR Supreme Soviet, in the Sejm of the Polish People's Republic, and in the legislative bodies of the FRG.

Undoubtedly, the ratification of the Treaty between the USSR and the FRG will usher in an essentially new and more fruitful stage of development of Soviet–West German relations in various fields. This, we believe, would be in the best interests of the USSR and the FRG and it would be of utmost importance for European peace.

The question of the ratification of the Treaties has given rise to a sharp struggle in the Federal Republic of Germany. Some politicians oppose the Treaties and even attempt to cast doubt on the very possibility of a real reconciliation and development of normal relations between the FRG and the socialist countries.

What do the opponents of the Treaties want? They make no secret of their plans. They hold that the Treaties are bad because they formalise the inviolability of the European borders, and they talk of 'revising' the Articles of the Treaties that bear on this subject. But is it not clear that the opponents of the Treaties will never find partners in talks to revise the borders? This is no matter for discussion either now or in the future. The borders of the socialist countries are inviolable and here the Treaties simply reflect reality.

The opponents of the Treaty do not hide the fact that they wish to weaken the sovereignty of the German Democratic Republic. Here, too, they would like to return to the past. The German Democratic Republic has been steadily

177

advancing along the socialist path for almost 25 years now. It takes an active part in international life. Those who shut their eyes to this and would not draw the proper conclusions are only capable of driving their policies into a blind alley. It is high time they realised that the situation in Europe cannot be normalised without taking into full account the position of the GDR as an independent and sovereign socialist country.

The FRG now faces a crucial choice which will determine the destinies of its people and the attitude to it of other countries for years ahead. This is a choice between co-operation and confrontation, between a *détente* and the aggravation of tensions, and, finally, this is a choice between a policy of peace and a policy of war.

As for the Soviet Union, we are sincere and earnest in our approach to the question of improving our relations with the FRG, although for obvious reasons this is no simple question for our country. The hardships of the past war and suffering which Hitlerite aggression inflicted on our people are still alive in the memory of the Soviet people. But we believe that the grim past should not forever remain an insuperable obstacle to the development of our relations with West Germany. We also take account of the fact that the bulk of the West German population are for improvement of relations with the Soviet Union and the other socialist countries.

Speech at the 15th Congress of the Trades Unions of the USSR. 20 March 1972

Esteemed citizens of the Federal Republic of Germany,

It is a pleasure for me to speak to you at a time of my first visit to your country. My coming here at the invitation of Federal Chancellor Willy Brandt, our talks — all this already indicates that relations between our countries are developing successfully.

My first immediate contacts with Chancellor Brandt were linked with a big event in the history of relations of our countries, and — it can be said boldly — in the political development of Europe. We met for the first time in Moscow in

178

1970 in connection with the signing of the treaty between the USSR and the FRG. Affixing their signatures to a document containing a realistic recognition of the present situation in Europe, and adopting a solemn pledge not to resort to force or the threat of force in relation to each other, the Soviet Union and the Federal Republic of Germany embarked on a new path in their relations.

I shall tell you frankly: it was not so easy for the Soviet people, and, therefore, also for their leaders, to open this new chapter in our relations. Much too vivid yet among millions of Soviet people are recollections of the last war, of the heavy sacrifices and dreadful destruction which Hitler's aggression brought us. We were able to step over the past in relations with your country because we do not want its return.

The Soviet Union has long been bound with the socialist German state, our ally, the German Democratic Republic, by ties of very close, sincere and unselfish friendship.

We approach our relations with the Federal Republic of Germany from positions of goodwill and peaceableness. We are sincerely ready for co-operation which – we are convinced – can be very beneficial to both sides and to universal security. We desire a lasting peace, and believe that the Federal Republic of Germany is also interested in peace and needs it.

We know that it was not simple for Chancellor Brandt's Government to arrive at this treaty. The cold war has its own inertia, the overcoming of which requires certain effort. All the more so, since supporters of a dangerous confrontation of the two worlds have not at all disappeared yet from the political scene.

That is why the people in the Soviet Union appreciate the realism, will and farsightedness displayed by the leaders of the Federal Republic of Germany, above all, Federal Chancellor Willy Brandt, in working for the conclusion and enforcement of the treaties with the Soviet Union and the Polish People's Republic, which marked the beginning of new relations of your country with socialist Europe.

In this connection, I would like to give due credit to all supporters of good-neighbourly relations between the FRG and the Soviet Union. Many of them, having gone through the battle with fascism, spared no effort in working for peace, for friendship between our peoples. The Soviet Union highly values their contribution to this noble cause.

Our meeting with Chancellor Brandt in Oreanda in the autumn of 1971 was an important landmark in the successful development of our relations on the road charted by the Moscow treaty. In a quiet and businesslike atmosphere, free of the tyranny of diplomatic protocol, we had the possibility of mapping out further prospects of development of relations between the Soviet Union and the Federal Republic, as well as certain spheres of possible co-operation between our countries on an international plane.

The implementation of the plans mapped out has started. We may already say confidently that the development of peaceful and mutually beneficial relations of co-operation between the Soviet Union and the Federal Republic is no longer an abstract hypothesis, a theoretical plan or emotional wish as it appeared not very long ago, but stark reality which exists and is gaining in scope and strength.

Of course, the possibilities of extending such relations between our countries are far from exhausted. We are at the outset of this process. The course of our talks with Chancellor Brandt confirms that there are good possibilities for the future, including opportunities in the field of economic relations. In addition to expanding conventional trade, there are also opportunities for making long-term large-scale deals based on economic co-operation between our countries and aimed at carrying out important joint projects.

Such deals are not short-term, time-serving or more or less of a chance nature, but open the way to joint activity in important sectors of the economy, designed to give both countries a guaranteed benefit for many years to come. This means, among other things, the possibility of a more rational organisation of production and, of course, steady employment for the workers of your country. And of particular importance is the fact that such co-operation helps to lay a reliable foundation for good-neighbourly relations between our two countries.

Both the Soviet Union and the Federal Republic of Germany are countries with a highly developed level of science, technology, and culture. Our scientists have something to show and tell their colleagues. The population of our two countries will take, I am sure, a great interest in each other's masterpieces of literature, music, theatre and fine arts. This is vividly borne out by the interest shown by your public in the Days of the Soviet Union now being held in Dortmund.

As you know, our countries have signed a number of concrete agreements on economic and cultural relations and air communications, which demonstrate both sides' mutual understanding and readiness to co-operate.

But no matter how important the good relations are for both our states and for their peoples, it is no less important that their establishment and development are today a component of a broader process of a radical improvement of international life in Europe, and not only in Europe. A change is taking place from a quarter of a century's period of cold war to relations of peace, mutual respect and co-operation between the states of the East and the West. This is precisely the objective of the peaceful coexistence policy pursued by the Soviet Union in relation to states of the opposite social system. In our days it has found its most complete expression in the now universally known Peace Programme approved by the 24th CPSU Congress, as well as in the materials of the Plenary Meeting of the CPSU Central Committee this April. There we find written down, among other things, that our country pursues the aim of effecting a radical turn to relaxation and peace on the European continent. I would like to say that the Soviet Union, its Communist Party and all our people will vigorously and consistently strive to attain this aim.

The Europe that has more than once been the hotbed of aggressive wars which brought about colossal destruction and the death of millions of people must forever recede into the past. We want its place to be taken by a new continent – a continent of peace, mutual confidence and mutually advantageous co-operation among all states.

Among the positive elements of present-day European development is, no doubt, also the gradual improvement of the Federal Republic of Germany's relations with its neighbours in the East – Poland, the GDR, Czechoslovakia and other socialist states in Europe.

We attach great importance to the businesslike, constructive co-operation we have established with the Federal Republic of Germany, France, the United States and other states in such an important field as the preparation for an all-European conference on security and co-operation.

There still remain in the world quite a few urgent and explosive problems awaiting solution. For example, the conflict has not yet been settled in the Middle East where Arab lands continue to be in the hands of the invaders and that is why dangerous tensions remain there. Opponents of a *détente* and of the cessation of the arms race can be found in other areas as well. However, mankind's horizon is brightening. The war in Vietnam has ended. Soviet–American relations continue to develop favourably. On the whole, it can be said that today our planet probably stands closer to a firm and lasting peace than ever before. The Soviet Union uses all its influence to promote this beneficial trend.

Our peaceable foreign policy is an expression of the very essence of our society, an expression of its profound internal requisites. The 250-million-strong Soviet people is engaged in carrying out the spectacular projects of peaceful construction. In the north and south of our vast country, in Siberia and in Central Asia, we are building huge power stations, hundreds of plants and factories, and developing irrigation systems in areas which in magnitude could compete with many European states. Our aim is to ensure that tomorrow the Soviet people will live even better than today. Soviet people feel tangibly the results of these collective efforts.

Naturally, all this does not mean that we in the Soviet Union have solved all the problems, and have no difficulties. Problems which we still have to tackle exist and apparently will exist always and at all times. Yet, the distinguishing feature of the problems arising before us is that they are connected with the confident growth of the country, of her economic and cultural potential, and that we are looking for a solution to these problems exclusively along the lines of further peaceful construction, of boosting the cultural and living standards of the people, and developing our socialist society.

I would like to add that our plans are by no means plans with an eye to autarchy. We are not following a policy of isolating our country from the outer world. Quite the contrary, we proceed from the fact that it will develop under the conditions of growing all-round co-operation with the outer world, and not only with the socialist countries, but, in large measure, also with the states of the opposite social system.

Speech on West German television. 21 May 1973

Our two-day meeting with French President Georges Pompidou has just ended in Pitsunda. The thorough-going talks with the head of the French Republic were held, as before, in a spirit of goodwill, realism and mutual respect. They no doubt helped the two sides to bring still closer their stand on a number of important questions and in this way to improve the conditions for the interaction of the Soviet Union and France in the international arena, with the aim of further extending international *détente* and promoting co-operation between countries on an equal basis.

It was once more convincingly proved that the greater the sphere of our concerted efforts, the more effective can be the contribution of each of our countries to the solution of major problems of present-day international relations. I can say that the Pitsunda talks have led to a further drawing near of our views on the need to complete the conference on European security as soon as possible. Our positions on the approach to the solution of the Middle East problem are also close. The closeness or coincidence of points of view was shown on some other major problems, too.

In addition to international problems, we exchanged opinions on ways of further broadening relations between our countries on a government level. As is known, the adoption of the document on the principles on which relations between the Soviet Union and France should be built and the signing of the protocol on consultations have laid a good foundation for our relations. Today Soviet–French relations are extensive and varied. They cover different spheres, such as politics, the economy, science and culture. With every passing year something new is added to them and new vistas open up.

In short, the Pitsunda meeting is fresh proof of the firmness of traditional Soviet–French friendship which conforms to the vital interests of the peoples of our two countries and to the cause of strengthening peace and international security.

Speech at a meeting to mark the 20th anniversary of the Opening Up of Virgin Lands. Alma-Ata, 15 March 1974

Meetings and talks between the leaders of the Soviet Union and the FRG have become a good tradition in recent years. They have invariably enriched relations between our countries and made it possible to make fresh advances in the development and deepening of mutually beneficial co-operation.

The determination of the present Federal Government to implement consistently, in relations between our states, the political course which took shape while the Brandt–Scheel government was in office and which found its expression in the Moscow Treaty has been duly appreciated in the Soviet Union. This document may rightly be called an historic one. The treaty has laid a basis for a radical improvement of relations between our countries, between the FRG and the states of the socialist community. It originated many positive processes both in Europe and outside it.

The development of all-round co-operation with the FRG is a principled long-term line in our policy. It organically stems from the decisions of the 24th Congress of the CPSU, from the Peace Programme adopted by it. We have always been convinced that a turn in Soviet–West German relations is possible, that the sense and will of people, the development of the political situation will break the barriers impeding its implementation. Nowadays this turn has become a *fait accompli.*

A solid and firm foundation underlies our new relations. One can, of course, only talk of the significance of the work done and admire its results. But there is little use in it. The task now is, apparently, to expand and deepen what has been achieved, clothing it in a strong fabric of mutually advantageous links in most diverse fields. Opening a new chapter in the mutual relations of our states and giving it a new positive meaning also calls for much strength, persistence and, I would say, political courage.

It is quite obvious that improvement of relations between the USSR and the FRG is not detrimental to anyone. Moreover, not only the peoples of our countries benefit by it. It is deeply consonant with the processes of *détente* under way in Europe and outside it.

Never before in history has the situation in Europe been so favourable for the establishment of a lasting peace as today. Confidence in this is based on real factors and increasingly wins the minds of Europeans. In these conditions the responsibility of the governments and political leaders for the expansion and deepening of the processes of *détente*, for a businesslike and sober approach to the settlement of the still remaining problems acquires even greater significance.

We were free from illusions when we started reshaping relations between our countries. In fact, there have been and still are difficulties. And this is understandable. The shaping of new relations between the USSR and the FRG is far from being a simple job. Regrettably, it is at times even more complicated by recurrences of the policy that has nothing in common with the spirit of the times. The influence of the forces, whose views are alien to the state and social realities in Europe and who are rooted in the years long past, can still be felt in the FRG.

But history has made its choice. And it is no accident that it is not the forces of the past that determine nowadays the policy of the FRG.

The peoples of our countries remember their past experience too well and therefore treasure the salutary changes achieved. The Second World War brought so much suffering and grief to our generation that hardly fell to the lot of fathers and grandfathers. It is no simple thing to draw a line under the tragic events of the past. But this is necessitated by solicitude for the peaceful life of peoples and their future. The generations which never heard the rumble of guns must not experience the horrors of war.

We are confident that the people of the FRG, just as our people, want peace in their country, want good relations with their neighbours. The Federal Government can rest assured that any of its efforts aimed at the improvement of relations with the socialist states, at the enhancement of the role of their country in the development of peaceful co-operation on the continent, will always meet with our understanding and support.

The exchange of opinions and consultations on a rather wide range of questions now holds an important place in relations between the USSR and the FRG. This is a useful practice. We are ready to develop and deepen it, specifically, through a more regular exchange of opinions on the general problems of relaxation and co-operation in Europe and all over the world.

We know what interest you, Mr. Federal Chancellor, show in economic co-operation with the Soviet Union. This, indeed, is an extremely important field in relations between our countries. Quite a lot has already been done in this field. This year, our trade exchange will approach the 2000-million-rouble mark. This means that it will almost have trebled since 1971. Yet, in this aspect our countries, perhaps, are merely at the beginning of the road.

It seems that the key to intensive development of our economic relations is implementation of large-scale projects, development of industrial co-operation, joint work in developing natural resources and other new forms of economic exchange. In this we would be ready to go beyond the limits of bilateral relations, to invite third countries to participate in the implementation of joint projects. I hope that our talks will give the impetus to such undertakings.

185

There is no doubt that businesslike co-operation between the USSR and the FRG brings considerable advantages to both countries and can bring still greater advantages. But the importance of this co-operation goes beyond commercial advantage. It is known that there exist links between economy and politics. The wider and fuller economic co-operation, the greater mutual trust, the stronger and more versatile political contacts, the easier it will be to find a common language in international problems, too.

The intensive quest for the ways to mutual understanding and peaceful co-operation between states is, undoubtedly, the dominating trend in international life nowadays. One clear manifestation of this trend is the holding of the European conference. The experience of collective solution of many problems of vital importance for our continent is accumulating in the course of its work.

This experience already leads us to an important conclusion: it is necessary to learn to value what reflects the common views of states and to leave out what lies beyond the limits of reality and has nothing to do with the central issue.

The attempts to bring back the past, to bring back the things that are obviously unacceptable can lead to procrastinations and nothing else. The Soviet Union would like the conference to be a complete success. We favour its speediest conclusion so new horizons for co-operation, on an all-European scale, can be opened up. You, Mr. Federal Chancellor, will probably agree that there are things to which we should give thought together.

The success of another forum, the Vienna talks on reduction of armed forces and armaments in Central Europe, that is in the area of their greatest concentration, may serve to further consolidate peace. Rather considerable differences in the principled approach of the sides to the questions discussed are manifested at the talks so far. Some participants in the talks clearly show a striving to obtain unilateral advantages. If there is a wish to reach agreement, it would be better to give up such strivings. It can hardly be regarded as realistic to seek to build one's security at the expense of the security of others. The progress of the talks in Vienna is one more problem on which we could exchange opinions.

So there is no lack of important problems on which the Soviet Union and the Federal Republic could act in unison for the benefit of peace and international co-operation. Obviously, it would be worth one's while to concentrate on them.

In reality, however, a situation forms from time to time where instead of advancing forward, attempts are made to create obstacles for mutual understanding in areas where, it seemed, obstacles have already been overcome. This, in effect, is what is happening with the West Berlin issue which was settled when the quadripartite agreement was concluded. This agreement, as it is generally admitted, makes it possible to solve successfully practical problems related to West Berlin. A better agreement in the present conditions could hardly be achieved. Strict observance of the agreement is what is needed so that the West Berlin issue should no longer cloud the political atmosphere in the centre of Europe. We would like to think that the Federal Government proceeds from the same viewpoint.

Speech at a dinner in the Grand Kremlin Palace in honour of Helmut Schmidt, Federal Chancellor of the Federal Republic of Germany, Moscow. 28 October 1974

We are grateful to you, Mr. President, for the invitation to come to France, a country with which we are on friendly relations, and to pursue Soviet–French contacts at summit level. Since 1966 such contacts have become a permanent and, it can be said, a determining element in relations between the USSR and France. We have had four working meetings in the past 2 years.

This is our first meeting since you became President of the Republic of France. But you have long been known in the Soviet Union and are known there for the considerable contribution you have been making personally to the development of Soviet–French relations, above all in the economic sphere. We hope that our meeting will be useful and fruitful. It will be in the interests of the peoples of both our countries.

We have reason to favourably assess the development of Soviet–French relations. Joint efforts have enabled us to establish a sound foundation for mutually beneficial co-operation. This pertains to the economy, to our scientific, technical and cultural relations. Certainly there are matters that must be resolved and certain complexities to be overcome.

We have come here earnestly seeking to promote Soviet–French co-operation by joint efforts. And we understand the French side is desirous of this, too.

It is gratifying for us to note here that in many respects Soviet–French relations have served as a good example for other countries. It is no exaggeration to say that the joint efforts of the Soviet Union and France have done much to improve the political climate in Europe, and not just in Europe.

Our countries take an identical or close position on a number of key issues pertaining to the present-day international situation. And this means there is scope for further constructive co-operation in the interests of further promoting *détente*.

As is known, on some matters our viewpoints do not coincide completely. This is no secret. All the more reason, to our mind, to meet, hold consultations, to bring our viewpoints closer together. We feel that one of the most important tasks of our meeting is to further expand the sphere of co-operation between our countries in international affairs.

International life in our times is complex and contradictory. The trend towards consolidation of peace and security of nations is gaining ground, *détente* is in progress. At the same time hot-beds of war still exist, the situation in the Middle East remains explosive, armaments are piling up and are being improved. The scientific and technological revolution affords unprecedented opportunities for prosperity for all of mankind. At the same time energy, food and other problems are becoming more acute in many countries.

We have not set ourselves here the task of analysing the reasons for these phenomena and of proposing ways of settling outstanding problems. Every one of them requires the special attention and joint efforts of many states.

One thing is certain: in order to successfully resolve all these problems it is imperative to ensure a durable peace, to develop and intensify *détente*. As for the Soviet Union, we can firmly and definitely declare that it has always been, and always will be, a reliable partner in the effort to achieve these goals.

It is in practical deeds that adherence to the ideas of relaxation, co-operation and peace is tested. The security and co-operation conference is the most important practical step in this regard in Europe.

Next year it will be 30 years since the guns were silenced in Europe, since the bloodshed ended. We in the Soviet Union, just as you in France, will never forget the past war, the grimmest and bloodiest war in the history of mankind.

We feel it is the common duty of all who want to see that the tragedies of the past are never repeated to do everything possible to reliably ensure the basis of peace in Europe. The speediest conclusion of the work of the European conference at the most authoritative level will be, we are convinced, a very important step in this direction.

There is no goal more important and worthy than that of ensuring clear, peaceful skies over our entire planet. Every effort should be made to achieve this. It is from this standpoint that we positively assess the results of the recent talks in Vladivostok with President Gerald Ford of the United States.

And it is from this standpoint that we view the development of relations between the Soviet Union and France. The better these relations, the more extensive our co-operation and the greater our mutual trust, the better it will be for the cause of durable peace in Europe and throughout the world.

The past years have confirmed the fruitfulness of the policy of all-round development of Soviet–French friendly relations, have shown convincingly what potentialities they have. Now it is a matter of making the most of these potentialities, of following up our principled agreement with new, specific steps. I would like to assure you, Mr. President, that the Soviet Union will not be lacking in goodwill.

The friendship of the Soviet Union and France is a valuable attainment for the peoples of our countries and it is up to us to strengthen and develop it. The Communist Party of the Soviet Union, our government, and the Soviet people as a whole are guided by this.

Speech at a dinner given by President Giscard d'Estaing of France. Rambouillet, 5 December 1974

Permit me once again to greet you, Mr. Wilson, and to express satisfaction at your visit. We are happy to have this opportunity to exchange opinions with you and Foreign Secretary Callaghan both on questions of the further development of Soviet–British relations and on a number of international problems.

Frankly speaking, the need for such an exchange of views is felt all the more strongly since there have been no contacts on a sufficiently high level between the Soviet Union and Great Britain for a fairly long time now. It can even be stated that over the past few years the development of mutually advantageous co-operation between our two countries has, to a certain extent, slowed down. Let us not analyse now the causes of such a situation. It is clear, however, that today we do have things to talk about.

In many parts of the world a struggle is at present under way between opposing trends – a line for international *détente*, the strengthening of peace and the development of co-operation among states, and a line for reviving the 'cold war' spirit, a new whipping up of the arms build-up, and interference in the affairs of other countries and peoples. But of decisive significance is, we feel, the profound and ever more clearly expressed will of the peoples – and, I emphasise it, of the peoples, above all – for peace, and their determination to see to it that the tragedy of a new world war shall never repeat itself.

Fully in keeping with these aspirations of the peoples are the significant positive changes that have taken place in recent years in international affairs, notably in relations between the Soviet Union and other socialist countries, on the one hand, and such states as France, the Federal Republic of Germany and the United States, on the other. I should like to stress most emphatically, Mr. Prime Minister, that the leaders of the Soviet Union are fully determined to do all in their power to impart an historically irreversible character not only to international *détente* proper, but also to a real turn to the long-term, fruitful and mutually beneficial co-operation of states with different social systems on the basis of full equality and mutual respect. That is what we in the Soviet Union mean by peaceful coexistence. And it is towards that goal that the Soviet Union has always urged other states.

As I see it, Great Britain, too, could be a good partner of ours on this path of strengthening peace and peaceful co-operation. Her voice carries no small weight in world affairs. Not in all things and not at all times have our positions been similar, but surely we have no right to forget our record of fruitful co-operation. In particular today, shortly before the 30th anniversary of the great Victory of the powers of the anti-Hitler coalition and the freedom-loving peoples over the Hitlerite aggressors and enslavers, there are grounds to recall that the Soviet Union and Great Britain have the experience of a combat alliance in the fight for a just cause. You and I, Mr. Wilson, like other people of our generation, remember well enough that this was an alliance not only of governments; it was also a combat alliance of our armies and our peoples, and an historic example of successful co-operation, regardless of differences in social systems.

The present day of our planet, on which we are all living as ever closer neighbours, is marked by a struggle to remember the memory of those who gave their lives in the battle against aggression and for the right of people to live in conditions of peace, independence and freedom. It would be, perhaps, no exaggeration to say that never before have such vigorous efforts been made on a broad international scale to strengthen peace and peaceful co-operation among states. But there is still a lot to be done.

Let us take Europe, for instance. Here a good start has been made. The European Conference on Security and Co-operation is working, though not at a very fast pace. This forum of thirty-three European states, with the participation of the United States and Canada – a forum unprecedented in the continent's history – is called upon to lay a durable foundation of peace and good-neighbourly co-operation on European soil for a long historical period. No small amount of work has already been done, but far from all that is necessary is as yet being done. The immediate task now is to successfully and fittingly complete this great endeavour which we are sure can and must serve as the starting-point for a new, truly peaceful and constructive epoch in the life of Europe.

We believe that Great Britain could play no small part in ensuring that a constructive course is adopted by the European Conference. The Soviet Union would welcome that.

The significance of the contribution made by any state and its leaders to the solution of the major tasks of building a lasting peace is determined, we believe, by the ability correctly to assess the historical scale of these tasks. Today it is more important than ever before to be able to single out the main thing the peoples are looking forward to and hoping for, and to separate this from the superficial situations engendered by shortsighted political manoeuvring aimed at obtaining various momentary advantages for some participants in negotiations to the detriment of others.

This applies also to the Vienna talks on the reduction of forces and armaments in Central Europe. The persistent attempts of some countries there to lead matters towards obtaining one-sided advantages, attempts to 'outplay' the other side are unfortunately still seriously impeding the progress of the Vienna talks.

L. I. BREZHNEV ON FOREIGN AFFAIRS

The peoples of the world expect that international *détente* will soon be embodied in concrete deeds contributing to a better life for millions of people. Such deeds include curbing the arms build-up, reducing the scale of the military preparations of states and their military expenditures, and broadening economic and other kinds of peaceful co-operation between them. Today, with the serious economic difficulties besetting many Western countries, progress in these matters is, I believe, becoming an increasingly urgent task in the eyes of public opinion.

As before, a paramount objective is the achievement of a peaceful settlement in the Middle East. The situation in that area remains explosive. And it cannot, indeed, be otherwise so long as the aggressor holds the foreign land he has seized, so long as the rights of the peoples are flouted. The peoples of the Middle East need a just and lasting peace as much as the very air they breathe.

One sometimes hears arguments to the effect that a complete peaceful settlement in the Middle East is hard to achieve and that, instead, one should be content in the next few years with partial arrangements.

What can be said on this score?

Naturally, partial measures, such as the withdrawal of the occupationists from this or that part of the captured Arab territory and its return to the Arabs, are in themselves useful, but only if they constitute steps towards the earliest possible genuine peaceful settlement and are not used as a pretext for freezing the situation as a whole, for delaying a peaceful settlement, and for weakening the unity of the Arab countries.

There are some who seem to want to offer the Arab peoples something in the nature of a soporific in the hope that they will calm down and forget about their demands for the restoration of justice and the complete elimination of the consequences of aggression. But a soporific lasts only for a short time, and on awakening the same real life and all its problems are still there to be faced.

Practical experience attests to this quite eloquently. It will be recalled that partial bilateral measures were already carried out in the Middle East. Have they eased tension there? Unfortunately, not. Have they given the peoples of the Middle East tranquillity? No, they have not. Have they lessened in any way the onerous and dangerous arms build-up in which the Middle East countries are involved? It is well known that they have not.

All this indicates that there is no substitute for a genuine and enduring peaceful settlement. And its postponement is inadmissible unless complete

192

neglect is displayed for the destinies of the countries and peoples of the Middle East (naturally, including Israel, whose people can hardly be interested in living endlessly in a country converted into a military camp), and for the destinies of universal peace.

That is why the Soviet Union is resolutely in favour of the earliest resumption of the work of the Geneva Peace Conference. Of course, the voice of representatives of the Palestinian Arab people must be heard at the conference on an equal footing with others, for the just solution of the Palestine problems is a key element of a lasting peaceful settlement.

In discussing ways to strengthen universal peace, mention cannot fail to be made of the ever growing importance of preventing the further spread of nuclear weapons in the world, enhancing the effectiveness of the international treaty on this subject, and increasing to the utmost the number of its participants.

In short, there are quite a few problems in the present-day world which cannot but preoccupy the peace-loving states and for whose solution it would undoubtedly be useful to pool the efforts of those states, including our two countries – the Soviet Union and Britain – and to improve our co-operation in foreign-policy matters, including regular consultations at various levels.

A no less urgent topic is, we feel, the question of further developing and deepening Soviet–British relations in the economic field. Here we can lean on the already accumulated good experience. Economic ties between our two countries have been successfully developing for many years on the basis of equality and considerable mutual advantage. This has always been valued in the USSR – and not only for economic reasons. Soviet people invariably harbour feelings of comradeship and class solidarity towards the British working class. Our people remember that in the first and most difficult years of the Soviet state's existence the British proletariat came out against the imperialist intervention in the affairs of our country, proclaiming the slogan 'Hands off Soviet Russia!' The working people of the Soviet Union have always been in solidarity with the struggle of the working class and all working people of Great Britain for their rights and vital interests. And we are gratified to know that, in the event of a further expansion of Soviet–British economic co-operation there will be new job opportunities for thousands and thousands of workers in your country, and a new impetus for the development of its economy.

While positively evaluating the experience of the past, we believe at the same time, Mr. Prime Minister, that the political climate and the technological and economic possibilities of our times are putting on the agenda the question of a larger-scale and longer-term mutually profitable co-operation of our two countries in many economic spheres.

The realisation of such co-operation could become one more example of the way in which the policy of peaceful coexistence is filled with concrete material content and yields tangible benefit to millions of people.

Speech at the luncheon in the Kremlin in honour of Harold Wilson, Prime Minister of Great Britain. 14 February 1975

Esteemed Mr. President,
Esteemed Mme. Giscard d'Estaing,
Esteemed guests,
Comrades,

We are glad to greet you, the President of friendly France, as a guest of the Soviet Union.

Soviet–French summit meetings have always been given great political content and each of such meetings has moved forward relations between our states. The present meeting with you, Mr. President, acquires special meaning in view of the fact that the success of the European conference opens up new horizons in European and world politics.

Almost 10 years ago, in our talks with General de Gaulle, we defined the main factors that rendered the drawing together of the Soviet Union and France significant on a broad international scale. It was then established that the Soviet Union and France, proceeding from their national interests and great responsibility for the destinies of the world, regarded the fundamental problems of European and international security as problems of paramount importance in their relations. Subsequently these problems have invariably been at the centre of our talks with President G. Pompidou and with you, M. Giscard d'Estaing, when we met at Rambouillet in December last year.

Time is an impartial judge, and it has passed its judgement: the aims of co-operation set by the Soviet Union and France have proved to be in accord with the dictates of the modern age and the aspirations of many peoples.

Every new major event in Soviet–French relations leads one to ask what it is that prompts our two countries to continue their attempts to draw closer together and to deepen mutual understanding. I think you will agree with me, Mr. President, that this source is, above all, the traditions of friendship between the Soviet and the French peoples, friendship tested by hard trials at crucial moments of history.

My personal impression and the impression of my colleagues who have visited your country is that the French people clearly see the peaceful role of the Soviet Union, of the Soviet people in international affairs. We in the Soviet Union, for our part, believe that France, the French people, are impelled by a desire for peace. Such mutual confidence is a firm foundation for the development of Soviet–French co-operation now and in the future.

The strong point of this co-operation consists in the fact that apart from friendly sentiments and sympathies which the peoples of the two countries have towards each other, it is permeated with political, state realism. What I have in mind is, above all, the fact that both our countries proceed in their policy from a recognition of the situation that has arisen in post-war Europe, from the need for peaceful coexistence between states with different social systems, from the principle of impermissibility of interference in the internal affairs of other countries. It is quite logical that much of what has been developed in the process of Soviet–French co-operation was later accepted in wider international practice.

A decade in international affairs is both little and much. It is not much if viewed in terms of history. But it is a great deal if it is measured in terms of the concentration of effort to promote peace and relaxation of tension and in terms of all that is good that has been done during the period.

Indeed, important positive changes have taken place in relations between states, in the general political climate and in the sentiments of broad public circles.

This was clearly manifested at the Conference on Security and Co-operation in Europe. At this Conference there were outlined tasks of truly historical scope. Those who would like to call into question the realities of present-day Europe – territorial realities, realities of post-war development, realities of relaxation of tension – had the ground cut from under their feet. An extensive programme of co-operation in the name of the noble goals of peace and progress of the peoples was worked out.

I think that you and I and all those who sat at the conference table in Helsinki and signed the Final Act of the Conference see more clearly than others the responsibility which rests on the participating states for the implementation of the agreements reached. It will take, of course, much effort, mutual and constant efforts, to further reshape relations between states in accordance with the principles approved in Helsinki, to deepen economic, scientific and technical ties, intensify co-operation in the fields of culture, education and information, and to widen contacts between people.

Materialisation of *détente* is now becoming the most vital demand in international relations. We believe that our countries, our peoples, can actively facilitate the attainment of this aim. The businesslike, constructive nature of the contacts between political leaders and statesmen, systematic consultations, close economic co-operation, various joint scientific–technical projects, including those in the most advanced spheres of human knowledge, and the great scope of cultural contacts – all these are the tangible results of the work of recent years. At the same time, undoubtedly, there are possibilities that have not yet been explored for the further deepening and enrichment of Soviet–French relations. And we are convinced that the deepening and widening of Soviet–French co-operation, the drawing of ever broader sections of the population into it, would meet with a favourable response on the part of the Soviet and French peoples.

Materialisation of relaxation is simply inconceivable without *détente* in the military sphere, too. I think that the conditions for this have become more favourable.

A lessening of military confrontation in Europe, limitation of armaments, and disarmament are a sphere of international relations where goodwill and initiative of the states are now particularly necessary. Ever more urgent, in our view, is the reaching of a broad international agreement envisaging strict commitments of states not to develop new types of weapons of mass destruction or new systems of such weapons. Life itself confronts the states with the necessity of defining their role in the solution of these problems, which are of vital importance for all the peoples.

Mr. President,

We have always considered that the strength of the policy of France lies in its independence. An independent France can make a substantial contribution to the strengthening of international peace. The Soviet Union is open to friendship and co-operation with France.

It goes without saying that in the course of co-operation between states with different social–economic systems, with different ideologies, the specific features arising from these class differences cannot be removed. It would probably be an illusion to believe that one could change the general approach of each of the countries to the problems which it, proceeding from its system, its international ties, understands and solves in its own way.

Relaxation of international tension does not eliminate the struggle of ideas. This is an objective fact.

At the same time it is indisputable that the Soviet Union and France, the peoples of our two countries, have fully realistic and broad mutual interests. Through their friendship and co-operation, the USSR and France have already done much that is beneficial for Europe and the world and, given mutual desire, can do still more in this direction. The question now is essentially this: what new things, things that are attractive for themselves and for others, can the two countries achieve at the present stage by developing and deepening their interaction in the field of *détente* and peace? With what new elements can they enrich their bilateral relations?

Concrete replies to these questions can be given only by joint purposeful search. We should like to hope that consideration of mutual interests, the experience accumulated in the development of Soviet–French relations will make the search fruitful.

May our talks and their results bring satisfaction to the peoples of our countries, to all who cherish the interests of peace, equal co-operation and *détente*.

Permit me to propose a toast to the further development of co-operation and the strengthening of friendship between the USSR and France!

Here is to our joint creative search in this noble field in the interests of international peace and security!

Here is to your health, Mr. President!

Here is to the health of Mme. Giscard d'Estaing and of all the French guests!

Here is to the prosperity and happiness of the French people!

Speech at the dinner in the Kremlin in honour of Valery Giscard d'Estaing, President of the French Republic. 14 October 1975

You have put to me quite a few questions. I shall try to answer them.

I should like, first of all, to greet French televiewers as my old acquaintances. This is not our first meeting. This time, as you see, my dear friends, a French journalist has come to the Kremlin and we are now in my study, in the midst of a working day. Therefore, the question about what I do seems quite a natural one. I shall try to answer it, although it will not be easy to do so.

The type of work I do and that carried out by the Political Bureau of the Central Committee are determined above all by the role played by the Communist Party in this country.

The Party here unites the front-ranking, the most active and politically conscious part of the working class, farmers and members of the intelligentsia. It maps out its policy on the basis of a scientific approach to and a painstaking analysis of the real requirements of life and the needs of the people. It unites all sections of society and all nationalities, and arms the people with willpower and a readiness and an ability to fight for the ideals of communism, the most progressive and just society.

The supreme guiding principle of the Party's work is everything for the people, everything for the welfare and happiness of the people. That is why the people regard the Party's policy as their own and entrust it with the leading role in society.

As far as I know, many in the West have no clear idea of our political system. Wrong ideas about it are sometimes voiced. It is asserted, for example, that the Party replaces other bodies, both state and public ones. This is wrong, of course.

Our state organs – the Supreme Soviet of the USSR, the Council of Ministers of the USSR, governmental bodies on the republican and local level – have a clear-cut sphere of competence defined in the Constitution. These organs enact and enforce laws and are responsible for the proper functioning of the economy and the advancement of science, culture, education and health service.

Public organisations have their own fields of activity: the trades unions are concerned primarily with the protection of the interests of the working people and with the organisation of their work and holidays; the Komsomol is in charge of the education of the younger generation, and so on. But, I repeat, it is the Party that is the guiding spirit in society and the political organiser of the affairs of the Soviet people.

As you see, our system is different from yours. Also different is the practice of leadership in the Soviet Union from that in the capitalist countries. The range of questions which concern the Political Bureau and myself, as General Secretary, is much broader than that handled by the leaders in the West. We keep in the field of vision practically all aspects of life of the people, everything that takes place on the territory of this country. This includes the ideological life of the Party and of society, economy, social problems, and the development of socialist democracy. It is impossible to list everything here. International affairs also claim no small amount of our attention.

If one speaks of the main direction of our work at present, it consists in the implementation of the decisions of the 25th CPSU Congress, above all, the ensuring of a further rise in the material and cultural standards of the people and an improvement of their working and living conditions.

As is known, our Congress has approved the guidelines for the new, tenth 5-year economic development plan. The current 5-year period differs in many ways from the preceding ones. We have set ourselves the task of carrying out deep-going qualitative changes in the structure and the technical level of economy and of radically altering its entire pattern.

We even call it a 5-year plan period of quality and efficiency. This means introduction of the most advanced technology, raising the levels of skills and know-how, promoting a more conscientious attitude to work, thus securing higher labour productivity and better quality of goods.

Of course, we do not overlook the quantitative aspect of the matter. This country now accounts for 20 per cent of the world's industrial output (though only 6 per cent of the world's population live in the Soviet Union). But we want to increase our industrial output by another 36 per cent over this 5-year period. You can imagine what this means and what efforts must be made to attain such a level!

Much is being done in this country to make agriculture a highly developed sector of economy. That our country's climatic conditions are anything but benign is well known. A substantial proportion of the country's territory belongs to the so-called critical farming regions where crop yields are not stable. That is why the development of agriculture that we are now undertaking requires a tremendous effort.

Last year's harvest was poor on account of a very dry year. Neither does the weather favour us this year. But we've successfully coped with the difficulties involved. Millions of people in rural communities – collective

199

farmers and workers on state farms, which are called *sovkhoz* in our country – have responded with exceptional enthusiasm and initiative to the call of the Party: to combat the bad weather conditions this year by energetic work and flawless organisation of all jobs. As a result, we shall have a very good harvest of grain crops.

We have made a good start with this 5-year period. We are far ahead of the plan in the main indices. But there are still unsolved problems and difficulties. We believe that we have the resources needed to run the economy better and carry out more successfully the great and complex tasks confronting society.

As you see, the Political Bureau and myself have plenty to do. On top of this, time has to be found for visiting republics and regions and meeting with people more often. For there is no substitute for personal contacts, for personal impressions. My experience confirms this.

I have visited Kazakhstan recently where I met with many people and took part in a meeting of the republic's executives. Things are going well there; the morale of the people is high and to see this is always gratifying for me as General Secretary of the Party's Central Committee.

I cannot help mentioning one more experience. On this last trip to Kazakhstan, as during my many previous visits to other regions of the country, I came to realise again and again that what the Soviet people are particularly concerned about is the achievement of a lasting peace. They are grateful to the Party and the Soviet state for their consistent policy which upholds and promotes peace and peaceful co-operation among states.

We remember that co-operation between the Soviet Union and France has played a notable part in ensuring the successful work of the European Conference. And we believe that good relations between the Soviet Union and France can in future too be a main element in the building of a lasting peace and security in Europe, and not only in Europe.

For many years we have been steadfastly pursuing a policy towards broader co-operation with France. This policy was vigorously followed in the past decade and was reaffirmed at the 25th CPSU Congress.

Soviet–French co-operation has brought tangible benefit to both countries and, at the same time has introduced much that is fresh and new into the conduct of international affairs, of relations between states with different social systems.

Economic, scientific and technological co-operation between the USSR and France embrace today such fields as space exploration, electronic computer technology, and the development of unique machinery and equipment.

Perceptible changes have taken place in the trade between the two countries. In the past few years their trade has been growing at a rate of about 30 per cent annually, which, in fact, is greater than the average growth rates of foreign trade both for France and the Soviet Union. So one can speak with confidence about good prospects for the development of trade relations between the Soviet Union and France. The same is true of cultural relations and relations in other fields.

Still there are many unused opportunities for strengthening Soviet–French co-operation, above all, political co-operation. We sincerely believe that the Soviet Union and France have major common interests, especially in such matters as elimination of the threat of war, curbing the arms race and turning Europe into a continent of lasting peace. We are convinced that our countries, by co-operating more actively with each other, could be able to make an ever greater practical contribution to the solution of these vital issues. The Soviet Union is most definitely ready for this.

I would like to speak of one more aspect of our relations to which we attach great significance. In the Soviet–French declaration which President Giscard d'Estaing and I signed in Moscow in 1975 both sides spoke in favour of promoting and strengthening the feelings of friendship between the peoples of the Soviet Union and France. This is really a very important question.

We have strictly acted and will continue to act in conformity with this understanding. Not a single Soviet statesman, not a single press organ of this country has ever uttered an unfriendly word against France, her people or those who act on their behalf. We cherish the growing friendship and co-operation between the Soviet and the French peoples, which is of great value to both. We would like to hope that such an approach would also develop in France.

Speaking about the prospects of our co-operation, the main thing, we are convinced, is the consistent and steady advance along the ascending line.

The current 'Soviet Week' sponsored by French television is a good example of how the mass media can promote understanding among nations.

Interview on French television given in Moscow. 5 October 1976

Our relations with France, I would call them many-sided, which also include the questions of foreign policy, continue to develop successfully, even though, of course, it is by no means on all international questions that we occupy common positions with the leadership of that country.

It is not ruled out that I may visit France again on the invitation of President Giscard d'Estaing in accordance with the established practice of exchanging visits. I believe this visit would not only offer a fresh opportunity for discussing questions of mutual interest, but also would promote the traditionally friendly co-operation of the two great nations.

Now about relations with the Federal Republic of Germany. Recently elections to the Bundestag took place there. During the election campaign the activity of forces attacking the government's 'Ostpolitik' from badly concealed anti-Soviet, revanchist positions noticeably grew. This prompted us to make a statement about our policy towards the FRG to clarify the Soviet Union's stand.

To emphasise the readiness of both the USSR and the FRG to develop good relations between them. Chancellor Schmidt and I have in principle reached an agreement about my next visit to the Federal Republic. A short announcement on this has been published.

Although the government coalition lost some ground, its victory at the elections, in our opinion, confirmed that the majority of the FRG's population stands for peace and the relaxation of tension, for the further improvement of relations with socialist states. This, apparently, creates favourable conditions for the normal development of mutually advantageous relations between the USSR and the FRG. Our stand is clear: we are for this.

Speech at the Plenary Meeting of the Central Committee of the Communist Party of the Soviet Union. 25 October 1976

Not so long ago I appeared on television in a broadcast to France. That was in October of last year, when Soviet Union Week was being held on French television. And now French Week on Soviet television is ending. It looks as though, in this respect, France and the Soviet Union are the trail blazers of a new form of regular exchanges between countries with different social systems. It will be good if such an initiative becomes a tradition.

And in general, we can speak of a wealth of accumulated traditions in Soviet–French co-operation. I have in mind the practically annual summit meetings, the regular consultations with the aim of broadening mutual relations and exchanging opinions on urgent world problems, the doubling of trade turnover from one 5-year period to another, and the extensive exchange of cultural values which already has a long history.

We want the intensity of contacts between the peoples of our countries to mount consistently and their forms to become ever more diversified and productive. We shall come to know each other better and better and this leads to mutual trust.

We know that the course for the continued development of good relations between our countries is widely endorsed by the people of France, for whom the Soviet people cherish feelings of sincere friendship. We attach special importance to the growing contact between our peoples because we see this as a major guarantee of the durability and depth of the great changes that have taken place in Soviet–French relations during the last decade.

I expect to meet with President Giscard d'Estaing and other French statesmen and political figures in Paris in 3 weeks' time. I hope that this meeting will give us an opportunity to take a new step forward in strengthening Franco–Soviet co-operation, peace and world *détente*.

I wish you good health, esteemed televiewers.

An address over French television. 29 May 1977

Question: Mr. General Secretary, this will be your second visit to France since Valery Giscard d'Estaing was elected President of the Republic. Could you tell us, what changes have taken place in the relations between our two countries since the meeting at Rambouillet in December 1974?

Answer: The time that has elapsed since the meeting at Rambouillet is only a part of the considerable distance the Soviet Union and France have travelled together. It began with the meeting of Soviet leaders with General de Gaulle in 1966. It was then that a turn came about in relations between the Soviet Union and France and a course was taken for the development of co-operation between the two countries in various fields. Since then fairly good results have been achieved both in the sphere of bilateral relations and as regards co-operation of our countries in international affairs.

I note with satisfaction that this positive process has continued after the meeting at Rambouillet.

Among the many agreements and protocols signed between our countries during this period I would like to mention specially here the agreement on the prevention of an accidental or unsanctioned use of nuclear weapons. This is important not only for our two countries; there is every ground to regard it as a notable contribution to the cause of world peace. It would be good if this agreement should be followed by other actions by our countries aimed at eliminating the risk of a nuclear conflict, at slowing down and putting an end to the arms race.

I have already had occasion to speak of the successful development of Soviet–French economic relations. This is a kind of material foundation for relations between countries. Some time ago we set and carried out the task of doubling the volume of our trade. Now we are advancing further, towards trebling it. Judging by the results of the past 2 years, this, too, will be achieved.

I cannot but note here, however, that on the whole France's share in the volume of the USSR's foreign trade and the Soviet Union's share in the foreign trade of France are still below the possibilities of our two countries.

Many good words can be said about the scientific, technological and cultural ties between our countries. These ties benefit the peoples of both countries and help improve mutual understanding and create a friendly atmosphere between them. We have achieved a good deal in this respect; take, for example, our joint research in several important fields of science and technology, the now traditional Weeks of the USSR on French television and Weeks of France on Soviet television, and the regular exchange in the field of the performing arts.

In short, we in the Soviet Union take a positive view of the distance covered and believe that a good basis has been laid for long-term and stable relations between our countries in the future. It is now important not to lose momentum in the development of our co-operation, but to build it up. We in the Soviet Union sincerely desire this.

Question: Of late, Left-wing forces in France have been scoring decided victories with every new election. Their coming to power next year has become a definite possibility. Would that change anything in terms of Soviet–French relations?

Answer: This question relates solely to France's domestic problems. It is a matter for the French people, and the French people alone, to decide.

As to the future of Soviet–French relations, we look forward with optimism, for we are deeply convinced that their further development completely corresponds to the vital interests of the peoples of the USSR and France.

Answers to questions from Le Monde. *15 June 1977*

Thank you, Mr. President, for your cordial words about the Soviet Union and the Soviet people and for your favourable assessment of the development of relations between our countries, an assessment with which we fully agree.

The roads of Soviet–French co-operation and the growing friendship between the peoples of our countries have again taken us to Paris. This friendship also rests on long-standing traditions and the invigorating force of what has been jointly done over the past 10 years. A great deal has indeed been achieved during this period.

We have always appreciated the aspirations of France and her freedom-loving people towards independence in politics and towards security. We appreciated the bold actions taken by France in this direction at one time. Like other socialist countries, the Soviet Union has come to regard France as a reliable partner in implementing the policy of *détente* and the strengthening of peace.

We want co-operation between the Soviet Union and France to grow steadily in scope and depth and, I would say, be consonant with the requirements of our epoch. The possibilities for this do exist.

We maintain permanent political contacts. We hold close positions on many international problems awaiting solution. And each new Soviet–French summit meeting serves to bring our views closer and to strengthen trust.

The growing economic ties serve as a good basis for our political co-operation. Over the past 11 years trade between the USSR and France has grown almost ten-fold. But this is not the limit. We are in favour of trade continuing to grow and become more balanced and, in particular, for the volume of French purchases of Soviet machinery and equipment to increase. It would also be beneficial to look at the more distant prospects of our economic and industrial ties and to lay the basis for co-operation in these fields not for 1 year and not even for 5 years but, say, right up to the year 1990. This would impart stability to such co-operation and would increase the effectiveness of our scientific and technological ties.

The exchange of cultural values has already become an every-day feature of the life of our peoples. Soviet people are well familiar with the works of great French authors, painters, and composers, with the achievements of the French theatre and cinema and, of course, they appreciate them. It gives us pleasure to see that the French people, for their part, take a lively interest in what has been created by the workers in culture and art in our country.

The particular value of Soviet–French co-operation is, in my belief, that it is aimed at *détente* and the strengthening of peace in Europe and in the world.

The basic document 'Principles of Co-operation Between the Union of Soviet Socialist Republics and France' signed in 1971 says: 'The two sides shall give every assistance in the solution of the problem of general and complete disarmament, and first of all, nuclear disarmament.' I think that it is our joint duty to act in such a way that this principle, like all the others in this document, is translated into practical deeds to the greatest degree possible by both our states.

The road to general and complete disarmament may still be long, but it is necessary to ensure a continuous advance towards this goal, so that there shall be no halting on the way, so that every year and month shall bring new practical steps in some field related to curbing the arms race, reducing the arsenals of states and lessening the danger of nuclear war.

This means that the leaders of states must also devote constant and unremitting attention to these questions. It is clear, therefore, that such questions hold no small place in our exchanges of views these days with President Giscard d'Estaing and other French leaders. And I would like to express satisfaction over the fact that we are, it seems to me, increasingly finding a common language on these issues.

Mr. President,

The Soviet–French 'Principles of Co-operation' also read in part that 'The USSR and France shall exert efforts for the speediest possible attainment of a political settlement in the interests of universal peace in areas where peace is being endangered or violated'.

Life convincingly shows how topical this task is. Today, too, one can find many points on the world map where serious problems in relations between countries and peoples and conflicts potentially dangerous to peace exist.

Of course, our countries may hold different views on a certain situation or the causes that have given rise to it. It seems to us, however, that the great responsibility of France and the Soviet Union, as permanent members of the United Nations Security Council and as countries playing a major part in international affairs, impels them to take joint actions in favour of peace. It is in our common interests – and here they coincide with the interests of all peoples – not to allow complicated political situations to grow into international conflicts.

Our common conviction in this respect has also found clear reflection in the Soviet–French declaration on the further development of friendship and co-operation, which you, Mr. President, and I signed in Moscow in 1975.

The Soviet Union and France have the means to speak out most energetically in favour of strengthening and advancing the noble cause of *détente*. Their words will carry weight and will no doubt become an appeal to others, to all governments, states and peoples without exception and will have an important stimulating effect in international life.

Mr. President,

Our countries belong to different social systems. Each has its own friends and allies. We understand many problems differently, but for all this our co-operation has become a stable and very useful element in international life. I believe that our talks with you, Mr. President, and the agreements which there is every reason to expect will be reached, will reaffirm this.

Speech at a dinner at the Elysée Palace.
21 June 1977

We are happy to greet you, Mr. President, and other outstanding representatives of the state and public life of friendly France, here at the Soviet Embassy.

It is a particularly great pleasure for us to receive you in the new Embassy building. The construction of this building is also one of the signs of growing relations between the USSR and France. You are the first guest here, Mr. President. We consider this to be very important. And I would like to wish that the life of this new Soviet house in the capital of France be marked by ever growing friendship between our countries and peoples.

Our 3-day visit to France is coming to an end today. These have been pleasant, memorable and politically eventful days. We highly assess the importance of the talks we have had these days with the President of the French Republic and members of the French Government. A great deal of important work has been done through our joint efforts.

The topics of our talks covered a number of pressing problems arising from the present world situation. Naturally, the results reached concern not only the sphere of bilateral co-operation, but have wider importance.

The President and I have signed a special document in which we have tried to find a common answer to the question of what the content of the policy of *détente* is and in what direction this policy is, in our opinion, to develop in present conditions.

In proclaiming our shared understanding on this major aspect of international politics, we are looking to the future. Perhaps this time, too, France and the Soviet Union will set a good example to others by their co-operation.

The Soviet Union has always attached great importance to the problem of strengthening security, promoting *détente* and developing co-operation in Europe. We therefore welcome the Belgrade meeting of representatives of states which took part in the European conference. We want it to be a constructive and successful meeting, and we are pleased to see that on this, as on other issues, there are unmistakable signs of mutual understanding between the Soviet Union and France.

We are also pleased to see that, in addition to the efforts already made on a broad international scale to reduce the danger of nuclear weapons proliferation, we have succeeded in defining the avenues of co-operation between the Soviet Union and France with a view to solving this problem. This is the essence of another important document which was signed today. The fact that this document expresses the common view of two nuclear powers imparts special weight and authority to this problem.

The present talks have opened up broad vistas for the expansion of co-operation between our two countries also in other major fields of international affairs. It is important in particular that the Soviet Union and France have reaffirmed their determination to act in such a way that the seat of war danger in the Middle East is at last eliminated, securely eliminated, on a just, principled and, hence, sound basis.

Naturally, questions on the further development of friendly and mutually beneficial ties between the Soviet Union and France figured prominently in our talks. The new joint political document covering a wide range of questions which was signed today, as well as the agreements on co-operation in a number of specific fields, will most certainly be beneficial to the peoples of our two countries and, I am sure, will be approved by them.

There is every reason, therefore, to be satisfied with the results of the present talks. Owing to these results we can view the future of Soviet–French co-operation with greater confidence. It now remains to implement the accords that have been reached. We are prepared to do this and believe that the French side has similar intentions.

Speech at a lunch at the USSR Embassy in France in honour of President Giscard d'Estaing. 22 June 1977   '333

Question: In connection with your visit to the FRG we would like to know how you appraise the present state of relations between our two countries and the prospects for their development.

Answer: I believe that the relations between our countries are developing successfully along many channels. We maintain that the prospects are good, provided, of course, that they do not run into artificial obstacles.

As regards your question, I cannot help recalling the treaty between the Soviet Union and the Federal Republic signed in Moscow in August 1970. For both our peoples, the past was far too tragic to underestimate the daring turn taken then.

The treaty was a major event of international scope. It laid a cornerstone in the edifice of *détente*. It gave impetus to the positive development that had long been expected. Several other agreements followed it, including multi-lateral ones.

A long road has been covered since then. The FRG concluded important treaties with the Polish People's Republic, with the German Democratic Republic and the Czechoslovak Socialist Republic. Relations between the USSR and the FRG are now qualitatively different. Co-operation is a norm. There is definite confidence in each other's words and in the signatures on joint documents. Members of government, parliamentarians, political and public figures meet; many delegations travel back and forth. There are cultural and tourist exchanges being organised. Briefly then, a great deal of experience in different relations has been accumulated.

It is understandable that summit meetings had and continue to have a determining part in building up and strengthening fruitful relations between the USSR and the FRG. Each time they provide something new, something positive, help untangle difficult problems and take decisions which signify further progress. So it is not surprising that there is now a great deal of interest in your country and in others in our coming talks in Bonn with President W. Scheel and Chancellor H. Schmidt. I will be pleased to meet Chairman W. Brandt, with whom we began clearing the road to good relations between both countries.

Relations with the FRG are a part of the Soviet Union's many-faceted and essentially worldwide relations. But they are an important part. Even in European affairs, a great deal depends on the positions of our two countries and on their understanding; in a wider context, the state of relations between the FRG and the USSR is a sensitive indicator of international *détente*, of peaceful coexistence in Europe and not only in Europe.

I want to make the point once more: the policy of good-neighbourly and mutually beneficial relations with the Federal Republic is a fundamental long-term policy of our Party and state.

Can it be said that there are no problems, no difficulties in relations between the USSR and the FRG? Of course not. Problems do exist, though they are not all of the same character.

First there is the objective aspect — the very fact that we live in countries that have different social systems gives rise to many complexities in different areas of our relations. But it is necessary to learn to live in peace and to co-operate, because there is no reasonable alternative to peaceful coexistence between states.

However, there are difficulties and obstacles of a different type. They are deliberately created by forces which are aggressively hostile to socialism, and which yearn for the cold war period. These are the forces who, using con-cocted pretexts, regularly organise anti-Soviet campaigns, provoke complica-tions, attempt to interfere in our internal affairs, and try and stir up the arms race. The actions of these forces, which are rather influential in the FRG, obstruct the smooth progress of relations between our two countries, and lessen the possibilities of our co-operation in international affairs.

We are confident that today all problems of interstate relations can be resolved if they are approached calmly and prudently, with a desire to understand the partner, to avoid passions building up, and differences being aggravated. Given goodwill on both sides, one can view the future with optimism.

Question: Some people in the FRG make statements suggesting that com-mercial relations with the USSR have 'reached the ceiling'. What is your opinion on this question?

Answer: I do not think this is so. Take the figures describing the growth of trade between the USSR and the FRG. They make a rather impressive picture. Trade in 1977 was 2.5 times greater than in 1973 and 5.5 times greater than in 1970. The FRG is our leading trade partner among the capitalist countries. We have many mutually advantageous agreements. A good example is the contract for the export of Soviet natural gas to the FRG in exchange for pipes. It is important not only because of its proportion, but because it is calculated for a long period of time – to the year 2000. It can be said to symbolise our two countries' mutual desire for stable and solid economic relations.

In the USSR West German companies are helping build the Oskol Electrometallurgical Combine, the world's biggest of its kind and Sheremet-yevo Airport. Some time ago I visited the Baikal–Amur Railway area – truly the 'construction project of the century'. Trucks bought in the FRG are doing good work there. Many of your people like the Lada automobile built at the Volzhsky Motor Works. And there are many more examples.

But to say that we are completely satisfied with the state of economic relations with your country would not be the truth. Everything in the relations between FRG companies and our organisations does not always go the way we would like it to go. We realise this and, on our part, are doing our best to take the necessary measures in good time. We hope that the Federal Republic will help surmount the difficulties we encounter. For instance, we expect that the restrictions on imports of Soviet goods will at long last be lifted, and a more favourable customs policy established.

I have had occasion to say that the economies of our two countries could in some respects supplement each other. The growing international division of labour opens up great opportunities for all countries and also holds great promise for the steady progress of our economic relations in our mutual interest. We can go beyond existing forms of economic relations, we can seek new forms, and show enterprise which is naturally founded on prudent calculations and on the idea of mutual benefit.

Soviet exports to the FRG make up 0.09 per cent of the overall social product of the USSR. West German exports to the USSR make up 0.6 per cent of the gross social product of the FRG. So it is impossible to agree that 'the ceiling has been reached' in commercial relations between our two countries.

Question: What personal expectations do you have for your visit, also remembering your first visit in 1973?

Answer: I remember with pleasure my first trip to the Federal Republic, the meetings and talks with statesmen and representatives of parties, trades unions and the business community.

I hope that this time these favourable impressions will be even stronger, and, most important, that it will be possible to do something useful and necessary for both peoples for the cause of peace.

In conclusion, I would like to cordially greet the readers of your newspaper and extend my good wishes to them and to all citizens of the Federal Republic of Germany.

Replies to questions from Vorwärts, *weekly of the Social-Democratic Party of Germany. 4 May 1978*

Esteemed Mr. Federal President,

Esteemed Mr. Federal Chancellor,

Ladies and gentlemen,

Comrades,

I would like to sincerely thank our hosts for the invitation to visit the Federal Republic of Germany, for the cordiality with which we are received here, for the warm words you have spoken, Mr. President.

It is pleasant to again meet statesmen, politicians, members of parliament and businessmen of your country. Especially those with whom 8 years ago we undertook the difficult job of sharply turning relations between our countries towards mutual understanding and good-neighbourliness.

The Moscow Treaty, mentioned here by Mr. Scheel, was truly an outstanding event. It made the Soviet Union and the FRG and also all the peoples of Europe richer, richer in their faith in the preservation of peace in the present and the attainability of a peaceful future.

The results of our bilateral co-operation during the past years have been both weighty and tangible. They can be seen in the developed political contacts, in the extensive economic ties that are steadily growing in scope, in the growing contacts between people.

I do not want to say that the time has come to fold one's hands and admire these accomplishments. There was a time when history was not miserly in preparing problems for us to inherit. Later, they were multiplied and deepened by the policy of cold war which, fortunately, has in the main receded into the past.

But now, too, there are enough things to worry about. Problems arise to this day. Perhaps of another type, but still they arise. And not every one of them has a patent medicine within easy reach or a ready article in our agreements. But it is necessary to advance all the time. We are obliged to by the memory of what has been and by responsibility for what will be. It is from this viewpoint that I approach our meetings, those which have taken place already or which are still to take place. I believe that our partners are similarly minded.

It is said that man can get used to almost anything. In war he gets used to danger, in good times to prosperity and, while he is not sick, even to health. Peace has reigned in Europe for more than 30 years now. This has never happened before. And people have begun to grow accustomed to peace, as though it is something to be taken for granted, as though *détente* has not

213

passed through many trials.

This penetration of peace into the fabric of daily life is the best reward for all who pressed for *détente* without sparing their energy. But at the same time it is a warning: it would be most dangerous to become complacent, to let events develop by themselves. I have already said and I repeat again with the full force of conviction: it is necessary to struggle for peace; *détente* should be consistently deepened and made irreversible. In this question there should be no observers on the sidelines and no dependants. It concerns everyone equally.

Peace will truly become firm when it becomes the main goal and criterion of the policy of all states, when not fear of the neighbour but a conscious striving to honestly co-operate with one another, to reach agreement without detriment to anybody's security, will determine the approach of governments to problems that arise. Fear is a poor adviser and suspiciousness is of no service to peace.

We know well that in the FRG, just as in other Western countries, millions of people, including many prominent statesmen and politicians, sincerely want lasting peace and good co-operation with the Soviet Union and other countries of the socialist community.

But we also know that in the West in general, and in your country as well, there are opponents of *détente*. Some of them believe that apprehension about and animosity towards the Soviet Union and other socialist countries should be constantly present in the policy of their states, even if this increases the risk of a new war. Others, perhaps, are simply deluded, accepting at face value the words of those who ascribe to the Soviet Union evil intentions it does not have.

The most impassable mire is the mire of prejudice. The most difficult barrier is the barrier of mistrust. Should we surmount it, mankind will acquire unprecedented strength and means for the establishment of a peace reliable as never before in the past.

Mistrust nourishes such a monstrous creation of present-day international life as the race in the manufacture of means for the mass annihilation of people. By its essence this race is senseless. It is impossible to win this race. But it is easy to bring about mankind's destruction. It is time to stop.

So let us stop. Let us no longer build up armaments. Let us start real steps to reduce armed forces and armaments both on a world scale and in Europe, in particular in Central Europe. Let us reach agreement on the renunciation of the production and deployment of new systems of weapons of mass annihilation. By way of a binding mutual agreement let us preclude the appearance of the neutron weapon, which it is intended to present to the peoples of our continent like the ominous gift of the Danai.

The Soviet Union has just made a set of proposals on the full ending of the further quantitative and qualitative growth of the armaments and armed forces of states possessing a large military capability. We are convinced that no task is more ripe and urgent now than that of blocking all channels of the arms race, both nuclear and conventional. We call on all states, on all people of peace and goodwill, including, of course, our esteemed partners and friends in the Federal Republic of Germany, to co-operate in the solution of this task.

Esteemed ladies and gentlemen,

Judging by our first conversations in Bonn it can be said, I believe, with a justified sense of optimism that the meetings of the leaders of our two countries will serve our people and the cause of strengthening peace in good stead. We are sure that they will open additional spheres of joint effort, will put into circulation new, as yet untapped reserves and possibilities.

My country is vast. It spreads over two continents. It is populated by dozens of nations and nationalities forming a single, close-knit family. This is a peaceful, industrious people, lavishly endowed with talents and possessor of a kind soul. This people does not covet what belongs to others. Its intentions are noble. It is ready to live in peace and accord with all peoples, including your people.

Allow me on this May day of spring to wish the citizens of your country well-being and prosperity!

Speech at a dinner given by W. Scheel, President of the Federal Republic of Germany. 4 May 1978

Esteemed Mr. Federal President,
Esteemed Mr. Federal Chancellor,
Ladies and gentlemen,

I have the pleasure of heartily greeting as our guests the leaders of the

Federal Republic of Germany, leaders of political parties, prominent representatives of the trade unions, business circles, the press, all those who have accepted our invitation.

This is the second day of our stay in the Federal Republic. Like the first day, it is full of intensive work. Both sides have submitted for discussion everything that they deemed substantially important in their mutual relations and in the sphere of world politics. The path of our discussion has not avoided any sharp corners. After all, realism is the only reliable basis for constructive work. And we, I believe I can say this for both sides, wish to build the edifice of our relations not on sand, but on solid ground.

Getting ready for the trip here, I asked myself repeatedly what the recent years have added to the relations between our two countries, how tangible are the changes achieved.

The great thinker and founder of scientific socialism, Karl Marx, the 160th anniversary of whose birth falls today, once said that every step of genuine progress is more important than a dozen programmes. How true these words are. There is no substitute for concrete deeds, and it is precisely the deeds that speak out so eloquently in the given case.

The seventies, I think, have shown convincingly how much that is new and unquestionably useful has been brought about by the normalisation of the relations between our two countries. And I mean the deeds beneficial both for each of them and for the situation in the world arena as a whole.

Let us take for a start the material basis of this – economic relations. Big changes have occurred in this sphere. After all, we had to start from a rather low and clearly insufficient level for two such countries as ours, if not from scratch. And the results are already tangible. It is enough to recall that over the past 4 years the USSR has delivered to the FRG more than 27 million tons of oil and oil products, 100 million roubles' worth of chemical products, 2 million cubic metres of cut timber, 120,000 tons of cotton, and many other commodities. Deliveries of Soviet natural gas are increasing yearly. About 200,000 million cubic metres of gas will have been delivered before the year 2000.

During the same 4-year period we have imported from the FRG equipment and machinery alone worth more than 3500 million roubles.

West German equipment and technology are becoming a traditional component of several of our major economic projects and industrial enterprises. And Soviet orders, raw materials and fuel help you, in turn, to keep your plants and factories busier, which, as I understand, is very important in conditions of high unemployment.

Then take the cultural exchanges. It goes without saying that they play no small role in the creation of an atmosphere of greater mutual understanding between nations, among the masses of ordinary men and women. And considerable progress can be noted in this domain too.

The other day I asked for concrete figures on our cultural exchanges. And what do you think? The mere listing of the mutual exchanges that took place during the past 4 years occupied five full pages. They included fine art exhibitions, performances by many ensembles and companies, theatre presentations with the participation of noted directors and actors, concerts with famous singers and musicians, various meetings of creative intellectuals.

If we take international aspects, the changes for the better here are, probably, even greater. Improvement of the FRG's relations with her immediate or close neighbours – the GDR, Czechoslovakia, Poland, and other European socialist states – is unquestionably mutually beneficial. This is definitely sensed by many in the Federal Republic. The successful development of these relations is also borne out convincingly, and specifically, by the results of the recent visits paid to the FRG by Edward Gierek and Gustav Husak.

The admission of the FRG and the GDR to the United Nations is an important element in the normalisation of the world situation in general.

Finally, the radical change in the relations between our two countries, I would say, together with the experience of Soviet–French co-operation, served as the starting-point for progress towards so notable a landmark in the history of international relations as the All-European Conference in Helsinki with the participation of the United States and Canada.

I should like to believe that our current negotiations and meetings will leave their trace in the work to improve and expand the relations between the USSR and the FRG, will help consolidate the improvement of the European and world climate. In any case, this is the goal that we are pursuing. And I should like to add that the successes of our joint work in this direction will be the weightier and the more lasting the more the peoples of our two countries realise that the fundamental interests of the Soviet Union and the FRG are inalienably linked with the safeguarding of peace, that the citizens of our countries should never again peer at each other through gunsights, that the future of Europe rests only with peaceful co-operation. If we achieve such a cardinal change in people's hearts, nobody and nothing will ever divert us from this road. This is why truthful and well-intentioned information about each other is important. It is important to bring up the people, primarily the young, in the spirit of respect for other nations, to get rid of ideas and concepts that drag nations into the past like a lead weight. A huge responsibility rests here with the mass information media, schools and universities.

Ideological disputes, the struggle of ideologies will of course continue. But we are against ideologies being made to serve military staffs and ideological struggle being turned into psychological warfare. Our principle is peaceful, honest competition of ideas and social practice. People should not settle their relations, including ideological matters, on the battlefield. Neither you nor we need to compete in who presents the other side in a darker light. If our goal is co-operation and confidence, we should try to act correspondingly.

Rounding off my speech, I wish to sincerely thank Mr. Federal President and Mr. Federal Chancellor for the attention and hospitality accorded us in the Federal Republic. We can already say that the visit has been useful, comprehensive and necessary.

For my part, I wish to convey to you, Mr. Federal President, and to you, Mr. Federal Chancellor, an invitation to pay an official visit to our country. We shall be glad to accord hospitality to you, to continue contacts with you in the interests of further deepening the relations between the Soviet Union and the Federal Republic of Germany.

Allow me to propose a toast to the close mutual understanding and fruitful co-operation between the USSR and the FRG!

Speech at a lunch given in honour of FRG leaders. 5 May 1978

Good evening, dear TV-viewers.

I was very pleased to accept the suggestion that I talk to you tonight. My second visit to your country is near its end, and we are quite satisfied with its results. Our talks with President Walter Scheel, Chancellor Helmut Schmidt, Vice-Chancellor Genscher, and our meetings with Willy Brandt, Chairman of the Social Democratic Party of Germany, and other statesmen and political leaders of the FRG, have been very necessary and useful.

When leaving for Bonn this time, we considered that our task would be to define, on the basis of the 1970 Moscow Treaty, together with the leaders of the FRG, the main lines of further bilateral co-operation between our countries for the years ahead, and to also map out the ways we can interact in strengthening peace and international *détente*. In my opinion there has been a great deal achieved in this direction during the visit. There are grounds to hope that its results will give relations between the Federal Republic of Germany and the Soviet Union greater stability and broader scope. We are now at a very responsible juncture in the development of events in the international arena. The Soviet Union and the FRG are in a position to do a great deal to eliminate the difficulties which *détente* has come up against as it develops. It largely depends on our countries whether or not the positive processes which began in international relations in the first half of the 1970s are consolidated and deepened.

It is no secret that these processes have slowed down somewhat today. I shall not refer to all the reasons, and there are quite a few of them. But the main reason is that the monstrous arms race has not yet been curbed. This is extremely alarming; after all, this race cannot go on endlessly. It is relentlessly eroding the edifice of political *détente* and, if not stopped, can jeopardise the very future of the human race.

So our country, the Soviet Union, considers that its most important task in international affairs is to prevent mankind from drifting towards war, to uphold and strengthen peace – universal, just and lasting. This is our constant policy. It is independent of any time-serving trends; it is formalised in the Constitution of the Soviet Union. We are unswervingly pursuing this line in every way. Soviet diplomacy is subordinated to it. It is supported by all the people of our country. Whenever we draw up our plans, we keep the prospects of peace in mind.

More and more people, including citizens of the FRG, are visiting the Soviet Union every year. And anyone who takes an unbiased look at our life will certainly confirm that the entire atmosphere in our country is permeated with the people's deep commitment to peace, with the desire to live in peace with all nations.

When we say that we Soviet people want peace, we speak from the heart. I have travelled far and wide in the country. Recently, for instance, I revisited

Siberia and the Far East, covering thousands and thousands of kilometres and meeting many people. And whatever we talked about, the conversation inevitably turned to international issues. In the final analysis it all came down to the question of questions: whether or not it is possible to maintain and strengthen peace.

In the Soviet Union we have neither the classes, the social strata, nor the professional groups interested in war, or in preparing for war, or thinking of making profit out of it. There are the munitions factories and the army, of course, but neither the managers of those factories, the army commanders, workers, nor servicemen associate their well-being with war, or with military contracts. We would really like to convert our munitions factories to the manufacture of peacetime products, to gear them to the needs of peaceful construction for the great benefit of the entire society.

Our country is often compared to a giant construction site. This is not just a figure of speech. It is a fact. We are doing a great deal of building. And we are not simply building; we are transforming the very image of our country.

You have probably heard about the Baikal–Amur Railway. It is a railway more than 3000 km long. It is being laid across permafrost, across the virgin taiga, it is being cut through cliffs. Building it means not only that the distance to the Pacific will be greatly lessened, but also that an area big enough for several countries to fit in will be opened. And all this has been started literally from scratch. Or take the development of the Tyumen oil deposits in Western Siberia. We embarked on this tremendous project less than 15 years ago. And now 1 out of every 2 tons of Soviet oil is extracted in the region. On the Ob River there we are developing an area of about a million square kilometres.

Or, finally, the projects for the real rebirth of our Russian Non-Black-Earth Zone. This is a matter of transforming the very heart of Russia, so to speak. Just think about it: we have decided to build up, practically anew, highly productive agriculture on an area approximately as big as France. All the work, including the draining and irrigation of huge areas, will finally be completed only by 1990. But even by 1980 one-sixth of the Soviet Union's agricultural output will come from this land.

Our initiatives and plans are intended for decades ahead. We are working not on one or two but on dozens of projects, each of whose scope is greater than the plans of certain states. And the ultimate aim of every one of them is to improve the well-being of millions of people, of our entire country.

We are working on increasingly bigger and greater labour-consuming tasks in the social sector as well. I will give the following example. For the first time, we have formalised the right to housing in our new Constitution. This right cannot be merely declared; there is a great deal of work being done to make it a reality. In our country, eleven million people move into new flats every year. Rent in our state-owned apartments is extremely low. Set 50 years ago, it has not been raised since. All this means that society and the state are meeting a growing proportion of housing expenditures. Or another example. Our national health service is free and is probably the most extensive in the world. One-third of all the world's doctors are Soviet doctors. But guaranteeing our constitutional right to health protection demands major new capital investment, social measures and research. There are a great many similar examples.

None of these tasks are easy at all. We have quite a few complicated problems and quite a few short-comings, but we are solving all these problems through the growing activity and initiative of millions of people. And we will certainly solve them given the single condition that a new war is prevented, that a lasting peace is ensured on the solid foundation of peaceful coexistence. In the light of this it is not hard to see that the element of peace in our policy is not theatrical posturing, but the very essence of our life. This is the guarantee of the firmness and stability of the international policy of the Soviet Union whose objectives, I think, are clear, understandable and near to everyone: they are peace, disarmament and international security.

These are the objectives behind the important concrete proposals which the Soviet Union puts forward in the international arena. To begin with, what we want is at least to suspend the increase in the armaments and armed forces of countries which have a large military capability. This is the essence of our recent initiatives.

Esteemed citizens of the Federal Republic of Germany.

The end of the first 10-day period of May is a special time for our countries and for our peoples. At this time every year we celebrate the end of World War II fighting in Europe. Of course, we mark this in different ways and to a great extent our feelings are not alike in this context. We can understand why. But the different attitudes and feelings are not the only thing. There is also something in common – and this, I think, is much more substantial and much more important at this time. Our peoples suffered enormous and irreparable losses in the last war. And although new generations have grown up today – most likely now every second person in the USSR and the FRG knows about war only from books – the past compels us to draw a lesson from recent history, confirms us in our desire to live in peace, to prevent a new tragedy.

I think it is time that the responsible political leaders of all countries without exception tell each other and their peoples: there must be no war! Say this and do everything so that it will never really break out, but time compels us: every lost day, every delay, every procrastination may cost the human race, each one of us, all too dearly.

This, esteemed TV-viewers, was what guided us during the discussions in Bonn. The documents adopted there are extremely important.

Thus, the Joint Declaration we have signed with Chancellor Schmidt expresses the determination of both countries to promote political co-operation between the FRG and the USSR on a strong andpermanent basis. This applies to bilateral affairs and to major international issues, primarily peaceful coexistence, *détente* and curbing the arms race. We have also signed an Agreement providing for the development of economic contacts with quite a long perspective – until the end of the current millennium. A solid material foundation is being built for peaceful co-operation between our two countries.

These have been good results. Now, in our eyes, what we have to do is translate the agreements we reached into concrete deeds, into real joint efforts in the international arena. Let us worthily continue the historic endeavour which began with the signing of the 1970 Moscow Treaty. Let us develop and enrich the fine traditions of co-operation in the interests of the peoples of our two countries, for the sake of the further strengthening of peace, of the development of fruitful co-operation in Europe and all over the world!

To end, I would like to extend our heartfelt thanks to our excellent hosts – Federal President Walter Scheel, Federal Chancellor Helmut Schmidt, to all those we have met and had talks with, and to all residents of the FRG – for their warm welcome and cordial hospitality.

I wish you all the best! Until we meet again!

Speech on FRG television. 6 May 1978

6.
RELATIONS WITH THE UNITED STATES OF AMERICA

Speaking of the Soviet Union's relations with the United States, it will be recalled that the Resolution of the 24th CPSU Congress formulated our objectives as follows:

'The Congress instructs the CC CPSU consistently to continue carrying forward into practice the principle of peaceful coexistence, to extend mutually advantageous relations with the capitalist countries. The Soviet Union is prepared to develop relations also with the United States of America, holding that this conforms with the interests both of the Soviet and the American peoples and those of world peace. At the same time, the Soviet Union will always firmly oppose the aggressive actions of the United States and the policy of force.'

As you see, the objectives are quite clear. They are in keeping with the class line of the socialist state's peace-loving policy. The Central Committee of our Party, the Soviet Government, follow this line consistently.

The negotiations we had with President Nixon in Moscow this spring were a big step forward in the development of Soviet–American relations.

What is especially important is that the two sides have jointly defined the principles that are to govern the relations between the USSR and the USA, and that they did so out of a conviction that no foundation other than peaceful coexistence is possible for the relations between the two countries in the nuclear age.

Report at a gala joint meeting of the CPSU Central Committee, the USSR Supreme Soviet and the RSFSR Supreme Soviet in the Kremlin Palace of Congresses. 21 December 1972

I think that the time that has passed since our Moscow meeting has convincingly proved the correctness of the course which we have jointly taken towards improving relations between the USSR and the USA, towards rebuilding them in accordance with the principles of peaceful coexistence, as laid down in the document which we signed a year ago. I think you will agree,

Mr. President, that we are on the correct road, for it accords with the vital interests of the peoples of our two countries and of all mankind.

That which has been done and that which is being done to put into practice the principles agreed on in Moscow concerning relations between our countries are of no small importance. Life is our best teacher. The results of our efforts of the past year show in what direction we should go on. They encourage us to make new big strides during the present meeting, to give greater stability to Soviet–American relations and thereby increase the contribution of our countries to the cause of peace and international *détente*.

Of course, rebuilding Soviet–American relations is no simple task. This is so not only because the USSR and the USA have different social systems, but also because it requires the overcoming of the inertia of the 'cold war' and of the traces it has left in international politics, and in the minds of people.

But the development of mankind calls for positive and constructive ideas. It is, therefore, my conviction that the more persistently and the more rapidly we move towards mutually advantageous development of Soviet–American relations, the more tangible will be its great benefits for the peoples of our countries, the faster the number of supporters of such a development will increase, who as we know already today constitute a majority. That is why we are in favour of building relations between the Soviet Union and the United States on an appropriate scale and on a long-term basis.

We have come here with the firm desire, jointly with statesmen in the United States, to give a fresh strong impetus to such a development of Soviet–American relations. This fully conforms to the Peace Programme adopted by the 24th Congress of our Party.

In its resolution this Congress most definitely emphasised the Soviet Union's readiness to improve relations with the United States. In this it proceeded from the belief that this is in the interests of both the Soviet and American peoples, and in the interests of universal peace.

I would like our American partners in the talks to realise fully that this decision of the supreme forum of our Party – the ruling party in the Soviet Union – is an expression of he profoundly principled position of the Soviet state, of our entire people, on questions of relations with the United States of America. It is exactly this that determines the policy we are pursuing.

In my talk with the President today I spoke about the feelings of all our people who support the decisions we took at our meeting last year.

Mr. President, the peoples of the world are expecting much from our new meeting. And I believe that it is our duty to justify these expectations. The first talks that we have had with you here at the White House confirm, I think, that this is the desire of the two sides. In this connection I would like to express the hope – indeed, the belief – that our present meeting will play an important role in further strengthening mutually advantageous co-operation between our countries and in improving the international climate as a whole.

And here is another point. It is well known that the process of improving Soviet–American relations, which has begun, has aroused widespread interest around the world. The overwhelming majority of the opinions expressed on the subject indicate that the peoples and governments of other countries welcome this improvement. This is only natural. They regard it as a factor promoting an improvement of the international situation as a whole, as a major contribution of the Soviet Union and the United States to strengthening universal peace.

To all who are aware, if only slightly, of the actual course of events, of the nature of the development of Soviet–American relations, it is absolutely clear that the improvement of Soviet–American relations is in no way detrimental to the interests of any third country.

Of course, the development of good relations between the USSR and the USA will have, and is already having, a considerable influence on international affairs. But this influence is of a kind that promotes the cause of strengthening peace, security and international co-operation. In building, through joint efforts, the new edifice of peaceful relations, it is not at all our intention to turn it into an ivory tower, fenced off from the outside world. We want this spacious building to be open to all who are for peace and for the well-being of people.

Mr. President, contemporary political practice shows how difficult and strenuous at times are the tasks involved in the implementation of the foreign policy of states. But when our thoughts and practical deeds are aimed at achieving the noble goal of peace, this is a burden that, far from being heavy, imparts strength and confidence.

Speech at a dinner given in honour of Leonid Brezhnev by President Richard Nixon. 18 June 1973

I have heard that the American political vocabulary contains the expression 'to win the peace'. I feel that this is an historical moment when this expression can perhaps be used most appropriately. We jointly won the war. Today our concerted efforts must help mankind win lasting peace. The possibility of a new war must be excluded.

The results of the two summit meetings between the Soviet Union and the United States and all that has been accomplished in the year between these two meetings demonstrate convincingly that important progress has already been achieved. It transpired that a reasonable approach, acceptable to both sides, could be found to many questions that had seemed unresolvable. Only recently it was perhaps difficult even to imagine that such progress was possible.

The best proof that Soviet–American relations are not standing still, but are developing, is the important document which President Nixon and I signed the other day – the Agreement Between the Union of Soviet Socialist Republics and the United States of America on the Prevention of Nuclear War. I don't think I shall be accused of exaggerating if I say that this is a document of historic importance.

The Union of Soviet Socialist Republics and the United States of America have concluded an agreement aimed at preventing the outbreak of nuclear war between them, an agreement to do all in their power to prevent the outbreak of nuclear war in general. The tremendous importance of this for the peace and tranquillity of the peoples of our two countries and for improving the prospects for a peaceful life for all humanity is obvious.

Even if this, our second meeting, had no other results than this, it can be said in all justice that it will occupy a worthy place in the history of the development of Soviet–American relations, and international life as a whole.

Now the whole world can see that both our states, after signing last year the fundamental document on 'The Basic Principles of Mutual Relations Between the Union of Soviet Socialist Republics and the United States of America', regard it not as a mere declaration of good intentions, but as a programme of vigorous and consistent action – a programme which they have already started to implement and firmly intend to continue implementing.

Nor is it of small importance that our countries have agreed on basic principles for further work to prepare a new, wider agreement on limiting strategic armaments, and for a much longer term. This means that this exceptionally important work, which began in May 1972 in Moscow, is moving ahead. It means that political *détente* is being matched by relaxation in the military sphere. This will benefit all peoples and the cause of peace generally.

Representatives of our two states have also just signed new agreements on Soviet–American co-operation in a number of specific fields. Together with the agreements signed earlier in the course of the past year, they constitute an impressive body of documents dealing with the co-operation of our two states, of two great nations, in most diverse fields – from the peaceful uses of atomic energy to agriculture, from the expanses of space to the depths of the ocean.

Of course, the Soviet Union and the United States are self-sufficient countries, so to speak. And this, in fact, has been the case up to now in our relationship. But at the same time both we and many Americans realise well that rejecting co-operation in the economic, scientific, technological and cultural fields means a rejection of considerable additional benefits and advantages which could be derived by both sides. What is more – this would be an absolutely purposeless rejection, which could not be justified on any sensible grounds.

This particularly concerns economics. Now, I think we all agree that it is not sufficient merely to overcome the anomaly, generated by the cold war, of the complete freezing of Soviet–American trade. Today life faces us with much bigger questions. I have in mind, first of all, such forms of economic relations as stable, large-scale ties in a number of economic branches, and long-term scientific and technological co-operation, something that in our age is of great importance. The contacts that we have had with the officials and businessmen of your country confirm that it is precisely along these lines that there is the main prospect for the further development of the economic co-operation between our two countries.

One occasionally hears the allegation that the development of such co-operation is of a one-sided nature, and is to the advantage of the Soviet Union alone. But such a thing could be said only by one who is entirely ignorant of the actual situation, or who has deliberately turned a blind eye to the truth.

The truth of the matter is that from the development and deepening of economic co-operation in general, and the long-term, wide-scale deals over which talks between Soviet organisations and major American firms are either under way or have been successfully concluded, both sides must derive real and tangible benefits. We have had clear confirmation that this is so as far as they are concerned from representatives of US business circles with whom

I happened to talk, both here in the United States and earlier in Moscow. President Nixon and I also discussed this very point in our talks.

To this I would like to add that the leadership of the Soviet Union, just as, I understand, the Government of the United States, is attaching great importance to the fact that the development of long-term economic co-operation will also have favourable political consequences: it will consolidate the turn for the better that has become apparent in Soviet–American relations as a whole.

There are also good prospects, as we see it, for a broad development of Soviet–American exchanges in the cultural field. Both our countries have much to give each other in this respect. To live in peace it is necessary to trust one another, and to trust – each must know the other better. We, in any case, want Americans to know, as fully as possible, and truthfully, our way of life and our way of thinking.

On the whole we can say that much has already been accomplished in the development of Soviet–American relations. But we are still standing at the very beginning of a long road. We must show constant concern to protect and nurture the fresh shoots of good relations. Tireless work is needed to determine the most necessary and most suitable forms of co-operation in various spheres. Patience is needed to understand this or that specific feature of the other side and to learn to do business with each other in a good spirit.

I think that those who support a radical improvement in relations between the Soviet Union and the United States may look ahead with optimism, for this goal is in the interests of our two peoples and in the interests of peace-loving people throughout the world.

The general atmosphere in the world depends in great measure on the climate prevailing in the relations between our two countries. Neither economic and military might, nor international prestige confer upon our countries any additional rights, but instead invest them with special responsibility for the fate of world peace, for preventing war. In its approach to its ties and contacts with the United States, the Soviet Union is fully aware of this responsibility.

We regard the improvement of Soviet–American relations not as an isolated phenomenon, but as an integral and very important part of a wide process of a radical clearing of the international atmosphere. The world has outgrown the rigid armour of the cold war, in which attempts were made to confine it. Man wants to breathe freely and peacefully. And we shall welcome it if our efforts to improve Soviet–American relations help draw into the process of *détente* more and more states, be they in Europe or Asia, in Africa or Latin America, in the Middle or the Far East.

We consider it a highly positive fact that the normalisation of Soviet–American relations will make it easier to carry out such a big and important task as strengthening peace and security in Europe, including the holding of an all-European conference.

The improvement of Soviet–American relations has undoubtedly played a part in helping to end the long Vietnam war. Now that the agreement on ending the Vietnam war has come into force and both our countries, together with other states, have signed the agreement reached at the Paris Conference on Vietnam, we deem it especially important that this success be consolidated, and that all the peoples of Indo-China be given the chance to live in peace.

There are still areas of dangerous tension in the world. In our talks, President Nixon and I touched on the Middle East situation which is still very acute. We believe that justice must be ensured in the area as soon as possible and that a lasting peace settlement must be achieved – a settlement that will restore the legitimate rights of those who suffered in the war and ensure the security of all the peoples of this vast area. This is important for all the peoples of the Middle East, and it is important for ensuring universal peace.

In a word, the elimination of conflicts that have flared up and the prevention of new crisis situations are essential for the creation of truly reliable guarantees of peace. And our two countries are called upon to make a worthy contribution to this. The President and I gave these questions much attention during our talks of the last few days.

I would like to stress here that, when discussing questions of bilateral relations and general international problems alike, we invariably took into account the fact that both the Soviet Union and the USA have allies and commitments concerning this or that country. It should be made quite clear that both the spirit of our talks and the letter of the agreements signed take this fully into account.

The main point of our discussions and agreements in the field of international affairs is the firm resolve of both sides to make the good relations between the USSR and the USA a permanent factor of international peace.

Speech on American television. 24 June 1973

Today we can say that thanks to the growing might and international influence of the Soviet Union and of the entire socialist camp, thanks to our active foreign policy and to the actions of the peace forces, the relaxation process is well under way and international security has become more reliable. As a result, international conditions for communist and socialist construction and for the people's social progress have become much more favourable. This enables us to concentrate, to a still greater extent, on peaceful, creative work, and we are naturally gratified by such a course of events.

We stand for lasting peace. And this presupposes not merely the renunciation of war as a means of settling controversial international issues, but also the establishment of definite mutual understanding and trust between states, the development of co-operation on the basis of full equality and mutual advantage.

It is precisely from this angle that we approach the development of relations between the Soviet Union and capitalist states, including such big states as the USA, France, the FRG, Japan. Speaking of our relations with the United States, for instance, we regard their improvement as an organic component of the overall process of a radical change in the international climate on our planet. And this part is very important, but by no means for the reason that these two states allegedly possess some 'exclusive' rights in international affairs or some claim to joint ruling of the destinies of the whole world. Such inventions contradict the very nature of the Soviet Union's policy, our manner of thinking and actual developments in the international arena. The gist of the matter lies elsewhere. By force of the military, economic, scientific and technical potential of the Soviet Union and of the United States, the state of the relations between them objectively affects the international situation as a whole, especially as regards the problems of war and peace.

The Soviet Union has of late concluded quite a few treaties on matters of principle and major agreements with a number of capitalist states and we shall not sin against the truth if we say that all of them serve one and the same noble cause – the cause of relaxation, peace and the development of peaceful co-operation. Indeed, does not the process of relaxation gain momentum when the Soviet Union and France, the Soviet Union and the United States agree on principles of peaceful relations or when we conclude with the Federal Republic of Germany an agreement which settles many issues which for years past contaminated the European atmosphere? Do not the agreements on the mutual limitation of the most powerful and the most dangerous weapons or on the prevention of nuclear war, concluded by the Soviet Union and the United States of America, serve the interests of universal peace? The answer is self-evident, I think.

True, one sometimes hears assertions to the effect that the agreements signed are allegedly unsatisfactory since they do not wholly solve the existing problems – once and for all, so to say. It is claimed that only a general agreement on universal and complete disarmament, on the banning and destruction of nuclear weapons and on the disbandment of military blocs would bring about a real change in world politics, and that what is being done now are only half measures.

One can only wonder at the naïverty of such an approach. It would be good, of course, to have universal and complete disarmament, including the solution of the problem of nuclear weapons and military blocs. The Soviet Union has long been persistently working for these ends. Unfortunately, our Western partners are not yet prepared for such a solution. But do we have to sit idly and wait for the manna to drop from the sky? Not at all. The principle of 'everything or nothing' can by no means be applied in modern politics. We should always try and make progress, using every possible opportunity available to us.

Those who do nothing and miss the chance to make a real – even though small – step forward prejudice the cause of peace. Our Party and our country are guided by Lenin's principle: 'We should like to see a minimum of general assurances, solemn promises and grandiloquent formulas, and the greatest possible number of the simplest and most obvious decisions and measures that would certainly lead to peace.'

What has lately been done has already led to noticeable positive changes in the world situation. Incidentally the experience of the development of our relations with certain capitalist countries confirms that the Leninist principles of peaceful coexistence are a reliable way of broadening economic contacts. In turn, large-scale and long-term economic agreements cement peaceful relations among acquiescent countries. We think that there is considerable opportunity for more progress here – proceeding, of course, from mutual advantage and universally recognised norms of equal co-operation free of discrimination.

The Soviet Union has always insisted on the peaceful coexistence principles becoming an indisputable norm of the entire international life on all continents.

> *Speech at the joint celebration meeting of the Central Committee of the Communist Party of Uzbekistan and the Supreme Soviet of the Uzbek SSR, devoted to the presentation to the Republic of the Order of Friendship Among the Peoples, in Tashkent. 24 September 1973*

Everyone knows how much has been done in recent years to achieve a turn in international relations from the cold-war atmosphere poisoned with mutual animosity and distrust to normal, reasonable forms of inter-state intercourse based on the principles of peaceful coexistence. This process which requires constant political struggle has already resulted in substantial achievements which, we can safely say, are of historical significance.

The results of the recent Soviet–US summit meeting are further proof that the process of easing international tension is continuing and intensifying. The main thing, we feel, is that both sides in all clarity reaffirmed their determination to carry on the great cause started in 1972 and 1973: to do everything possible to further lessen and then completely eliminate the risk of a military clash between the USSR and the USA, a clash which would be tantamount to the outbreak of a world nuclear-missile war. Also clearly evident was the mutual desire to develop and deepen the peaceful mutually beneficial Soviet–US co-operation in various fields.

The concrete results of the Moscow talks are known to all. Here I should like only to emphasise once again the importance of that part of the talks which has a direct bearing on curbing the arms race and on strengthening universal peace.

The Soviet Union and the United States of America signed a protocol envisaging further substantial limitation of anti-ballistic missile systems of the two countries. This is doubtless a useful step. It is useful not only from the standpoint of the development of the peace-time economies of the two countries but also from the point of further growth of trust between them and, consequently, a general improvement of the international climate.

The outlines of further steps to limit strategic offensive arms also began to shape up as a result of our talks with President Nixon. I want to emphasise the far-reaching scope of the envisaged measures: the interim agreement on this matter, which, as is known, is to remain in effect till 1977, is to be followed by a new, longer-term agreement to be in force till the year 1985 and provide for both quantitative and qualitative limitations of nuclear-missile weapons. It is understandable that it is not an easy matter to conclude such an agreement. We hold, however, that the work which has already been done, including what was done during the latest summit meeting, will help to solve the tasks that face us.

The USSR and the USA also agreed to considerably limit at an agreed-upon time their underground nuclear weapons tests and to discontinue altogether the most powerful test explosions. We consider this agreement as a step towards an eventual all-inclusive, universal ban on nuclear weapons tests.

It is also evident that the Soviet–US agreements against the use of the most dangerous lethal means of chemical warfare, as well as means of affecting the environment for military purposes, are of benefit to the cause of peace. This is a question of great importance.

We feel, comrades, that this entire complex of practical actions, which is a good example of limitations set by powers on their military preparations, is in the interests of all who strive for consolidation of peace on earth. This is why the constructive results of the Soviet–US talks have met with such widespread, positive response in the world.

I can say, comrades, that we would have liked to achieve something more and were prepared to go further. The Soviet Union is ready, in particular, to conclude an agreement on complete cessation of all underground tests of nuclear weapons. We also feel it would be useful to agree upon the withdrawal from the Mediterranean of all Soviet and US ships and submarines carrying nuclear weapons. Regretfully, no agreement on this score has so far been achieved. But we are convinced that the implementation of these proposals of ours would be a new real contribution to the strengthening of peace and would be regarded by the peoples of many countries with great satisfaction. We hope that the time will come for agreements on these matters to become possible.

There is no denying, the setting up of normal and, I would say, friendly relations between the Soviet Union and the USA is of vital importance for the cause of peace. But international relations are up to all countries, big and small. They all enjoy equal rights and each is called upon to make its contribution to the consolidation of universal security.

Speech at a ceremonial session of the Sejm of the Polish People's Republic to mark the 30th anniversary of the resurrection of Poland, Warsaw. 21 July 1974

Versatile bilateral relations and co-operation between our countries are expanding quite well on the political and legal basis created by the joint efforts. These relations encompass the sphere of economy, various branches of technology, ever more lively exchange in cultural values and reciprocal visits of representatives of various state and public organisations. These relations, undoubtedly, are useful by themselves, in a purely practical way in every specific field. But they are even more valuable due to the fact that they create better conditions for mutual understanding and growth of trust between our peoples. And this is especially important.

The time is ripe for outlining jointly the new steps that will enable us to advance forward, relying on the basis we have created. It is precisely in this, as I understand, that both of us see the main task of our meeting, Mr. President. Certainly, in the first turn, our attention was attracted by such a vitally important problem as achievement of an agreement of further limitation and then reduction of armaments, especially such armaments that it is now customary to call strategic ones. This is necessary if we really wish to promote elimination of the threat of an outbreak of a missile-nuclear war with all its disastrous consequences for peoples. To make international *détente* really firm, it is necessary to consolidate it by *détente* in the military field. Further progress in this direction will be of great importance for universal peace. I think we have done a good job in this respect here in Vladivostok.

This is our first meeting, Mr. President, and we are pleased with the fact that it is held in the Soviet land, so we have an opportunity to show, to some extent, hospitality for President Ford. Though, of course, you are just starting familiarising yourself with our country, Mr. President, we are sure you will be able to learn still more about our country.

The fact that our first meeting has a purely working nature and is held in less than 6 months since the previous Soviet–American summit meeting is indicative of many things. Meetings and talks of the leaders of our two countries become regular. Without losing their great significance in essence, they are no longer anything extraordinary. They are becoming, as it were, a norm of development in Soviet–American relations. And this, to my mind, is a substantial achievement in itself.

Over the past 2 or 3 years, quite a lot has been done by joint efforts to rebuild relations between the Soviet Union and the United States of America on the basis of peaceful coexistence, in the interests of the peoples of both countries and universal peace.

Our states have pledged themselves to act in such a way as to prevent an outbreak of a nuclear war. This is a great undertaking. The first steps have been made to arrest the strategic arms race. The transition of our countries to a constructive dialogue in this extremely important field has become a serious factor of consolidation of international security and universal peace.

And one more important point. We in the Soviet Union are convinced that the USSR and the USA, being guided by the interests of peace and acting jointly with other peace-loving states, can and must actively promote settlement of acute international problems that still remain unsolved, promote liquidation of dangerous seats of tension and conflicts. Certain things have been done in this respect in the past. But, we believe, co-operation of our two countries for consolidation of peace and security of peoples could be much more effective.

It is known that much yet remains to be done so as to really clear the way for development of commercial and economic relations between our two countries on the basis of equality. This is needed ever more so since it means not merely mutual material benefit, but creation of a sort of material basis for the steady improvement of Soviet–American relations as a whole.

As I understand it, Mr. President, we have established the common view that it is necessary to exert all the efforts to ensure the steady progressive development of Soviet–American relations, to make this process irreversible.

It is worthwhile to work for this purpose, sparing no efforts, and we are glad that our meeting enabled us to take new essential steps in this direction.

Speech at a dinner in honour of Gerald Ford, President of the United States of America, Vladivostok. 24 November 1974

The turn for the better in our relations with the United States of America, the biggest power of the capitalist world, has, of course, been decisive in reducing the danger of another world war and in consolidating peace. This has beyond question contributed to the improvement of the international climate in general, and that of Europe in particular. Acting in complete accord with the guidelines set by the 24th Congress, we have devoted very great attention to the objective of improving relations with the United States.

As a result of the negotiations with US President Nixon in Moscow and Washington, and later of the meetings with President Ford in Vladivostok and Helsinki, important and fundamental mutual understanding has been reached between the leaders of the Soviet Union and the United States on the necessity of developing peaceful equal relations between the two countries. This is reflected in a whole system of Soviet–US treaties, agreements and other documents. Unquestionably the most important of these are 'The Basic Principles of Mutual Relations Between the Union of Soviet Socialist Republics and the United States of America', the Agreement on the Prevention of Nuclear War, and the series of strategic arms limitation treaties and agreements. What is the main significance of these documents?

In all, they have laid a solid political and legal foundation for greater mutually beneficial co-operation between the USSR and USA in line with the principles of peaceful coexistence. To a certain extent they have lessened the danger of nuclear war. Precisely in this we see the main result of the development of Soviet–US relations in the past 5 years.

There are good prospects for our relations with the United States in future as well – to the extent to which they will continue to develop on this jointly created realistic basis when, given the obvious difference between the class nature of the two states and between their ideologies, there is a firm intention to settle differences and disputes not by force, not by threats or sabre-rattling, but by peaceful political means.

In recent years our relations with the United States have been developing in many areas. There is a frequent exchange of delegations, including parliamentary, and cultural exchanges have become more active. Many Soviet–US agreements have been concluded, envisaging expansion of mutually beneficial co-operation in various economic, scientific, technical and cultural areas. Most of them have already come into force and are being put into practice to the obvious benefit of both sides, and, more important still, of mutual understanding between the Soviet and US peoples.

The essentially positive development of Soviet–US relations in recent years is, however, complicated by a number of serious factors. Influential forces in the United States, that have no interest either in improving relations with the Soviet Union or in international *détente* as a whole, are trying to impair it. They portray the policy of the Soviet Union in a false light and refer to an imaginary 'Soviet threat' to urge a new intensification of the arms race in the USA and in NATO. We may recall that there have also been attempts to interfere in our internal affairs in connection with the adoption by the USA of discriminatory measures in the field of trade. Naturally, we could not and will not suffer that sort of thing. That is not the kind of language one can use with the Soviet Union. By now, I think, this is clear to all.

It is no secret that some of the difficulties stem from those aspects of Washington's policy which jeopardise the freedom and independence of peoples and constitute gross interference in their internal affairs by siding with the forces of oppression and reaction. We have opposed and will continue to oppose such actions. At the same time I want to emphasise once more that the Soviet Union is firmly determined to follow the line of further improving Soviet–US relations in strict accordance with the letter and spirit of the agreements reached and commitments taken, in the interests of both peoples and peace on earth.

Report of the CPSU Central Committee to the 25th Congress of the Communist Party of the Soviet Union held in Moscow. 24 February 1976

Suffice it to say that things are practically at a standstill in such an important area of Soviet–American relations as the drafting of a new long-term agreement on the offensive strategic arms limitation, although there was already agreement on the main content of this document at the top level in late 1974.

The American side, which has received our latest proposals on the unresolved questions already in March of this year, has not given its answer yet. We are given to understand that the reason for this lies in the complexities of the situation in an election year. We can only regret that an issue on which depend the strengthening of peace and security of the two great nations and the general improvement of the world situation for years ahead is approached in such a way.

But on the whole, our relations with the United States so far continue to develop in a positive direction. The Treaty on Underground Nuclear Explosions for peaceful purposes was signed recently. Mutually advantageous co-operation is taking place in many fields of science and technology. Cultural exchanges have acquired quite a wide scope. Economic relations are also somewhat expanding, despite the obstacles created by discriminatory trade legislations in the United States. Obviously, were it not for these obstacles, our economic relations with each other would have acquired a totally different scope.

During the election campaign the rival candidates – President Ford and Mr. Carter – have repeatedly made statements on foreign-policy issues and on relations with the Soviet Union.

But these statements were mostly of a general and, not infrequently, contradictory nature. On the whole, both contenders appear to be in favour of a further normalisation of the international situation and of developing good relations with the USSR. But one hears also their statements of a different type: calls for a further arms race, for the pursuance of a policy from 'positions of strength', for the so-called 'tough line' towards the Soviet Union, etc.

Nevertheless, whoever might be in office in Washington after the elections, the United States apparently will have to reckon with the actual alignment of forces in the world which in recent years have prompted the American ruling circles, after making a sober analysis of the existing situation, to seek ways of coming to an understanding with the world of socialism. In any case, one thing is absolutely clear: our policy towards the extensive development of relations with the United States, and lessening the threat of a new world war, remains unchanged.

Speech at the Plenary Meeting of the Central Committee of the Communist Party of the Soviet Union. 25 October 1976

Esteemed members of the Council, we met here in the Kremlin 2 years ago. I remember that meeting and also the good conversation I had with prominent representatives of the American business world in Washington in 1973.

I would like to say that I consider such contacts important, above all, from the political point of view, because I well understand the great role that is being played – or can be played – by businessmen in establishing peaceful co-operation between states and between peoples. A similar viewpoint is expressed in the letter from President Ford, which was given me today.

In the general process of normalising Soviet–American relations during the past few years, proper attention has also been given to questions of trade and economic relations. As you know, our countries have concluded several important inter-government agreements on developing trade and economic, scientific and technological co-operation. On the whole, a fairly good organisational foundation has been established and mutually useful contacts in various fields between our countries have started to develop and multiply.

Whereas we noted that trade turnover between the USSR and the USA approached the 1000 million dollar mark in 1974, it stood at 2000 million dollars already in 1975 and will probably exceed 2500 million dollars this year. We have concluded several important contracts with American companies, including contracts for supplying us with almost 1000 million roubles' worth of various equipment over the next few years.

Prospects for the future could be quite good if the American side creates normal conditions for them. On the whole, we expect that our trade with the industrialised capitalist countries will increase by more than 30 per cent in the current 5-year period, that is, from 1976 to 1980. According to the estimates of our organisations, the volume of our trade with the USA in industrial goods only, including raw materials, could reach approximately 10,000 million dollars, if not more. We would be ready to develop economic, technological and industrial co-operation with you, including the conclusion of contracts on a compensation basis, in many industries: the automobile, oil and gas, chemical, pulp-and-paper, machine-tool building, electrical engineering, non-ferrous metallurgy, shipbuilding and other industries.

But naturally this will be possible only if a solution is found to the main question, that is, if the USA will put an end to discrimination against the Soviet Union in trade and extending credits. Promises that the US administration gave as far back as 1972 have remained unfulfilled to this day. Of course, this is a serious obstacle to the development of trade between us and of economic relations in general.

Esteemed gentlemen, I ask you to take into consideration the fact that we are not at all raising the question of extending any privileges, any special benefits to the Soviet Union. All we want is that the USA should trade with us on the same legal basis as it trades with most other countries. This means that we want to receive the same treatment which we extend to your country, that discrimination should not be allowed.

But if the present situation persists it does not bode well for Soviet–American trade. I will speak with absolute frankness with you businessmen.

In spite of the general results which look favourable so far, the volume of our economic contacts with the USA is virtually decreasing under present conditions. In many dealings we now naturally prefer partners who trade with us on a normal, equal basis. Discrimination also impedes the sale of our goods in the USA, increases the imbalance of trade and diminishes our interest in the American market.

According to some estimates, the upshot in the last 2 years was that American companies had lost orders from this country worth a total of 1500 million to 2000 million dollars. You are the best judges of whether this is much or little, but I think such amounts are not to be found in the street.

We are living to a large extent on what might be called old capital. For example, almost all the equipment for the chemical complex, the KAMAZ, the iron-ore pellet plant and a number of other projects has been supplied under contracts signed before the United States adopted its discriminatory trade legislation.

It therefore rests with the American side to rectify the abnormal situation. We are prepared to continue developing economic links in many areas and are prepared to trade with large and medium-sized firms, but only on the basis of full equality and mutual benefit. And, of course, we resolutely reject any attempts to link trade with political conditions and we will not tolerate any interference in our internal affairs. This must be made clear once and for all.

Those who believe that discrimination in economic relations could influence our policy or arrest our economic development are seriously mistaken. The Soviet Union has never allowed itself to become dependent in these matters on the benevolence of Western partners. We are successfully carrying out the great tasks of our Tenth Five-Year Plan, both in industry and in agriculture. And we will certainly fulfil them. The hard work and creative enthusiasm of millions of Soviet people are a guarantee of that. Our close co-operation with the fraternal socialist countries is developing remarkably well. There is good progress also in the development of our economic links with many capitalist countries which honour in practice the principles of equality and the spirit of Helsinki in trade as well.

Given normal conditions for trade between the USSR and the USA we believe the prospects for its development are not bad at all. The volume of trade could well increase beyond the level envisaged earlier.

All this goes to show that in speaking about economic relations one cannot ignore the general state of political relations among states. In that respect our policy as regards our relations with the United States of America is perfectly clear and consistent. It is linked with the main principles of the peaceful foreign policy of our Party and our state. Our policy towards the United States is not based on considerations of expediency and looks not months but years and decades ahead. We want to see really stable peaceful relations take shape between the USSR and the USA in the interests of our peoples and universal peace, and not to the detriment of any third countries. The 25th Congress of the CPSU reiterated with all clarity our readiness to promote good, mutually beneficial relations with the USA.

This reminder is not irrelevant today because, of late, especially in connection with the recent election campaign, trends have emerged in the United States which, let us face it, run counter to the task of improving American–Soviet relations. Once again, as in the time of the cold war, there are calls for pursuing 'a tough line' with regard to the USSR and acting from the 'position of strength'. Some are persistently making the allegation that there exists a military threat stemming from the Soviet Union and that our country is interested in continuing the arms race. There are even attempts to stir up fears about Soviet 'preparations for a first nuclear strike' against America. Who needs to utter this rubbish and to what purpose, I do not know. But it is a fact that there is such talk.

It would seem that the absurdity of these concoctions should be clear. This is at odds with the entire policy of the Soviet Union which is aimed at decreasing and ultimately eliminating completely the threat of nuclear war, ending the arms race and developing peaceful co-operation among states.

The whole world knows of the concrete and urgent proposals of the Soviet Union aimed at curbing the arms race and achieving disarmament. I may mention here such proposals as banning the development of new types and systems of mass destruction weapons, complete and universal halting of nuclear weapons tests, and the conclusion of a world treaty on the renunciation of the use of force in international relations. To back up our proposals with deeds we recently again cut our military budget.

As regards to the Soviet–American dialogue, we have proposed to the United States that our two countries abandon work to develop new generations of nuclear-powered submarines such as your 'Trident' and new heavy bombers like your B-1 and corresponding types of Soviet submarines and bombers. We have proposed the withdrawal by both the USA and the USSR of nuclear armed ships from the Mediterranean. All these proposals remain standing.

The latest evidence of the peaceful nature of our policy is the recent proposal of the Soviet Union and its Warsaw Treaty allies addressed to all the participants in last year's conference in Helsinki, including the United States, that they sign a treaty pledging not to be the first to use nuclear weapons one against the other. We are awaiting a reply to this proposal and hope it will be a positive one.

The talk about alleged sinister plans of the Soviet Union with regard to the United States is pure invention. And malicious invention at that. For it provides a cover for unbridled inflation of military budgets and further arms build-up. And that is a dangerous thing. It is not to be ruled out that by raising a hue and cry about imagined Soviet intentions some quarters in the United States are actually nurturing plans of a 'first strike' without considering the consequences.

As for the Soviet Union, I must reiterate emphatically that it has been and

244

remains a convinced opponent of any such adventurist concepts and of nuclear war in general. We honour the agreement with the USA on the prevention of nuclear war and proceed from the assumption that the American side will honour its commitments under the agreement.

We set great store by what has been done by our two countries jointly to lessen the threat of nuclear war. We are prepared to go further along this road in co-operation with the new US Administration if it is prepared to act in the same spirit. The Soviet Union thinks that there is a need to intensify efforts to bring about the conclusion of a new agreement on limiting strategic offensive weapons on the basis of the accord reached in Vladivostok long ago. We believe it is high time to put an end to the 'freezing' of this important question imposed by Washington almost a year ago. The Soviet Union is prepared to discuss new possible steps to effectively prevent the proliferation of nuclear weapons on our planet and other measures aimed at reducing the threat of nuclear war.

Esteemed guests,

While economic links depend on the political atmosphere their development in turn helps create a healthier and more stable political climate. Businessmen can do a great deal in this direction not only for their firms but for their nation as a whole, for peace and the prosperity of mankind. With this in mind, I extend my sincere wishes of new successes to the US–USSR Trade and Economic Council whose constructive activity we in the USSR value highly.

Speech at the dinner in the Kremlin to mark the 4th Session of the US–USSR Trade and Economic Council in Moscow. 30 November 1976

Question: What message would you like to convey to the American people for the New Year?

Answer: For the Soviet people the coming year will be a jubilee year. It will be the year of the sixtieth anniversary of the Soviet state, which was born under the star of Lenin's famous Decree on Peace. Of course, in the coming year we would like to see new major steps taken to maintain and strengthen peace, to further enhance peaceful coexistence as the only reasonable and the only acceptable norm in relations between states.

History has proved that our two countries, when they act reasonably and take into account their responsible positions in the modern world, can make an important contribution to the cause of peace and the development of mutually advantageous co-operation.

I am glad to avail myself of this opportunity to convey to the women and men of America cordial New Year greetings on behalf of all the peoples of the Soviet Union and on my own behalf.

Question: What do you consider to be the most important measures of co-operation the USSR and the USA could take in 1977 to serve the cause of world peace and to strengthen Soviet–American relations?

Answer: I believe that our countries could do a lot in this respect. I shall only mention what is most important: we are in favour of the earliest possible completion of the work on a Soviet–American strategic arms limitation agreement on the basis of the understanding reached in Vladivostok in 1974. On our part, there has never been, nor will there be any obstacle to this agreement which is a matter of concern to all mankind. A Soviet–American agreement would undoubtedly represent at this time a very important step towards effectively ending the arms race. The solution of this task is most directly connected with the main goal of our time – to prevent a nuclear war. Conversely, delay of the agreement, while the development of even more horrible types and systems of weapons continues, is fraught with new threats to peace, international stability and security. Judging by recent statements of President-elect Carter, the US side is also aware of the urgency of this matter. Let us hope that this promises early success.

I must say that we in the Soviet Union are baffled by the position of certain circles in the West, both in the United States and in other NATO countries. They behave as if nothing has happened in recent years, as if nothing has changed and the world continues to be in a state of cold war. They instigate one noisy campaign after another about an allegedly increasing 'military threat' from the USSR, demand more and more military appropriations and are intensifying the arms race.

We believe that things should not continue in this way. Having achieved the relaxation of political tension, we have also made it possible to deal seriously with cardinal issues of arms limitation and disarmament. I would like to reaffirm most definitely: the Soviet Union does not threaten anyone and has no intention of attacking anyone. It makes no sense to be frightened by mythical threats; it is better to discuss in a businesslike and constructive manner the problems and opportunities which exist here. The continuation of the arms race cannot be justified by assertions that arms limitation allegedly carries a risk to national security. Today a far greater risk to universal security lies in inaction, in letting the unrestrained arms race go on.

We would like very much to see the year 1977 become a real turning-point in ending the arms race. It would then surely find a worthy place in history.

Question: Would you welcome the opportunity to confer early in the new year with the new American President at a mutually convenient location?

Answer: Experience, including that of Soviet–American relations, has shown the usefulness and fruitfulness of summit meetings when each participant strives for a constructive, businesslike dialogue. That is why we are for the continuation of this practice. The timing of the next Soviet–American meeting will naturally be determined by mutual agreement and will depend on progress in appropriate issues.

In conclusion I would like to repeat what has been said at the 25th Congress of the Communist Party of the Soviet Union: our country is firmly determined to follow the line of further improving Soviet–American relations which is in the interests of both the American and Soviet peoples, as well as in the interests of universal peace.

Answers to the questions of Joseph Kingsbury-Smith of the Hearst Corporation (USA). 29 December 1976

We are prepared to co-operate with the new Administration in the United States in order to take a new major step forward with regard to relations between our countries.

First of all, it is necessary, we are convinced, to complete in the nearest future the drafting of an agreement on limiting strategic arms on the basis we had agreed upon in Vladivostok back in late 1974. Some statesmen in Washington now express regret over the fact that such an agreement still has not been signed. But regrets cannot recover lost time, and it is important that practical conclusions should be drawn from this.

In the United States, too, the question is being asked as to what will happen if such conclusions are not drawn. An influential US newspaper recently noted that in such an event the Soviet Union and the United States would start producing a new generation of nuclear weapons which would be practically impossible to control.

Such a prospect does not suit us. I repeat: time is short, and the conclusion of the agreement must not be postponed.

It goes without saying that the Soviet Union is prepared to go further as regards questions of limitation of strategic arms. But first it is necessary to consolidate what has already been achieved and to carry into practice what was agreed upon in Vladivostok, all the more so since the term of the Interim Agreement expires this October. Then we could immediately proceed to talks on more far-reaching measures. Otherwise, should we add new questions to the ones currently under discussion, we might only further complicate matters and delay the solution of the problem as a whole.

The need is urgent to prevent more surely the proliferation of nuclear weapons, to make more effective the non-proliferation rules and regulations defined in the known treaty. We are prepared to hold businesslike talks on this matter.

Speech in the city of Tula. 18 January 1977

First of all, about Soviet–American relations to the positive development of which we have always attached and continue to attach great importance. I would say that here the situation at present is determined by three basic factors. The first is the sound foundation in the form of the important treaties and agreements on co-operation in various fields concluded in 1972–1974. The second is a state of certain stagnation. The American side at first explained it by the election campaign in the United States; but the first two months the new Washington Administration has been in power do not seem to show a striving to overcome this stagnation. And, finally, the third factor – the existence of important objective possibilities for further developing equal and mutually advantageous co-operation in various spheres for the good of both countries and of universal peace.

In this connection I will mention several concrete and, we believe, quite attainable tasks. First, the completion of the drafting and the signing of a new agreement on the limitation of strategic offensive arms, which was already agreed upon in the main in 1974, and further advance on this basis to mutual arms reduction with strict observance of the principle of equality and equal security of both sides. Then there are possible joint initiatives of the USSR and the United States in the field of banning and liquidating the most dangerous lethal types of chemical weapons, and other measures restraining the arms race and strengthening the security of nations. There is also the extensive development of mutually advantageous trade and economic ties on the basis of a removal of discriminatory barriers created by the United States, and entry into force of agreements on these questions signed a long time ago. Lastly, these tasks include concerted actions by our countries to achieve a just and lasting peace settlement in the Middle East.

We are for actively utilising all these possibilities. But there are also circumstances obstructing further improvement and development of Soviet–American relations. One of them is the whipping up of a slanderous campaign about the mythical 'military threat' posed by the USSR. I have already spoken on this matter recently. Another circumstance is the outright attempts by US official bodies to interfere in the internal affairs of the Soviet Union.

Meanwhile, Washington's pretensions to teach others how to live are, I am sure, unacceptable to any sovereign state, not to mention the fact that neither the situation in the United States itself, nor US actions and policies in the world at large justify such pretensions.

249

I repeat: we will not tolerate interference in our internal affairs by anyone, no matter what the pretext. Any normal development of relations on such a basis is, of course, unthinkable.

The Soviet Union has always firmly upheld and will continue to uphold its sovereign rights, its honour and its interests. At the same time, a constructive, realistic approach by the other side will always meet with understanding on our part and readiness to reach agreement.

The US Secretary of State, Mr. Cyrus Vance, is coming shortly to Moscow for negotiations. We shall see what he brings with him. Everybody, of course, realises the importance of how Soviet–American relations develop further. We would like them to be good-neighbourly relations. But this requires a certain level of mutual understanding and at least a minimum of mutual respect.

Of course, we are confident that the interests of the peoples of our two countries and the interests of universal peace will prevail, and that relations between the USSR and the United States will eventually be resolved satisfactorily. The point is *when* this will be achieved and how much time will be lost in which many useful things could have been accomplished.

Speech at the 16th Congress of the Trades Unions of the USSR. 21 March 1977

It is natural, too, that we attach great importance to relations with the United States. There is much that divides our countries – from the socio-economic system to ideology. Not everyone in the United States likes our way of doing things, and we too could say a great deal about the way things are in America. But if differences are accentuated, and if attempts are made to lecture one another, the result will only be a build-up of distrust and hostility, useless to both countries and dangerous to the world as a whole. At the very inception of the Soviet state Lenin made it clear to the American leaders of the time that 'whether they like it or not, Soviet Russia is a great power' and 'America has nothing to gain from the Wilsonian policy of piously refusing to deal with us on the grounds that our government is distasteful to them'. This was true half a century ago. It is all the more true today.

Life itself demands that considerations of a long-term character, prompted by a concern for peace, be decisive in Soviet–American relations. This is the course we follow, and this is what we expect in return. There is no lack of will on our part to continue developing relations with the USA on the basis of equality and mutual respect.

> *'The Great October Revolution and Mankind's Progress': Report at a jubilee meeting of the Central Committee of the CPSU, the Supreme Soviet of the USSR, and the Supreme Soviet of the RSFSR to mark the sixtieth anniversary of the Great October Socialist Revolution. 2 November 1977*

In the conditions of peace, we are tackling major economic and social problems set by the 25th Congress of the CPSU. In the centre of our plans is a steady rise in the living standards of the Soviet people.

In considering the plans laid by the Party for the further development of our country and the problems of economic development, we cannot ignore, of course, the way the international situation develops.

The present state of affairs in the world is characterised by a turn for the relaxation of international tension. The consistent implementation by our Party of a Leninist foreign policy and the purposeful efforts of the Soviet Union, the fraternal socialist states and all the peace forces and peoples have played a tremendous part in the impressive achievements made on this way.

These successes did not come easy, they were achieved in intensive struggle. The struggle over the question of the further destiny of *détente* is going on, sometimes taking on point and gaining in intensity.

For all the significance of this or that problem, there is no more important task in present conditions, one touching the destiny of every person on earth, than the task of achieving real disarmament. The main problem now on the order of the day is to stop the arms race, to ensure progress towards reducing

251

and eventually removing the threat of a thermonuclear disaster. It is here, in this direction, that the basic question is decided, the question of how the world situation will develop further, and it is here that the most bitter struggle is unfolding.

It is no secret that both to the west and to the east of our frontiers there are forces which are interested in the arms race, in working up an atmosphere of fear and hostility. They sow doubts as to the possibility of taking practical steps to limit armaments and to achieve disarmament, and hamper efforts to achieve agreements in this field.

The activities of these forces have an adverse effect on the position of the USA and some other countries, partners of the Soviet Union in the talks on curbing and stopping the arms race.

As is known, a Soviet–American summit meeting took place in the Far East, in Vladivostok, in November 1974. It led to an accord on the conclusion between the USSR and the USA of a long-term agreement on the limitation of strategic offensive arms. Having assessed all aspects of the situation, the two sides then concluded that there was a possibility of finishing the drafting of the agreement in the next year, 1975.

Almost $3\frac{1}{2}$ years have passed since that time and the agreement has not yet been signed. I have already had cause to mention the reasons for this. The experience of the talks, the lessons of the agreements concluded earlier in this sphere, show that given proper awareness of the great importance of the problem and a real desire to reach agreement on the basis of equality and equal security, both sides are capable of resolving what would seem to be the most complex problems. And the documents that are being prepared now have been thrashed out and are largely agreed upon.

And if the final conclusion of this work is, nevertheless, being delayed, it is, evidently, for political reasons. The matter is that the United States government is both indecisive and inconsistent; it continually looks back over its shoulder at the circles which were against this agreement from the very beginning and which are doing everything they can to thwart it and to get their hands free for an uncontrolled missile–nuclear arms race. That is apparently the reason why the American side repeatedly made attempts during the talks to amend in its favour or to call into question what was agreed to earlier, and instead of conducting a businesslike discussion, has tried to raise all kinds of questions behind which is concealed only one thing – the absence of readiness to look for practical solutions. Moreover a tendency is being shown to link in some way the advance at the talks and the destiny of the agreement in general with other political problems in the hope of bringing pressure on the Soviet Union.

This position of the United States was manifested soon after the Vladivostok meeting. As a result of this the work on the agreement was then practically stalled and even set back in a number of aspects.

Great efforts have been required to bring the talks back on the track of the Vladivostok arrangement. But this has been finally done. Principled solutions of some remaining questions have been found and the range of questions to be worked upon has, on the whole, been considerably narrowed. This has been ensured largely due to the Soviet Union's patient and constructive stand.

It is understandable, however, that the remaining questions cannot be solved without the United States making steps to meet us halfway. But, frankly speaking, we do not see such steps of late. One gets the impression that some people in the United States are inclined to interpret our readiness to conclude an agreement as a chance for the USA to gain unilateral advantages.

This is the only way to explain the continued attempts at the talks to erode somehow, for instance, the understanding reached on limitations on cruise missiles or to impose unjustified limitations on Soviet missiles while leaving the United States full freedom of action for modernising and creating new types of practically all components of strategic arms.

We resolutely reject any attempts to impose unacceptable terms of agreement on us. We have said and we are saying now that the Soviet Union stands for the earliest achievement of an agreement, but only the kind of agreement that would be strictly in keeping with the principle of equality and equal security and that would embody in a real way this basic principle. We do not demand that the agreement give us any advantages at the expense of the other side, but we expect the other side to take a similar approach. There can be no other solution.

Further delay and all kinds of manoeuvres over the talks can only lead to missing the very opportunity of concluding an agreement and, hence, a chance for subsequent transition to more far-reaching steps to limit and reduce strategic arms. It is our firm conviction that such a prospect cannot suit anyone.

Therefore we should like to hope that proper conclusions would be made in Washington and that a course would be finally taken there towards a fruitful completion of the talks.

There are a whole number of other disarmament questions which are now being negotiated and whose solution is long overdue. Our constructive proposals on this score are well known, as is the broad series of concrete measures our country proposed for consolidating the relaxation of military tension in Europe. We intend to seek the realisation of all these measures.

A number of statements in favour of disarmament have been made lately in the West, the USA included. But the peoples of the world judge not by words but by deeds. The question of neutron weapons is very indicative in this respect. This is a weapon of mass destruction of a new type. Any talk about such weapons being allegedly defensive in character does not correspond to reality. These are nuclear offensive weapons, weapons designed chiefly to destroy people. This weapon increases the risks of a nuclear war.

Faced with a mass protest movement against the plans to develop and deploy these weapons in Europe, the USA and some other NATO countries are trying to mislead the peoples, pretending that they are ready to hold talks with the Soviet Union on this question while in fact they are trying to make it the subject of bargaining and tying this weapon to unrelated issues. Concealed behind all this is only one thing – a desire to get away from the clear-cut and concrete Soviet proposal for mutual commitment not to manufacture neutron weapons. Such manoeuvring does not testify, of course, to the seriousness of intentions to achieve disarmament. Nor does it facilitate advance towards this aim.

It is high time some leaders of the West thought in earnest about their responsibility to their own peoples, to all peoples, for the destinies of the world, and showed in deed the readiness to take effective steps towards curbing the arms race.

The Soviet Union, for its part, will continue its efforts to achieve a steady advance along the road of military *détente* and transition to real disarmament. Such is our firm policy and we shall continue implementing it steadily.

We do not threaten anyone. The talk about the so-called Soviet menace is a mere invention of the opponents of the relaxation of international tension and nothing more. We are improving our defences with the sole purpose of defending securely the gains of the Great October Revolution, of guarding reliably the peaceful work of the Soviet people, of our friends and allies. It is this noble aim that the Soviet Army and Navy serve.

Speech at Vladivostok. 7 April 1978

As you know, recently we had meetings in the Crimea with the leaders of the fraternal Parties of the socialist states, including Bulgaria, Czechoslovakia, the German Democratic Republic, Hungary, Mongolia, Poland and Romania, meetings which, one may say, have already become a tradition in summer time.

With each of those countries we have varied and fruitful relationships which progress from one year to the next. Co-operation between the fraternal countries has great new prospects. Practice raises new problems which should be tackled and resolved. We believe this to be a major Party matter. This concerns relations with our closest friends, allies and associates in the struggle for our common communist objectives.

So, we highly value bilateral meetings as a form of concerting our positions. They help outline the general line which is jointly laid down by the states participating in the Warsaw Treaty at the meetings of their Political Consultative Committee.

Much attention was paid at our talks to the key problems of the international situation, which, as you know, is a complex one. Its aggravation is caused by the unwillingness of the more hard-headed imperialist circles to take a reasonable attitude towards the new correlation of forces in the world, and also by schemes, which are absolutely unrealistic and dangerous to peace, to achieve military superiority over the socialist countries and to dictate conditions to them.

The Washington session of the NATO Council pointed the way to another upswing in the arms race, one which will extend over decades. This completely lays bare the real purposes of the organisers of the ballyhoo about the alleged 'military threat' to the West from the Soviet Union and the Warsaw Treaty. These inventions have become necessary to justify NATO's desire to get a longer and sharper sword and to try and return to the 'position-of-strength' policy.

Isn't this the reason why the elaboration of a mutually acceptable agreement with the United States on the limitation of strategic offensive armaments still cannot be completed? Meanwhile, the distance separating the stands of the sides on this problem as stated at the talks is not that wide and, given goodwill and statesmanship, can certainly be bridged. But, apparently, the solution of this question does not satisfy those in the United States who want another edition of the 'cold war' rather than lasting peace and mutually beneficial co-operation.

255

Virtually the same objectives are pursued by the vociferous propaganda campaign started in connection with measures taken by the Soviet courts against the illegal activities of certain individuals who are hostile to the Soviet system, among them paid agents of Western intelligence services.

This is a direct attempt to meddle in our internal affairs and therefore a flagrant violation of the letter and the spirit of the Final Act adopted in Helsinki. The USA acts in the same manner towards other socialist countries.

The opponents of *détente* are seeking to broaden the front of the offensive against it. The development of business contacts has begun to be held back in the United States under artificial, hypocritical pretexts. Things have gone so far that deals that have already been concluded are being nullified and signed contracts scrapped. The pointed curtailment of contacts in scientific, technical and other spheres has also begun. Washington has started unceremoniously – but, incidentally, rather unsuccessfully – pressurising its allies, demanding that they follow suit.

Apparently, certain influential circles in the USA are deliberately trying to provoke the Soviet Union in a bid to further aggravate the situation. This, comrades, is a serious matter. We will resolutely oppose encroachments on the rights and interests of the Soviet state, and will not fall for provocations.

Our policy towards the countries of the capitalist world, including, of course, the United States, was and remains a policy of peace, peaceful coexistence and peaceful co-operation. That is why we resolutely reject the practice of outside interference in the internal affairs of states and violation of their sovereign rights.

We regard it as the fundamental task of our foreign policy to do everything possible to end the arms race and to consolidate peace and the security of nations. And we believe that all states, big and small, nuclear and non-nuclear, have the right to reliable security.

So, let no one have any doubt that the Soviet Union and the other countries of the socialist community will continue to make a substantial contribution towards the accomplishment of these tasks, which are so important to the whole of mankind!

Speech on presenting the city of Baku with the Order of Lenin. 22 September 1978

7.
RELATIONS WITH ASIAN AND AFRICAN COUNTRIES

The idea of ensuring Asian security on a collective basis has aroused growing interest in many Asian countries. It is becoming increasingly clear that the road to security in Asia is not one of military blocs and groupings, not one of opposing the countries against each other, but one of good-neighbourly co-operation among all the states interested in such co-operation.

To our mind, collective security in Asia should be based on such principles as renunciation of the use of force in relations between states, respect for sovereignty and inviolability of borders, non-interference in domestic affairs and extensive development of economic and other co-operation on the basis of complete equality and mutual advantage. We have advocated the establishment of such collective security in Asia and will continue to do so; we are ready to co-operate with all countries for the sake of carrying out this idea.

Not long ago the visit to China of President Nixon of the United States and his talks with the Peking leaders attracted much public attention. What do we have to say on this subject?

First of all, the restoration of contacts between two states and normalisation of relations between them is quite natural. The Soviet Union has always been against the imperialist policy of isolation of the People's Republic of China; it has always favoured due recognition of China's role on the international scene. However, an assessment of the current contacts between Peking and Washington should take into account the basis of these contacts.

The parties to the Peking meetings have said little about what they discussed and what they agreed on to the peoples, to the world at large. Indeed, they made it clear that they would keep secret and 'not discuss' that which lay outside the limits of the official communiqué. Thus, facts and future actions of the United States and the People's Republic of China will reveal the true significance of the Peking talks.

However, one must not overlook certain statements by the parties to the Peking talks which give us grounds to believe that the dialogue went beyond the framework of bilateral relations between the USA and China. How else is one to understand, for instance, the statement made during the banquet in Shanghai that 'today our two peoples [i.e. American and Chinese] hold the future of the whole world in their hands'?

It is a well-known fact that even quite recently the policy of peaceful coexistence, which the Soviet Union has consistently followed since the time of Lenin, was referred to in Peking as 'revisionism' and 'betrayal of the revolution'. Now the principles of peaceful coexistence have been confirmed in the Sino–American communiqué. This is certainly to be welcomed. But it is important not just to lay down these principles on paper, but also to implement them.

In general, it should be noted that there are various views and guesses concerning the Peking meeting. But views aside, I repeat that the decisive word remains to be spoken by facts and actions. This is why we do not hurry to make our final assessment. The future, probably the near future, will show how things really stand, and then it will be time for us to draw the appropriate conclusions.

As far as our relations with the People's Republic of China are concerned, the principled position of our Party and the Soviet state was clearly outlined in the documents of the 24th Congress of the CPSU. The Congress resolution points out that our Party adheres to the position of consistent defence of the principles of Marxism–Leninism, all-round consolidation of the unity of the world communist movement and defence of the interests of our socialist Motherland. It goes on to say: 'The Congress resolutely rejects the slanderous inventions of Chinese propaganda concerning the policy of our Party and state. At the same time our Party stands for normalisation of relations between the USSR and the PRC, and restoration of good-neighbourliness and friendship between the Soviet and Chinese peoples. Improvement of relations between the Soviet Union and the People's Republic of China would meet the vital, long-term interests of both countries, the interests of world socialism, the interests of intensifying the struggle against imperialism.' This position remains fully valid today too.

Chinese official representatives tell us that relations between the USSR and the People's Republic of China should be based on the principles of peaceful coexistence. Well, if Peking does not find it possible to go further in its relations with a socialist state, we are prepared to conduct Soviet–Chinese relations on this basis today. I can say, comrades, that we not only proclaim such readiness, but we translate it into the language of concrete and constructive proposals on non-aggression, on settlement of border disputes, on improvement of relations on a mutually advantageous foundation. The Chinese leaders have known these proposals a long time. The next move is China's.

Speech at the 15th Congress of the Trades Unions of the USSR. 20 March 1972

Present-day Asia is a continent renovated in many respects, a continent which has broken the fetters of colonialism. The peoples of Asia are fully resolved to uphold their independence, to march along the road of national and social progress, along the path of fundamental revolutionary changes.

In short, Asia is a continent in development. But this process of development cannot but be extremely difficult, due to the tenacity of the reactionary forces and the opposition from imperialism and reaction. It is plain that stable peace, *détente* and good-neighbourly relations provide favourable conditions for the successful development of the process.

We all witness momentous changes for the better in Asia. The long and difficult war in Vietnam has ended in victory for the Vietnamese people. Agreement has been reached on the restoration of peace and national accord in Laos. Conditions have been established for relations between Hindustani countries to return to normal. New positive factors have developed in the situation on the Korean Peninsula, thanks to the KPDR's important initiative concerning peaceful, democratic reunification of the country.

Lastly, and this is very significant, the policy of peace-loving nations exercises an increasing influence over the situation in Asia. An outstanding place among those nations is held by such a great country as India, which today is celebrating the 26th anniversary of her independence. India spoke in support of the principles of peaceful coexistence at a time when many in the West kept repudiating this very notion.

I am now speaking only about the positive factors not, of course, because there are no negative ones. They exist and operate, as you well know. But as everywhere, a sound tendency which we support is forcing its way in Asia.

The Soviet Union is firmly convinced that Asia can and must live according to the laws of peace, and collective security is a real way towards this. Of course, both time and considerable effort will be required to achieve this aim. But we believe that the peoples of Asia will come to this.

Why do we come out in favour of collective security in Asia? We do so because we seek to exclude wars and armed conflicts, imperialist aggression on the Asian continent; we especially want every country and people to be guaranteed conditions for free development and national revival, and the spirit of trust and mutual understanding to reign in relations among Asian countries.

We have said many times and we repeat again: the Soviet Union stands for equal participation of all Asian states without exclusion in the collective security system. The system we are advocating does not and must not give anybody unilateral advantages; every Asian state is called upon to make a contribution to its establishment.

We propose the building of a collective security system not on unprepared ground. Many principles, on which it could be based, have been proclaimed in the historic decisions of the Bandung Conference, others are reflected in a number of international documents concerning Asia.

Our policy is aimed at the development of normal, good-neighbourly relations with all Asian states that for their part desire this. In this respect we attach great importance to developing wide many-sided co-operation on a mutually advantageous basis especially with such a big Asian country as Japan.

Speaking here, in Alma-Ata, 3 years ago, I stressed that the Soviet Union wanted good relations also with the People's Republic of China. During these years we did everything we could to normalise Soviet–Chinese relations. Unfortunately, however, we have not succeeded in making an appreciable advance in this respect. The reason is one – the policy of the Chinese leadership, based on frantic anti-Sovietism, on undermining activity against socialist countries.

We say openly that a turn for the better in relations of the PRC with the Soviet Union and other socialist countries is possible only if the Chinese leadership observes the principles of mutual respect of sovereignty and non-interference in internal affairs, if it gives up encroachments on the interests of socialist countries.

Our principled course, which combines a resolute struggle against the theory and practice of Maoism, as a trend inimical to Leninism, with readiness to normalise inter-state relations with the PRC, the course of the 24th CPSU Congress, remains invariable.

Today the ideas of peace and friendship of peoples penetrate ever deeper the conscience of the world public. Behind these ideas stand the prestige and growing might of our country, the increasing unity of the socialist community, and the solidarity of all fighters everywhere for national freedom and social progress.

We shall continue to work actively for international *détente*, for the elimination of hotbeds of military danger, for the stopping of the arms race. We shall continue to resolutely rebuff those forces which would like to turn back world development. And we are convinced that our righteous cause of the struggle for peace and social progress will triumph!

Speech at the joint celebration meeting of the Central Committee of the Communist Party of Kazakhstan and the Supreme Soviet of the Kazakh SSR, devoted to the presentation to the Republic of the Order of Friendship Among the Peoples. 15 August 1973

I have already spoken many times, including recently, about Asia. It may seem at first glance that positive trends are not as clearly pronounced here as in Europe. But Asia can be likened to a huge flywheel which, as it gains momentum, rotates faster and faster until there is no stopping it. The situation in Asia is gradually improving, and we are sure that this process will continue in the interests of the cause of peace and progress.

As in Europe, a great role can be played by the constructive policy of socialist states which are coming out for peace, sovereignty and independence of the peoples. The Soviet Union, the Mongolian People's Republic, the Democratic Republic of Vietnam and the Korean People's Democratic Republic make a great contribution to the strengthening of peace and to the development of international co-operation on the Asian continent.

India undoubtedly plays a prominent part in shaping the destinies of Asia. We have a Treaty on Peace, Friendship and Co-operation with that country. We regard this Treaty as a reliable basis for durable good, friendly relations. India has made a large and valuable contribution to the entire world politics, and its role will keep growing, we are convinced. Soviet–Indian friendship grows stronger from year to year, and there can be no doubt that the future will be marked by fresh steps in this direction for the good of both our countries and of the cause of universal peace.

We are pleased to state here that our more than half-a-century-old tradition of good relations with neighbouring Afghanistan is fully preserved now, too, when that ancient country has become a young republic. We wish it success in its advance along the road of national and social progress.

In consistently upholding the principles of peaceful co-existence between states having different social systems, we proceed from the fact that the application of these principles cannot be 'selective', so to say. They should spread to all states, big and small.

We consider it a very important positive phenomenon that world politics is no longer the monopoly of a few powers, that ever more countries are being drawn into it as active participants.

Fresh evidence of this is the Conference of Non-aligned Countries just ended in Algiers.

Represented at the Conference, one of the biggest in the number of participants, were states very much unlike, big and small, ancient and quite young, situated in various parts of the world. But all arrived at the conclusion that it was essential resolutely to struggle against imperialism, against all forms of colonialism and racism, for freedom, independence and peace. There is no doubt that such a position and its consistent implementation will be conducive to the further growth of the non-aligned countries' influence in the world arena. For our part, we have every respect for the anti-imperialist programme drawn up in Algiers, and we wish the participants of the movement of non-aligned countries success in putting it into effect.

The part played by each state in the development of international relations is determined, in the first place, by the policy the given state is conducting. The prestige and influence of one or another country in world affairs depends on this in no small measure. In other words, the political watershed passes not between big and small countries, but along the line separating the policy of peace and progress from the policy of aggression and reaction.

Ever greater importance is gained by the countries that come out from positions of active struggle for strengthening peace, for equal international co-operation, and who proceed not from the current situation or narrow national calculations, but who consciously and in principle decide in favour of the overall strengthening of international security. Unfortunately, however, there exist countries which actually oppose the fresh wind of change in international life. Such a policy by no means enhances their prestige, and the part they play in international affairs is negative.

It must be said that this fully applies to the foreign policy of such a state as the People's Republic of China, whose leaders are still actively pursuing a line, and sometimes openly come out against relaxation of international tension, against the strengthening of peace and security, and the development of peaceful co-operation between states, especially in Europe and Asia.

Speech at the joint celebration meeting of the Central Committee of the Communist Party of Uzbekistan and the Supreme Soviet of the Uzbek SSR, devoted to the presentation to the Republic of the Order of Friendship Among the Peoples, in Tashkent. 24 September 1973

The peoples of Asia most certainly need lasting peace and constructive co-operation no less than, say, the peoples of Europe. It is probably safe to say that the people of Tokyo and Tashkent, of Hanoi and Teheran, Peking and Rangoon, Delhi and Colombo – all the hundreds of millions of inhabitants of the world's largest continent – have an equal stake in lasting peace and tranquil peaceful labour. This, I am convinced, is in the interest of them all.

It is often said that the idea of creating and ensuring security in Asia by collective effort is directed against China and all but pursues the perfidious aim of 'surrounding' or 'isolating' China. But these contentions are either the product of morbid suspicion or a reluctance to face the facts.

And the facts are that the Soviet Union and the other states favouring collective efforts to ensure peace and security in Asia have always maintained that all the states of the Asian continent without exception should take part in this big and important undertaking if they so desire. Nobody has ever raised the question of China's non-participation or, much less, 'isolation' (not to speak of the fact that it would be ludicrous to think of 'isolating' such a big country). As for the Soviet Union, it would welcome the participation of the People's Republic of China in measures aimed at strengthening Asian security.

Dear friends, of course, we would be going against the facts if we pretended that China's present actions on the international scene are consonant with the task of strengthening peace and peaceful co-operation between countries. For reasons they alone know, China's leaders refuse to halt their attempts to poison the international climate and heighten international tension. They continue to make absurd territorial claims on the Soviet Union, which, naturally, we reject categorically. They doggedly repeat the timeworn inventions of anti-communist propaganda about a 'Soviet threat', about 'a threat from the North', and, while dismissing all reasonable proposals for a settlement and for a treaty of non-aggression, continue to keep their people in an artificially created feverish atmosphere of war preparations. And all this is accompanied by the dissemination of preposterous, slanderous accusations against the USSR and other countries, by brazen attempts to interfere in our – and, in fact, not only our – internal affairs.

What strikes one is the total lack of principle in the foreign policy of the Chinese leaders. They say that they are working for socialism and peaceful coexistence, but in fact they go out of their way to undermine the international positions of the socialist countries and encourage the activity of the aggressive military blocs and closed economic groups of capitalist states. They style themselves proponents of disarmament, but in fact try to block all the practical steps designed to restrict and slow down the arms race and, defying world public opinion, continue to pollute the earth's atmosphere by testing nuclear weapons. They assert that they support the just struggle of the Arabs for the return of the territories seized by the aggressor and for the establishment of a just peace in the Middle East, but at the same time are doing their utmost to discredit the real assistance rendered to the victims of aggression by their true friends, the Soviet Union and the other countries of the socialist community. They call themselves revolutionaries, but cordially shake the hand of a representative of the fascist junta of Chilean reactionaries, a hand stained with the blood of thousands of heroes of the revolution, the sons and daughters of the working class, of the working people of Chile.

Of course, a policy of this kind does not help to strengthen peace and security. It injects an element of dangerous instability into international affairs. But the possibility of changing this policy depends wholly and entirely on the Chinese leaders. As regards the Soviet Union, we, I repeat, would welcome a constructive contribution by China to improving the international atmosphere and promoting true and equitable peaceful co-operation between states.

Speech at the World Congress of Peace Forces in Moscow. 26 October 1973

Allow me, dear comrades, to dwell briefly on international affairs. You are our close neighbours, friends and allies, and you are well aware of the principles, goals and main directions of the Soviet Union's peace-loving Leninist foreign policy. They are gone into quite thoroughly in the decisions of the 24th Congress of our Party, in the official documents of the Soviet state, in the speeches of Soviet leaders.

Our foreign policy is a persevering struggle for peace and security, against every type of imperialist aggression and diktat, against infringement on the rights of people, and is for the restructuring of international relations on the basis of just and democratic principles.

We are sincerely glad, dear comrades, that in this noble struggle People's Mongolia is marching shoulder to shoulder with our country, with all the fraternal socialist states. We are gratified to note that the Mongolian People's Republic is making a worth-while contribution to drawing up and implementing the co-ordinated foreign policy of the fraternal countries. Her voice in the international arena carries weight and prestige because it is the voice of peace and justice.

I would like to touch upon one question which of necessity concerns the USSR and the Mongolian People's Republic as states that are tied in with the life, affairs, interests and destinies of the Asian countries by thousands of bonds.

What is the right and sure way to lasting peace and good-neighbourly relations in Asia? This is a question that affects the interests of all Asian countries individually and as a whole.

The imperialist policy of dividing peoples and setting them against one another is being pursued today, too, although its outward forms change. The colonial past has, in some areas of Asia, left behind carryovers of national and religious animosity, distrust and mutual suspicion. As in the old saying 'The dead hangs on to the living', these evil remnants of the past impede the normal, healthy development of relations between some Asian countries.

This does not mean that Asian countries do not have common interests, or that Asian peoples cannot find a common language. On the contrary, comrades, we are confident that the time will come when the Asian peoples will live together in accordance with the laws of peace and good-neighbourliness.

The idea of peace and security in Asia based on joint effort is far from new. In the light of their own historical experience, Asian states have time and again suggested such principles and norms of relations which could serve as a basis for establishing peaceful, healthy relations among peoples.

In the fifties, the governments of India, the People's Republic of China and of several other Asian countries officially proclaimed their adherence to the principles of peaceful coexistence. The substance of the 10 principles approved at the historic Bandung Conference in 1955 was to make Asia and Africa continents of peace and co-operation. In recent years countries with a non-alignment policy have come up with consequential initiatives for strengthening peace in Asia, in particular at their 4th Conference in Algiers. One may recall many similar constructive proposals.

Thus the idea of ensuring Asian security and co-operation by collective effort is an outcome of political experience and quest of many states. To implement this idea, consistent and persevering practical measures will have to be taken by many states and attentive consideration given to many different views and positions.

The establishment and development of good and durable bilateral relations between Asian states is a very important factor in any guarantee of security in Asia. And we can say, with a clear conscience, that both the Soviet Union and the Mongolian People's Republic are also making a good contribution to this cause.

We, in the USSR, greatly appreciate the good relations which have developed between us and the Asian countries: with the socialist states of the DRV and the KPDR, the Republic of South Vietnam, with our great friend India, with Afghanistan, Burma and Sri Lanka, with Bangladesh and Pakistan, with Japan, Iran and Turkey, and with other states of the biggest continent on earth. We shall strive, as before, to develop and deepen these relations on a mutually advantageous basis and for the good of universal peace.

Of course, comrades, there is no magic cure that could resolve all Asia's problems overnight. But when past conflicts are left behind, when friendly relations between Asian states are consolidated, and bilateral and in some cases multilateral co-operation is established for creative purposes then we can truly say that these are elements from which the edifice of a lasting peace is being built on Asian soil.

Naturally, it would be good if such a large Asian state as the People's Republic of China would take part in this process in a befitting manner. Unfortunately, as you, comrades, are well aware, Peking's current foreign-policy course runs counter to *détente*.

The Soviet Union, on its part, works continually to normalise Soviet–Chinese relations. Our line, the line of the 24th CPSU Congress, remains unchanged. With regard to China, as with other countries, we firmly adhere to the principles of equality, respect for sovereignty and territorial integrity, non-interference in one another's internal affairs and the non-use of force. We are prepared to restore friendship and co-operation with the Chinese people, for whom the Soviet people have, as they always have had, sincere respect.

The desire of the nations for ending the threat of war, for a really lasting peace and fruitful co-operation is becoming ever more clearly and widely pronounced in conditions of international *détente*, which has already started. Progress in this direction requires persevering political struggle to overcome resistance in the many quarters that are either innately aggressive or simply inert in their thinking. However, the powerful trend towards *détente* and peace is making headway, after all, in spite of the many obstacles.

> *Speech at a meeting to commemorate the fiftieth anniversary of the 3rd Congress of the Mongolian People's Revolutionary Party, and the Proclamation of the Mongolian People's Republic, Ulan-Bator. 26 November 1974*

In the period under review the Central Committee devoted much attention to developing normal, and wherever possible also friendly, relations with the Asian states.

To begin with, a few words about our many-sided co-operation with India. We attach special importance to friendship with that great country. In the past 5 years Soviet–Indian relations have risen to a new level. Our countries have concluded a treaty of peace, friendship and co-operation. And even this short period has clearly shown its tremendous significance for our bilateral ties, and its role as a stabilising factor in South Asia and the continent as a whole.

Close political and economic co-operation with the Republic of India is our constant policy. Soviet people appreciate and, more, are in solidarity with India's peace-loving foreign policy and the courageous efforts of her progressive forces to solve the country's difficult socio-economic problems. We wish the people and government of India complete success in these efforts.

Events showed that the Soviet Union's approach to the problems of South Asia was correct. We welcomed the termination of the India–Pakistan armed conflict in 1971 and the important changes which occurred then and which were conducive to normalising relations between the states of that part of the world. We are pleased to note that we were to some extent able to contribute to this positive process.

Speaking of our relations with the Asian states in general, we must mention our good neighbour, Afghanistan, with which we have recently extended the almost half-century-old treaty of neutrality and non-aggression. Let me also mention Turkey, co-operation with which is gradually spreading from the sphere of chiefly economic to political questions.

The Soviet Union intends to continue its active participation in the search for ways of consolidating peace and security on the Asian continent, and of developing equal co-operation there as well. We shall work for this through bilateral contacts, and also on a multilateral basis. We have repeatedly set forth our views on this score and stressed our readiness to treat with the utmost attention any proposals prompted by a concern for lasting peace and security in Asia, and for assuring them by collective effort.

Report of the CPSU Central Committee to the 25th Congress of the Communist Party of the Soviet Union held in Moscow. 24 February 1976

You, Comrade Neto, had been in the Soviet Union before. Those were years when the Angolan people, under the leadership of the militant organisation which you headed, waged a courageous struggle for putting an end to colonial domination. It was precisely in those hard times that friendship between our peoples took shape and was strengthened.

Today the Soviet people for the first time welcome you and the members of your delegation as distinguished representatives of a sovereign country, of free and friendly Angola.

The Angolan people won a difficult but glorious victory. This victory is all the more striking because it was won in a struggle waged simultaneously against the old and the present-day colonialism. You inflicted a defeat on the internal reactionary forces and on the invaders – mercenaries and racists. Your people with honour withstood the pressure from the combined forces of the enemies of freedom. This is of historic significance for the whole of Africa.

The victory of Angola was won as a result of the staunchness and courage of your people, of your revolutionary vanguard. At the same time, it was a victory for internationalism and solidarity of progressive forces of the world. All freedom-loving peoples of Africa sided with you. From the very start of your struggle, the Soviet Union, Cuba and other socialist countries had actively helped you. On your side were the Communists and all sincere democrats of Portugal, all progressives of the world.

The events in Angola once again confirmed a great truth of our time; namely, that the determination of a people to defend its freedom, further fortified by international solidarity, is an indomitable force. Whoever really wishes to learn from revolutionary experience cannot but draw such a conclusion from these events.

The birth of People's Angola was a sign of the times. And it is only natural that it was enthusiastically welcomed by all who are for peace and national freedom. At the Berlin Conference twenty-nine Communist and Workers' Parties of Europe expressed unanimous support for the government and people of Angola, for their efforts to strengthen the independence of the country and ensure its advance along the road of progress. The formation of the young African state was also received with some understanding in those quarters in the West that are able realistically to assess contemporary developments.

Sovereign Angola has been accepted as a full-fledged member in the Organisation of African Unity, and in the non-alignment movement, and in this way it has become already now an active member of the international community.

Demands for ending the rule of racists in the south of Africa are growing and becoming increasingly insistent. This is also a dictate of the times, which is opposed only by representatives of extreme reaction.

We are firmly convinced that the problems of Zimbabwe and Namibia should be settled by the peoples of these countries themselves. The events of recent years in Africa show once again that only in this way can such problems be solved correctly, justly and really in the interests of the peoples themselves.

It is true that today, when Africa has shown its ability to do away with the remnants of colonialism and racism, some people purporting to promote this process are trying to substitute a fictitious for a genuine liberation of southern Africa, and, in effect, to preserve the positions of imperialism in that region and bolster up the tottering bastion of racism – the regime of the Republic of South Africa.

As regards the stand of the Soviet Union on this question, it is clear and unambiguous. We have said many times and want to repeat that we have no 'special interests' either in the south, or in the north, or in any other part of Africa; nor can we have any such interests. We seek no advantages for ourselves there. The only thing we want is to see that the sacred right of each people to decide its own destiny and choose its own road of development is recognised. This is a fundamental principle with us, from which our Party and the Soviet people will never depart.

We proceed from the belief that a people that is free cannot but wish that other peoples will be free and cannot but support true fighters for freedom. And we are convinced that the cause of peace on earth and international security will be advanced if all the nations of Africa, all the oppressed peoples without exception, achieve freedom and independence.

Dear Angolan friends,

We rejoice in your first successes in building a new life. It is an important fact that, having thrown off foreign oppression, your people are supporting the programme, put forward by the Popular Movement for the Liberation of Angola, of thoroughgoing social and economic changes designed to achieve the elimination of all forms of exploitation, including capitalist exploitation.

Of course, difficult is the road of a young state, especially one that has gone through such ordeals as befell Angola. We understand your desire to rebuild the war-ravaged economy as quickly as possible, to establish organs of people's power in the shortest possible time, ensure the growth of national culture and make every effort so that the working masses can taste the real fruits of the victory won. This undoubtedly will call for mobilisation of the energies and creative abilities of the people, a well-thought-out policy and great stamina.

Several matters, I believe, will promote the Soviet–Angolan co-operation. A good foundation has already been laid for its development. The negotiations to be held in the course of this visit, as we hope, will cement our friendship still further and provide a new impetus to extending and developing Soviet–Angolan relations.

We are prepared to develop the most sincere and friendly ties between the CPSU and the MPLA, between the Soviet Union and the People's Republic of Angola on the basis of mutual respect, equality, non-interference in each other's domestic affairs and comradely reciprocal assistance.

I am confident that all this fully meets the interests of the peoples of both countries and serves the noble aims of achieving peace, social progress, and a better future for mankind.

> *Speech at the dinner in the Kremlin in honour of Agostinho Neto, Chairman of the MPLA, President of the People's Republic of Angola. 7 October 1976*

The victory of the patriotic forces of Laos, and the fact that leadership in that country has been assumed by the Marxist–Leninist People's Revolutionary Party, is another important event. After taking power into their hands, the working people of that country have started the building of a new life. The visit to the USSR of the Laotian Party and government delegation in the spring of this year and the fruitful, comradely talk which Comrade Suslov and I recently had with the General Secretary of the fraternal Laotian Party Comrade Kayson Phomvihane, showed that the prospects for the development of Soviet–Laotian friendship were good. I think, comrades, that we have every ground to say that in Laos the family of socialist states has gained another new member.

Many events of major political significance have taken place in countries that have freed themselves from colonial dependence. Mention should be made first of all of the victory scored by the patriots of Angola over foreign imperialist interventionists and the forces of internal reaction.

The heroic struggle of the Angolan people met with the sympathy and support of a number of progressive African countries as well as of socialist countries, including the Soviet Union, and, as is known, also of Cuba. We gave selfless support to the just struggle of Angola's patriots, responded to the request of its lawful government, and we are proud of it!

Angola's victory has been an inspiring example for the forces of progress on the African continent. There has been an upsurge of the struggle of the peoples against the bastions of racism and reaction, against the stooges of world imperialism, such as South Africa and Rhodesia. The anti-imperialist forces in Africa have begun to feel more confident. We, too, could sense this when playing host in Moscow during the last few months to a number of high-ranking delegations of independent African countries, fighters for the freedom and progress of the peoples of that continent.

And the recent visit to the Soviet Union of the President of People's Angola, Comrade Neto, laid a firm groundwork for the further development and strengthening of friendship between our countries. The conclusion of the Treaty of Friendship and Co-operation between the USSR and Angola is a new step towards strengthening the great friendship between the world of socialism and the young emergent states, a big, a signal step!

Fruitfully developing are our ties with the young African Republic of Mozambique, fresh evidence of which was the visit to the USSR this summer of the President of the Republic, Chairman of FRELIMO Samora Machel.

Active steps are being taken on our part in support of the just demands by the developing countries of Asia, Africa and Latin America for the reconstruction of international economic relations on the basis of equality, for the removal of all forms of exploitation by capitalist states of their weaker partners in the Third World. The interests of socialist and developing countries coincide in this and in many other fields.

It goes without saying that, just as on the whole of our planet, a stubborn struggle between the forces of progress and the forces of reaction continues in the Third World. This is also borne out by the Fifth Non-Aligned Nations' Summit Conference held in Colombo in August. The non-alignment movement has become a notable factor in international life, an important link in the world-wide front of the peoples' struggle against imperialism, colonialism and aggression. The documents dealing with political and economic problems adopted at Colombo after long and, as it turned out, at times strenuous discussions confirmed that on the whole the non-alignment movement retains its progressive nature.

We have always attached great importance to our relations with Japan, our neighbour and one of the major states in Asia. We have always considered it possible and desirable to develop extensive and stable relations with Japan on the principles of mutual respect and advantage, relations permeated with the spirit of good-neighbourliness. As is known, we have spoken about this on many occasions, including during the 25th Party Congress.

The last time I had an opportunity to express certain views concerning the concrete prospects of long-term (10–15-year) economic co-operation between our two countries was in the Crimea in August, 1975, when I had a talk with a representative delegation of Japanese businessmen headed by Mr. Doko, Chairman of the Federation of Japan's Economic Organisations.

The reaction of the Japanese participants of the talk and the subsequent comments on it in Japan were favourable. This showed once again that there is a solid foundation for developing broad, stable and mutually advantageous relations between our two countries (in fact this has also been confirmed by practice up to this time).

Nevertheless we entertain no illusions, knowing well that it will take still much effort to achieve truly good Soviet–Japanese relations.

Speech at the Plenary Meeting of the Central Committee of the Communist Party of the Soviet Union. 25 October 1976

The enemies of Cuba, the enemies of socialism, are spreading the most absurd concoctions about the aims and intentions of socialist countries with regard to the emergent states. But no slander can refute facts.

And the facts are that the socialist countries are always on the side of the peoples who are confronted by imperialist aggression, diktat and violence; that the socialist countries are developing equitable relations with the young states and are assisting their economic growth as much as they can; and finally, that the policy of the socialist countries acts as a restraint on the forces of imperialism, the forces of the past which are trying to preserve the obsolete orders and to sow the seeds of enmity and conflict among the emergent states.

Sometimes our adversaries, and adversaries of the most varied kinds at that, present matters in such a way as to suggest that Asia, Africa and Latin America are simply an arena for rivalry between socialist and capitalist countries, and in the first place between the Soviet Union and the United States. All this is totally false. The peoples of these continents have long ceased to be passive objects of history. Actively and with all their strength, they are struggling for their rights and searching for their road to progress.

And it can be regarded as something quite natural when these peoples, who have undergone immense suffering and humiliation in the course of imperialist domination, should renounce the capitalist road and choose a socialist orientation. Behind that choice stands the will of the masses, against which the bullets of hired assassins, acts of subversion, blackmail and slanderous propaganda are helpless.

We welcome the progressive role played by the emergent countries, including the role of the non-alignment movement, in international politics, since this strengthens the preconditions for establishing a lasting peace.

Speech at the Kremlin dinner in honour of Fidel Castro Ruz, First Secretary of the Central Committee of the Communist Party of Cuba and Chairman of the State Council and the Council of Ministries of the Republic of Cuba. 5 April 1977

Question: Pondering the situation in Asia, one comes to realise that the Soviet policy in Asia has a great role to play. What is your opinion about relations with the People's Republic of China, prospects for the development of the situation on the Korean peninsula, and the policy pursued by South-East Asian nations, including Vietnam?

Answer: Historically, economically and geographically, our country was and remains inseparably bound with the Asian continent. It is only natural therefore that we earnestly seek to consolidate peace in that area. We believe that having become a dominant trend of world development, *détente* should not bypass the Asian continent where more than half of the world's population lives.

The historic victory of the Vietnamese people and the establishment of a large peace-loving state, the Socialist Republic of Vietnam, the settlement of the conflict in South-East Asia and the withdrawal of American troops from Indo-China – all these events created, in our opinion, more favourable conditions for ensuring a lasting peace and security in Asia through the joint efforts of all states on the continent. This is just the development of events in Asia that the Soviet Union favours.

As regards Soviet–Chinese relations, our position is well known. We want to normalise inter-state relations with China. The re-establishment of really good-neighbourly relations between our two countries would be of great importance for the USSR and the PRC and would also improve the international situation as a whole.

It is through the fault of the other side that there is no sign yet of any improvement in Soviet–Chinese relations. Unfortunately the new Chinese leadership is following the old, worn-out road, so to speak. It is common knowledge that a campaign of denunciation of the policy of *détente* continues and everything is being done to thwart any measures in the field of disarmament. Or take the thesis about struggle against 'hegemony'. Some people may fail to see anything dangerous in it. But is not this thesis being used as a cover to sow strife between states or, at least, to prevent improvements in relations between them? What is the purpose of all this? Are there not any hidden motives running counter to the interests of peace and co-operation? We have a fairly definite view about this anyway, and Japan knows what this view is.

As regards the situation on the Korean peninsula, we support the proposal of the Democratic People's Republic of Korea for a withdrawal of all foreign troops from South Korea and for creating favourable conditions for the country's unification on a peaceful and democratic basis without any interference from the outside. We are not alone in holding this view. Judging by the UN General Assembly resolution urging the creation of favourable conditions for the turning of the armistice in Korea into lasting peace and the speeding up of a peaceful reunification of Korea, most UN member-countries share it.

Question: What is your point of view on the questions of ... the national-liberation struggle in Asia and Africa, and the South–North problem?

Answer: Our stand on this question is clearly defined. The Soviet Union supports the demands of the developing countries for the restructuring of international economic relations on a just and democratic basis. This means, above all, that the process of eliminating colonialism must be extended to the economic sphere and that the oppression by the imperialist multinationals and the exploitation of the natural and human resources of the developing states by the developed capitalist countries must be ended.

Question: During the visit of former Prime Minister Tanaka to the Soviet Union it was recognised that the problem of northern territories was an 'outstanding' problem between Japan and the USSR. Is not the position held by the Soviet Union in the recent period on this question a departure from the above-mentioned understanding?

Answer: We well remember the negotiations with Japanese leaders that took place at that time. Those were, in our opinion, positive negotiations, in the course of which a wide range of questions concerning the relations between our countries, including that of a peace treaty between the USSR and Japan, were discussed. As you remember, the joint Soviet–Japanese statement of 10 October 1973 recorded an arrangement to continue the negotiations on concluding a peace treaty. The Soviet Union is prepared, unless, of course, the Japanese side lays down conditions which are known to be unacceptable, to carry through this important matter for our countries to its conclusion. Given a sober approach on the part of the Japanese side to the realities that have taken shape as a result of the Second World War, this could be done – and done quickly.

It is known that peace treaties, as a rule, cover an extensive set of questions, including that of the border line. This also applies to the Soviet–Japanese peace treaty. To say, then, that in the relations between our countries there is some 'outstanding territorial problem' is a one-sided and wrong interpretation.

Our position has repeatedly been stated at the talks with Japanese leaders and is well known.

If our understanding is correct, Japan is not as yet prepared to conclude a peace treaty. Taking this into account, we have made the suggestion that, while continuing the negotiations on a peace treaty, we should exchange opinions and sign a treaty of good-neighbourliness and co-operation which would embrace these fields of our relations which are already ripe for being placed on a firm treaty basis. It is our belief that this would constitute a sharp turn towards overcoming the remaining distrust and promoting reliable and mutually beneficial co-operation in all spheres.

We have called our proposal a treaty of good-neighbourliness and co-operation. After all, it is not the name, but the substance that matters. We are prepared to consider also the possible initiatives of the Japanese side in this direction. It is important that such a bilateral state document should serve the aim of establishing genuinely good relations between our countries in the interests of the Soviet and Japanese peoples and those of peace and security in the Far East and throughout the world.

Question: What can you say about Japanese–Soviet economic relations, the problems of fishing and co-operation in developing Siberia in particular?

Answer: I have already said more than once that Japanese–Soviet trade and economic relations have good prospects for development, particularly through mutually advantageous co-operation in developing the natural riches of the Soviet Far East and Siberia.

In the past 20 years trade between our countries has grown more than 70 times over. In 1976 this trade exceeded 2000 million roubles. Japan is one of the USSR's three biggest trade partners from among the developed capitalist countries.

There are grounds to believe that our trade will continue to grow and it can be expected that our aggregate trade will surpass 10,000 million roubles over the next five years. This will be promoted by the new 5-year trade and payments agreement which has been recently signed in Tokyo. I also think that the forthcoming 7th session of the Soviet–Japanese and Japanese–Soviet committees for economic co-operation could discuss on a more concrete plane the further expansion of trade and mutually advantageous economic co-operation.

I recall with satisfaction the business talk I had with the delegation of the Japan Federation of Economic Organisations led by its President, Mr. Toshio Doko, in the Crimea last August. We then advanced a number of proposals aimed at the further development of economic ties between the

Soviet Union and Japan. In particular, we touched upon the possibility of shaping a long-term programme of economic co-operation, covering 10 or 15 years, mostly through the more intensive utilisation of the resources of Siberia and the Soviet Far East. We also spoke about the expediency for our countries of concluding an agreement on the principles of economic co-operation to follow the pattern of the agreements which the USSR already has with Britain, France, Canada and some other countries and which justify themselves well in practice. Cannot the Soviet Union and Japan also develop their relations in this field on such a basis? I am sure that they can.

I would not like the readers of your newspaper to get the impression that the Soviet Union cannot develop the tremendous resources of Siberia and the Soviet Far East by its own efforts. It is quite clear, and this is proved by the entire history of our state, that we have every possibility of coping with this task. We use co-operation with other states only to accelerate the implementation of our plans for developing these areas. I do not know to what extent the voices which are sometimes heard in your country against extensive business co-operation with the Soviet Union meet the interests of Japan.

A few words about the problems of fishing which exist between the USSR and Japan. As is known, fishing has always held an important place in the complex of Soviet–Japanese relations. This is only too natural because our countries have been engaged in fishing in the same areas of the sea. In connection with a new situation which has arisen in the field of international fishing due to the establishment of 200-mile zones by many countries, it became necessary to bring Japanese fishing in the regions contiguous to the Pacific coast of the Soviet Union into correspondence with the decree of the Presidium of the USSR Supreme Soviet on temporary measures for the preservation of living resources and the regulation of fishing.

I must say that the Soviet fishing fleet is interested in utilising all catch, permissible from the viewpoint of science, obtained off the Soviet coast to compensate to some extent or another for the losses sustained by our fishermen as a result of the limitations introduced by other countries.

Nevertheless, realising the vital importance of fishing for Japan and its interest in continuing fishing in the waters adjacent to the Soviet coast, we expressed readiness to conclude a relevant agreement. Talks, although they were dragged out, have led to a mutually acceptable decision and, as is known, an agreement has been signed recently.

I would like to say the following in connection with these talks. It was noted in the Soviet Union that some people in Japan tried, clearly not without outside influence, to use the talks for unleashing an unfriendly campaign against the Soviet Union and presenting illegitimate territorial claims to the USSR. Such actions cannot bring anything but harm to Soviet–Japanese relations. They are only playing into the hands of those who do not want to see genuine good-neighbourliness and friendship between the Soviet and Japanese peoples.

Question: Is there a possibility that you and other Soviet leaders might be coming on a visit to Japan?

Answer: I accept with gratitude the invitation of your government to make an official visit to Japan and I shall use this invitation, provided the appropriate situation exists.

A few words in conclusion. Of late not everything has been developing in our relations as we would like to see it, as, in our opinion, is required by the interests of the Soviet Union and Japan . . . I would say that you and we have recently lived through a fairly difficult time when we had to decide in what direction Soviet–Japanese relations will develop further, whether they will follow the road of good-neighbourliness and co-operation or whether their further aggravation is inevitable. I believe that, due to the efforts of both sides, the only correct choice has been made, a choice in favour of the further development of co-operation. This fact is encouraging in itself and it gives us grounds to hope that our relations will continue to develop not from the positions of the past, but with an eye to the future.

I can say most definitely that we would like to conduct business with Japan honestly, on the basis of good-neighbourly co-operation and mutual advantage. The Soviet Union has not had nor has it any other plans in respect of your country which is our close neighbour.

Replies to the Editor-in-Chief, Shoryn Hata, of the newspaper Asahi Shimbun.
6 June 1977

Question: Many events have taken place in the world during this time. The arms race is continuing. Africa is being shaken by stormy movements. Do you expect a stabilisation of international relations or do you believe that *détente* is being threatened?

Answer: You mentioned Africa, and in a way that implied that the 'stormy movements' there impeded *détente* and created instability in international relations. But that is not the case at all.

The peoples of the African continent are carrying on a resolute struggle for their freedom and independence, for the right to choose their road of development without outside interference. They are waging a struggle against the shameful phenomena of racialism and apartheid. This is a just struggle and our country has always supported and will support such a struggle.

Instability in Africa is caused by something else. It is caused by external forces that are trying to prevent the African peoples from choosing the road they consider the most suitable for themselves. They are encouraging and inciting strife and provoking disputes over problems inherited by African peoples from the colonial times. It is this policy that runs counter to the demands of *détente* and principles of peaceful coexistence, and may lead to the emergence of new centres of international tension. It is in this that we see the cause of instability in Africa.

The Soviet Union is resolutely against interference in the internal affairs of African countries. We do not seek any advantages or privileges for ourselves in Africa. Our policy on that continent too is directed at building peaceful, friendly relations with all peoples, at helping them to advance successfully along their chosen road of independence and progress.

Question: The view is becoming increasingly widespread in the West that the way out of the economic and moral crisis experienced by our societies lies in the search for a new world economic order, that is, in changing relations between the industrially developed and developing countries. Do you share this view? To what extent could the Soviet Union take part in the search for and in guaranteeing the stability of this new order?

Answer: First, a clarification. You are evidently talking about the crisis that is gripping the capitalist countries. Neither the Soviet Union nor the other socialist countries are experiencing a crisis. True, to a certain extent we indirectly feel the consequences of the economic upheavals experienced by the capitalist world: for instance, in the course of our foreign-trade operations we have to take into account the process of inflation. But that is a different question altogether.

The restructuring of international economic relations on a democratic basis and the elimination from such relations of discrimination, diktat and inequality are important demands of the present epoch, and the Soviet Union is consistently working for this. We have made concrete suggestions on this matter, including proposals submitted to the United Nations. Our country forms its economic ties with the countries of Africa, Asia and Latin America, as with all other countries, on the basis of strict observance of equality, mutual advantage and non-interference in internal affairs. We are giving all possible aid to many newly free states in overcoming the economic backwardness inherited from the past.

We are convinced that the development of international economic relations on the just principles of equality and mutual advantage and the ruling out of discrimination would accord with the interests of every nation and with the interests of strengthening peace and international security, although this will not save capitalism from crises.

I will emphasise another point: the Soviet Union, like the other countries of socialism, naturally is not responsible either for the consequences of colonialism or for the harmful influence that the remaining inequality in economic relations has on the developing countries.

Answers to questions from Le Monde.
15 June 1977

Angola now occupies a worthy place in the ranks of progressive African states. It has proclaimed a programme of profound social and economic transformations, the ultimate aim of which is to eliminate exploitation in any form. We also greatly value the fact that your country consistently supports the strengthening of international peace and security and the complete elimination of colonialism and racialism.

The forces of reaction, however, are unwilling to accept the birth of another progressive state on the African continent. The very fact of the existence of the People's Republic of Angola is regarded by them as a threat to the last bastions of racialism and neocolonialism. The imperialist forces and their accomplices in Africa are now placing their main hopes on undermining the unity of African countries. To that end imperialism is resorting to the most sordid of methods. These include organising acts of banditry by groups of splitters, attempts in every way to incite internal conflicts in some countries and, of course, provocation of strife among African states. Imperialism is doing everything it can to prevent the peoples of the African countries from fully enjoying the fruits of a lasting peace and genuine independence. An example in point is the continuous provocations by internal and foreign reactionaries against the People's Republic of Angola.

I would like to call particular attention to one circumstance.

Many of the dangerous armed conflicts, including some very recent ones, have been caused by attempts to revise and forcibly change existing borders between states. A regrettable example is provided by the clashes between Somalia and Ethiopia, which have made the opponents of independence and progress of the African peoples so happy.

Of course, the frontiers of the present African states were in most cases not established by themselves, but by foreign colonialists who often deliberately sowed the seeds of discord among the peoples of the territories which they seized. But there can be no doubt that, as mutual trust and friendship among the peoples of the liberated states grow stronger, problems of this kind among them will be settled by mutual accord on the basis of good-neighbourly relations. Today, however, the most important thing, as we see it, is that the principles of the inviolability of borders should be universally observed in the interests of peace, security and progress of the peoples.

The European states have already taken an important step in this direction by assuming a corresponding obligation at Helsinki. In 1964 the member states of the Organisation of African Unity also agreed to respect each other's frontiers and observe their inviolability. This is recorded in the charter of the OAU. Adherence to that agreement and accession to it by all African states would be a good safeguard of a more durable peace on the continent and of friendship among all its peoples. This would be a good answer to the intrigues of foreign forces that seek to make African nations clash with one another for the benefit of their own imperialist interests.

The imperialists are making feverish attempts to strengthen the last bastions of racism and colonialism in the south of Africa. These ends are also served by setting up military strongholds of imperialist powers in Africa, such as the missile proving ground in Zaïre, attempts to form a military–political bloc in the Red Sea area, the development of nuclear weapons in South Africa with the help of NATO countries and Israel, and other activities.

The Soviet Union firmly stands for a lasting peace in Africa. We have supported the appeal of the African states to make Africa a nuclear-free zone. We strongly condemn all attempts to use the African continent as a military springboard.

Imperialist interference in African affairs can only bring more severe trials to the African peoples. No intrigues, however, can stop the historical process of the national regeneration of the former colonies. We are firmly confident of this.

The Soviet Union has for the past 60 years followed the road charted by the great Lenin. We are preparing to adopt a new Constitution of the USSR which will mark an important historical stage in broadening and deepening socialist democracy.

By building communism in their own country, the Soviet people are contributing to the internationalist cause of the struggle of the working people of the whole world for freedom, for mankind's progress and for a lasting peace on earth. They are also giving help and support to the People's Republic of Angola.

Soviet–Angolan co-operation, based on friendship, mutual respect and non-interference in each other's internal affairs, is, we believe, developing successfully. In a few days we are going to mark the anniversary of the Treaty of Friendship and Co-operation between the USSR and the PRA, which has greatly strengthened the political and legal basis of mutual relations between our countries. We have carried out and shall steadily carry out the commitments which the Soviet Union has undertaken under the treaty and the agreements signed between our governments.

We Soviet people sincerely want to see People's Angola as an independent, strong and prosperous state and wish the Angolan people fresh victories in strengthening the independence of their country and in building a free life!

> *Speech at a luncheon in the Kremlin in honour of Antonio Agostinho Neto, President of the Popular Movement for the Liberation of Angola (MPLA), and President of the People's Republic of Angola. 28 September 1977*

Your visit coincides with a period filled with great and happy events for our country, which has just adopted a new Constitution and is looking forward to its 60th anniversary. And we are glad that you are here with us at this time, for our countries are neighbours and our peoples are friends of long standing.

On the eve of the 60th anniversary of the Great October Socialist Revolution we recall here how its importance was assessed by outstanding representatives of India's liberation movement. Mahatma Gandhi wrote: 'There can be no doubt that behind the ideal of Bolshevism is the noble self-sacrifice of innumerable women and men, who gave everything for its sake. An ideal to which such spiritual giants as Lenin dedicated themselves cannot be barren. The noble example of their selflessness will be glorified throughout the centuries, making this ideal ever purer and more beautiful.' History has confirmed how true are these words written by the great son of the Indian people.

Not long ago the Indian people celebrated the 30th anniversary of India's independence. Three decades are a comparatively short period. But in these decades the independent Republic of India has achieved impressive progress in various spheres of life. As your sincere friends, we rejoice at this and wish the great Indian people new successes in the struggle for the strengthening of their national independence, for social progress and peace.

Relations between the Soviet Union and India, strengthened by the Treaty of Friendship and Co-operation, are fruitful and many-sided. They include co-operation in many economic, scientific, cultural and artistic fields, and this co-operation is extensive, stable and mutually beneficial. It also covers co-operation in the field of international affairs, which is aimed solely at promoting world peace.

The changes for the better in the international sphere, for the sake of which both our countries have done much, are manifestly of a large scope and of vital importance. But we clearly see, too, the dangers that still loom in the path of the policy of *détente*, of co-operation on an equitable basis, and of ensuring the security of the peoples.

Neither the Soviet Union nor, as we believe, India can remain indifferent to the fact that there appear, now in one part of the world and now in another, new situations of conflict and new centres of rising tension. We firmly adhere to the view that they must be eliminated as quickly as possible, and that any problems that emerge must be transferred to a plane where they can be resolved by peaceful means, at the negotiating table.

Developments on the continent of Asia are of immediate interest for both our countries. Our Indian friends, we believe, are well acquainted with the Soviet Union's point of view. We are convinced that one of the most reliable means of achieving *détente* and security in Asia consists in joint efforts by the Asian states in a form which they consider acceptable to themselves.

An agreement on curtailing military activities in the Indian Ocean would be in the interests of the peoples of Asia, and of the world at large. We are prepared to co-operate with India on questions concerning the Indian Ocean.

We have always considered peace to be indivisible. And today this is perhaps truer than ever before. A military conflagration in one area can spread in a matter of hours to other continents, eventually engulfing the whole planet. On the other hand, real progress in strengthening peace and good-neighbourliness in one part of the world can improve the entire international climate. We are confident, therefore, that peace-loving India duly appreciates the efforts towards strengthening peace in Europe.

Mr. Prime Minister, the Soviet Union will continue to do everything it can to make sure that its friendship with India develops in all fields. If the policy of the Indian leadership is the same, and we believe it is, then future Soviet–Indian relations will be good.

Soviet–Indian co-operation is developing in a political atmosphere that is calm and tranquil, with both sides strictly observing the principles of sovereignty, equality and non-interference in each other's affairs. Our relations provide a good example of peaceful coexistence of states with different social systems and are an important factor promoting peace and stability in Asia and throughout the world. As these relations develop, deep friendship between the peoples of the two great countries – the Soviet Union and India – is taking shape and growing stronger on the basis of mutual respect and mutual trust. And we are confident that this friendship will live on for ages to come!

Speech at a dinner given in the Kremlin in honour of Prime Minister of India Morarji Desai. 21 October 1977

8.
POSITION IN THE NEAR EAST

In recent years the Soviet Union has time and again – and I stress this – warned that the situation in the Middle East is explosive. Our stand on this issue has been clear and consistent from beginning to end. In keeping with the general principles of socialist foreign policy and in view of the fact that this region is in direct proximity to our frontiers, we are interested in seeing that a really durable and just peace is established in the Middle East and that the security of all the countries and peoples of that region and their right to build their life peacefully and in a manner of their own choosing are ensured. For that very reason the Soviet Union has always insisted that the territories seized by Israel should be returned to the Arab states and that justice should triumph in respect to the Palestinian people. This has been and shall remain the policy of the Soviet Union.

From the moment hostilities resumed in the Middle East early this month the Soviet Union maintained close contact with friendly Arab states and took all the political steps in its power to help end the war and create the conditions under which peace in the Middle East would be really lasting for all the countries of that region.

As is known, acting on the proposal of the Soviet Union and the United States of America, the UN Security Council twice, on 22 and 23 October, passed a resolution calling for a ceasefire.

On both occasions, Israel, while proclaiming compliance with the Security Council resolutions, in fact violated them treacherously, and continued its aggressive actions against Egypt. Capturing more and more of that country's territory, Israel completely ignored the Security Council demand that the troops be withdrawn to the positions they occupied on the evening of 22 October.

It is difficult to understand what the Israeli rulers are counting on by following this adventurist course, flouting the resolutions of the UN Security Council, and defying world public opinion. Apparently, outside patronage has something to do with it. But the people of Israel are paying a heavy price for this policy of the Israeli Government. Hopes of ensuring peace and security for one's own state through the forcible seizure and retention of the lands of others are wild hopes that are doomed to inevitable failure. Such a course will yield neither peace nor security for Israel. It will only result in Israel's still greater international isolation, arousing still greater hatred for it among the neighbouring peoples. The Arabs' courageous struggle and the growing solidarity of the Arab states show very well that they will never be

291

reconciled to the Israeli aggression and will never give up their legitimate rights. The Soviet Union supports the Arab people's just demands firmly and consistently.

The collective will of those who demand the establishment of peace in the Middle East must prevail over the recklessness of those who violate the peace. The experience of the past few days compels us to be vigilant. Urgent and firm measures are required to assure implementation of the ceasefire and troop withdrawal resolutions.

In view of the continuing violations of the ceasefire, the UN Security Council decided on 25 October forthwith to form a special United Nations force, which will be sent to the area of the hostilities. We hold that this is a useful decision and hope that it will serve its purpose in normalising the situation.

In the matter of normalising the Middle East situation, the Soviet Union is prepared to co-operate with all the interested countries. But, surely, co-operation is not benefited by such moves of the past few days by certain elements in the NATO countries as the artificial whipping up of sentiment with all kinds of fantastic rumours about the intentions of the Soviet Union in the Middle East. As we see it, a more responsible, honest, and constructive approach would be much more appropriate in the present situation.

I should like to stress that the Security Council's resolution of 22 October envisages more than a mere ceasefire: it envisages important measures aimed at eliminating the very causes of war. And this makes it especially valuable. The parties concerned are to begin immediately the practical fulfilment of all the provisions of the Middle East resolution adopted by the Security Council on 22 November 1967.

Let me remind you that this resolution, which stresses the 'inadmissibility of the acquisition of territory by war', provides for the withdrawal of the Israeli armed forces from territories occupied during the 1967 conflict. It demands respect for and recognition of the sovereignty, territorial integrity and political independence of all states in the region, and their right to live in peace. It also emphasises the necessity of a fair settlement of the 'refugee problem', that is, of ensuring the legitimate rights of the Arab people of Palestine.

It is not difficult to see that had all these provisions adopted in 1967 been translated into life there and then, there would have already been peace in the Middle East for 6 years. However, this did not take place. It did not take place because of the same short-sighted policy of Israel's ruling circles, encouraged by external forces.

In accordance with the letter and spirit of the resolution adopted by the Security Council on Monday, 22 October, the parties concerned are to start immediately, under the appropriate auspices, negotiations aimed at establishing a just and lasting peace in the Middle East. It is impossible to overestimate the importance of such negotiations. An historical responsibility devolves on their participants. Let me say that the Soviet Union is prepared to make and will make a constructive contribution to this matter. Our firm stand is that all the states and peoples in the Middle East – I repeat, all of them – must be assured of peace, security and inviolability of borders. The Soviet Union is prepared to take part in the relevant guarantees.

We feel that one of the most urgent tasks before all peace fighters and all peace forces in present-day conditions is to work for the immediate and full implementation of the Security Council resolution of 22 October 1973. This is necessary for the free and independent development of all states and peoples in the Middle East. This meets the interests of many states in Europe and Asia, Africa and America, for whom normalisation of the political and economic life in this key area of the world is of considerable importance. Finally, the acute situation which has arisen in the Middle East over the last few days and the risk of an extension of the conflict quite clearly show how important it is to settle this problem also for the sake of stronger world peace.

Speech at the World Congress of Peace
Forces in Moscow. 26 October 1973

The events of the past few weeks in the Middle East have become a vivid manifestation of the complexity of present-day international relations, a focal point, as it were, of the struggle in the world today, in which many forces are locked.

A lull has now set in there after a comparatively brief but fierce armed clash. Military operations have stopped. But the charred ruins are still smouldering, the graves of thousands of killed are still fresh, the hostile armies confront each other with their guns at the ready. It is clear that urgent steps must be taken to prevent a new bloodshed and establish a stable peace. But to achieve this it is necessary to take into account the lessons of the past.

What conclusions can be drawn from the recent events in the Middle East and around it?

The latest war, above all, has vividly brought out the impermissibility of preserving the situation generating the threat of war in the Middle East and the impermissibility of the further presence of the aggressor on the lands he seized by force. Unless there is a peaceful settlement in the very near future, unless all consequences of Israeli aggression are eliminated, another, still more dangerous military explosion may occur in the Middle East at any time.

The hostilities have clearly shown that the Arab world now is not the same as it was 6 years ago. They showed the increased might of the Arab states, victims of aggression, and dispelled the myth of invincibility of Israel's armed forces. At the same time the world witnessed effective solidarity of Arab states both in the military sphere and in the implementation of political and economic steps to defend their joint interests in the world arena.

The great effectiveness of the solidarity and friendly assistance extended to the Arab peoples in their just struggle by the Soviet Union and other socialist countries, by many states of Asia, Africa and other continents, was shown in practice. Israel's political and diplomatic isolation, a result of its aggressive policy, has been brought out most vividly these days.

At the same time the events of the past weeks once again showed the great benefit for universal peace of the work done in the past few years to normalise international relations, and to ease international tension, first and foremost, in the relations between the biggest states with differing social systems.

I think you will agree with me, esteemed Members of the Parliament, that matters would look quite different were it not for this factor of *détente* in the world, which emerged in the last 2 or 3 years. If the current conflict had flared up in a situation of universal international tension and aggravated relations, say, between the United States and the Soviet Union, the clash in the Middle East might have become much more dangerous; it might have assumed a scope threatening world peace.

It can be said for certain that in such a case there would have been no possibility of a joint initiative of the USSR and the USA, which was supported by other states and led to the well-known Security Council resolutions on the Middle East and which made the ceasefire possible.

The main task now is to achieve, at last, in the coming talks a firm peace settlement in the Middle East. It is necessary to this end to return the lands seized by Israel to their lawful owners, ensure justice in respect to the Arab people of Palestine, and to lay on this basis the foundation of firm peaceful coexistence and good-neighbourly relations between the Arab states and the state of Israel. Otherwise there will be neither peace nor tranquillity there.

All of the participants in the future talks will have an historic responsibility.

As for the Soviet Union, it has absolutely no selfish interests in the Middle East. Our profound interest is only that a really lasting and just peace be established at last in that troublesome area of the world situated not far from the borders of the Soviet Union. The Soviet Union will do its utmost to promote it.

Speech to the Indian Parliament. 29 November 1973

However, there is one problem in particular that we should touch on. I am speaking about the situation in the Middle East.

Exactly a year ago the aggressive policy of the leaders of Israel and their stubborn refusal to withdraw from occupied Arab lands led to a new military flare-up in that region, which could have developed into a threat to world peace.

The rebuff which Israel met with at the time, the growing unity of the Arab countries, the support for their just cause from the Soviet Union and other socialist states, from dozens of countries in Asia and Africa, and from large sections of the public the world over – all that, it would seem, should have taught the champions of aggressive policies in Tel Aviv a real lesson. The proposal we made together with the USA was approved by the UN Security Council and helped to bring about a cease-fire. An *immediate* political settlement of the conflict was on the order of the day, as clearly stated in the Security Council's resolutions. The Geneva peace conference was to solve this problem.

However, what happened in fact was that its work was replaced by group talks on the disengagement of the troops of the belligerents on individual fronts. As an initial step this was useful but it could not in any way substitute for a basic settlement and it did not, as is obvious to everybody now, solve the main problem – a complete settlement.

At present, the Israeli invaders are still holding and gradually absorbing the territories they have seized. And the leaders of the Israeli government, apparently enjoying the support of their traditional foreign backers, are trying in every way to avoid a resumption of talks on a peaceful settlement at the Geneva conference, and declare, as though to make it perfectly clear to the whole world, that Israel has not the slightest intention of going back to the 1967 borders.

The Arab states are quite rightly outraged by this. Naturally, as heretofore, the Soviet Union fully supports their just cause. Our large-scale and continually developing friendly co-operation with Syria, Egypt, Iraq and the leaders of the Palestine Liberation Organisation is a factor of no small importance for overcoming the aftermath of aggression, and achieving a just peace. We set great store by our contacts with the Arab leaders. Such contacts are especially necessary and useful in the present situation. This was confirmed, in particular, by our recent talks with Comrade Assad, President of Syria.

It is necessary, at long last, to implement the decisions of the United Nations Organisation and to ensure the liberation of the lands seized by Israel, the legitimate rights of the Arab people of Palestine and their right to their national hearth. This should be done without further delay, if we want to see a lasting peace in the Middle East. Postponing the solution of these problems and dragging out the present situation, which only benefits the Israeli invaders, means sitting on a gunpowder keg that can explode at any moment.

That is why the USSR is working resolutely for the speedy, effective resumption of work by the Geneva peace conference with the participation of all the interested parties, including the Palestinians. A just and durable peace must be established at long last in the Middle East. The security of all states in that region, including Israel, would profit from that, and we are convinced such a peace will be established, because it is the will of the peoples, because it is imperative in the interests of world security!

Speech at a meeting to commemorate the 50th anniversary of the formation of the Moldavian SSR and of the Communist Party of Moldavia, Kishinev. 11 October 1974

All these years, the Soviet Union has consistently supported the Arab peoples' struggle to eliminate the consequences of the Israeli aggression. Our country helped – and effectively, as the October 1973 war showed – to build up the military potential of the countries opposing the aggressor, that is, Egypt, Syria and Iraq. We supported the Arab political struggle both within the United Nations and outside it.

There is no war in the Middle East at present. But neither is there peace, let alone tranquillity. And who would venture to guarantee that hostilities do not erupt anew? This danger will persist as long as Israeli armies remain in the occupied territories. It will persist as long as the hundreds of thousands of Palestinians driven from their land are deprived of their legitimate rights and live in appalling conditions, and as long as the Arab people of Palestine are denied the possibility to create their national state. For Middle East peace to be lasting, the security of all the states of the region, their right to independent existence and development, must also be guaranteed. Is it not clear how serious a responsibility is assumed by those who, in pursuance of egoistic aims, are making a Middle-East settlement the object of political manoeuvre and use separate partial agreements to delay, or even entirely place in question, genuine solutions?

As regards the Soviet Union, its position is a constructive and principled one. As the co-chairman of the Geneva Conference, the USSR is prepared to co-operate in all efforts to reach an effective settlement of the conflict. We are prepared to participate in international guarantees of the security and inviolability of the frontiers of all Middle East countries either in the UN framework or on some other basis. Incidentally, it is our opinion that Britain

297

and France, too, could participate in such guarantees along with the USSR and the USA. This would only help matters.

We are for creating conditions that would facilitate the development of our relations with all Middle East countries. We have no prejudices against any of them. Finally, we are also prepared to participate in a search for a solution to such a problem as ending the arms race in this region. But it stands to reason that this must be tied in closely with a general settlement in the Middle East. To take up the problem before such a settlement is reached would place the aggressor on a par with his victims.

Report of the CPSU Central Committee to the 25th Congress of the Communist Party of the Soviet Union held in Moscow. 24 February 1976

We are for the implementation of the most vigorous measures to eliminate the seat of war in the Middle East. The bloodshed in Lebanon, stopped with such difficulty, has shown once again with what dangers a further delay in reaching a settlement of the Middle East conflict is fraught.

The Middle East needs a lasting and just settlement that would not impinge on the vital rights of any state and any people. Israel, of course, has the right to independence as a state and a secure existence. But the same right belongs also to the Arab people of Palestine.

The path to a solution of the Middle East problem lies – and we have said this on many occasions – through the Geneva Peace Conference on the Middle East. At present all the interested states appear to favour a resumption of the work of the conference. And this imparts still greater importance to co-operation between the co-chairmen of the Geneva Conference – the Soviet Union and the United States. Given the will, they can do much to help the sides involved in the conflict in seeking mutually acceptable solutions.

Speech in the city of Tula. 18 January 1977

The Middle East is another area that continues to attract attention. A noticeable increase in diplomatic activity has been observed there in recent weeks. Judging by everything, the resumption of the Geneva Conference is gradually, more and more becoming a realistic possibility. Such a course of events, naturally, can only be welcomed.

But the Conference in Geneva, of course, is not an end in itself. A fruitful and just outcome of its work is the most important thing. It goes without saying that the drawing up of peace terms in full detail is primarily a matter for the opposed sides themselves. But the Soviet Union, as a co-chairman of the Geneva Conference and a state situated in close proximity to the area in question, has views of its own concerning the main principles which should be observed in a future peace settlement and the direction it should take.

We consider, in particular, that the final document (or documents) on peace in the Middle East should be based on the principle that the acquisition of territory by means of war is impermissible, and on the right of all states in the area to independent existence and security. It goes without saying that the inalienable rights of the Arab people of Palestine must be ensured, including their right to self-determination and establishment of their own state.

We consider there is no question but that the documents on peace must provide for the withdrawal of Israeli troops from all Arab territories occupied in 1967. Such a withdrawal could be carried out not all at once, but in stages, in the course of, say, several months, within strictly defined time limits. The appropriate border lines between Israel and its Arab neighbours involved in the conflict should be clearly defined. These borders should be declared to be finally established and inviolable.

We proceed from the premise that as soon as the withdrawal of the Israeli troops has been completed, the state of war between the Arab states involved in the conflict and Israel will be at an end, and relations of peace will be established. Furthermore, the sides will undertake mutual obligations to respect each other's sovereignty, territorial integrity, inviolability and political independence, and to resolve their international disputes by peaceful means.

Demilitarised zones, which afford no unilateral advantage to either side, could be created on both sides of the established borders – with the consent of the respective states, of course. Either a United Nations emergency force or United Nations observers could be stationed within these zones for some stipulated period of time.

Evidently, the final documents of the Conference should also contain a provision for a free passage of ships of all countries, including Israel (after the ending of the state of war), through the Strait of Tiran and the Gulf of Aqaba, as well as a statement by Egypt concerning the passage of ships through the Suez Canal which is entirely under Egyptian sovereignty.

In our opinion observance of the terms of the peace settlement could be guaranteed, should the negotiating parties so desire, by the United Nations Security Council or, perhaps, by individual powers, for instance, the Soviet Union, the United States, France, and Britain. The guarantor states could have their observers in the United Nations contingents stationed in the respective zones.

Comrades, these are very briefly our tentative ideas on the possible foundations of a just peace in the Middle East. We are not forcing them on anyone, but we felt it would be useful to let them be known, because we, naturally, are prepared to hear the views of others.

We have already said that as far as a peace settlement in the Middle East is concerned, the relevant states could explore the possibility of facilitating an early stop to the arms race in that area. In general, the problem of international trade in arms seems to warrant an exchange of views.

> *Speech at the 16th Congress of the Trades Unions of the USSR. 21 March 1977*

The Syrian people have just celebrated their national holiday, the anniversary of the evacuation of foreign troops. This anniversary is also close to the hearts of Soviet people.

For our country was among the first to come out vigorously in defence of the freedom, independence and autonomous development of the young Syrian Republic. We firmly stood on these positions in the trying years of war that befell the Syrian people in its struggle against imperialist aggression. We still stand on these positions.

The countries of victorious socialism and the forces of the national-liberation movement are natural allies.

The aim of their alliance is to eliminate exploitation and imperialist plunder everywhere on earth and to enable peoples to settle their destinies and build a new life without outside interference; in short – to enable people to lead a better life in greater justice and have confidence in their peaceful future.

In making a broad assessment of political development, in analysing its main trends, one cannot fail to see the colossal transformations that are taking place in various regions of the world, changes in favour of peace, freedom and independence for peoples, and social progress.

The Middle East is no exception in this regard. Events here have been turbulent and often dramatic. At times the policy of different Arab countries abruptly changes direction. One thing is certain, however: if in the past colonialists had uncontrolled domination of the Middle East, today the Arab countries are politically independent. Their peoples are fully resolved to follow the road of social progress. And the changes are historically irreversible.

Why have things been moving lately, as it appears, towards a settlement in the Middle East and towards the convening of the Geneva Conference? Why is this the subject for discussion in the capitals of those countries where – and this is no secret to anyone – other methods have been preferred and practised?

Definitively, it is because the forces – in the Middle East itself and elsewhere – which are calling for an all-embracing settlement are so impressive that they cannot be ignored.

All the peace-loving nations strongly urge the elimination of the centre of tension in the Middle East.

For the Soviet Union, I can say definitely: our desire to establish a just and lasting peace in the Middle East is unswerving and consistent.

This clearly follows from the foreign policy decisions of the 25th CPSU Congress and the Programme it put forward for continuing efforts for peace and international co-operation and for the freedom and independence of peoples.

Our country works persistently so that peace and tranquillity may come to the lands of the Middle East and the consequences of the Israeli aggression be removed. We stand for a radical settlement. Our proposals in this respect are balanced and, what is most important, they are honest proposals.

And it is natural that our ideas about a possible basis for a just peace in the Middle East which we recently made public, have met with broad and favourable response from all over the world, and from the Arab peoples as well.

301

Clearly, peace built on aggression and the conquest of foreign lands cannot be just. And this means that it cannot be lasting either. We are for returning unconditionally to Syria and the other victims of aggression their homelands seized by Israel.

Likewise, no peace can be lasting if it flouts the vital interests of a state or a people in the Middle East. This refers, above all, to the Arab Palestinian people who are waging a courageous struggle to set up their own state. This refers, of course, also to the other peoples of the region, including the people of the state of Israel. They all have the right to state independence and a secure existence.

The time was reached long ago to give concrete consideration to all questions concerning a settlement at the Geneva Conference, of which the Soviet Union is a co-chairman. We are in favour of it being held without delay.

It goes without saying that the Palestine Liberation Organisation, the lawful representative of the Palestinian Arabs, must take part in its proceedings on an equal footing. We insist that not a single decision affecting the Arab people of Palestine be taken without the Palestinians or against their will.

> *Speech in the Kremlin at a dinner for Hafiz al-Assad, Secretary-General of the Arab Socialist Renaissance Party and President of the Syrian Arab Republic. 18 April 1977*

In the course of many years the Middle East crisis now flaring up, now abating, has been one of the sources of international tension. No one any longer doubts the urgent need for its peaceful settlement. In our opinion, the task now is to ensure the resumption of the Geneva Middle East Peace Conference, and without delay.

As to the essence of the Middle East settlement, our point of view, briefly, is as follows: a genuinely lasting and just peace in the Middle East can be established only on the basis of the withdrawal of Israeli troops from all the Arab territories occupied in 1967, and of respect for the right to independent and secure existence of all states and peoples of this region, including Israel and the Arab people of Palestine, on the basis of satisfaction of the legitimate right of the Palestine Arab people to create their own state.

For its part, the Soviet Union is prepared to do everything in its power to bring nearer such a peace.

Reply to the Editor-in-Chief, Shoryn Hata, of the newspaper Asahi Shimbun.
6 June 1977

Middle East affairs are an acute problem. Of late changes, moreover, unfortunately, of a negative character, have taken place in it. And they have taken place at the very time when it seemed that things were moving in a positive direction, towards the convocation of the Geneva Peace Conference, and when much had already been accomplished to this end, including that done by the joint efforts of the USSR and the United States as co-chairmen of the conference. Today, however, the situation has been sharply aggravated. The convocation of the Geneva Conference and the reaching of an overall settlement in the Middle East have become more difficult.

The course of recent events in the Middle East is well known. I should like to stress here only the following. The Soviet Union has been and remains a consistent advocate of an overall settlement in this region of the world with the participation of all the sides concerned, including, of course, the Palestine Liberation Organisation. A settlement that would envisage the withdrawal of Israeli troops from all the Arab territories occupied in 1967; the realisation of the inalienable rights of the Palestine Arab people, including their right to self-determination, to the creation of their own state; guaranteeing of the right to an independent existence and security of all the states directly involved in the conflict, both the Arab countries, neighbours of Israel, and the state of Israel; ending of the state of war between the Arab states concerned and Israel. Only if these fundamental provisions are implemented will peace in the Middle East really be durable and not turn into a precarious armistice.

We by no means consider that the road of unilateral concessions to Israel and separate negotiations with it, such as the notorious talks between the Egyptian and Israeli leaders, leads to this goal. On the contrary, it leads away from it, creating a deep split in the Arab world. This line has the purpose of thwarting a genuine settlement, and primarily of undermining the Geneva Conference even before it opens.

The lavish praising of the imaginary 'advantages' of the so-called direct talks, that is, of Israel's negotiations with each of the countries subjected to its attack, is actually nothing but an attempt to deprive the Arabs of the strength which lies in their unity and in the support given to their just cause by friendly states.

This is why the USSR stands for the convocation of the Geneva Conference, moreover, in conditions that would rule out the possibility of its turning into a screen covering up separate deals to the detriment of the interests of the Arabs and the cause of a just and lasting peace. This is our stand. It is fully supported by the Soviet people and approved by the peace-loving forces of the whole world.

Replies to questions put by a Pravda *correspondent. 24 December 1977*

The major problems that should be resolved if we want lasting peace and international stability include, of course, a just peace settlement in the Middle East. The situation there remains complex and potentially dangerous both to the countries in that area and to the international situation as a whole.

The reason for this is the stubborn refusal of Israel and the forces on which it relies to take account of the legitimate rights and interests of the Arab nations, and Israel's desire, militarily or diplomatically, but anyway from the position of strength, to impose its will on the Arabs.

Of late the heaviest wager towards this end has been laid on the method of behind-the-scenes separate deals with those who are willing to trade in the Arab interests. The scheme is absolutely clear: to split the Arabs, to set them against one another and to impose on one Arab country after another the conditions of settlement that suit the aggressor.

But any attempts to ignore the fundamental prerequisites of a bona fide solution of the Middle East problem, to exclude or circumvent one legitimate participant in the settlement or another, to sacrifice their interests and to dictate conditions to them can produce nothing except the illusion of a settlement. Whatever the 'framework' of the separate deal camouflaging the capitulation of one side and perpetuating the results of the aggression of the other, the aggression of Israel, it can only make the situation in the Middle East even more explosive.

This is demonstrated by the experience of the recent American–Israeli–Egyptian talks in Camp David. We have here another anti-Arab deal between Israel and Egypt, worked out with Washington's active participation.

Now attempts are being made to compel the other parties to the Middle East conflict to accept the conditions of this deal, worked out behind their backs and directly contravening their interests. Frankly, this task is far from easy. It is obvious even today that the Arabs resolutely condemn the separate deal in Camp David and angrily dissociate themselves from it. These sentiments are not hard to understand.

The experience of many years irrefutably proves that there is only one way for the genuine solution of the Middle Eastern conflict. This way consists in the complete evacuation of all the Arab lands occupied by Israel in 1967, complete and unambiguous respect for the legitimate rights of the Arab people of Palestine, including their right to form an independent state, and the guaranteeing of real security for all the countries in the region, including, of course, Israel. Such a comprehensive settlement can only be possible with the participation of all the parties concerned, including the Palestine Liberation Organisation. The sooner this is achieved, the sooner the Middle East will cease to be a seat of tension.

Speech on presenting the city of Baku with the Order of Lenin. 22 September 1978